READINGS AND CASES
in the Management of Information Security

READINGS AND CASES
in the Management of Information Security

Dr. Michael E. Whitman, CISSP
Kennesaw State University

Herbert J. Mattord, CISSP
Kennesaw State University

COURSE TECHNOLOGY
CENGAGE Learning

Australia • Brazil • Japan • Korea • Mexico • Singapore • Spain • United Kingdom • United States

COURSE TECHNOLOGY
CENGAGE Learning™

Readings and Cases in the Management of Information Security
Dr. Michael E. Whitman, Herbert J. Mattord

Senior Acquisitions Editor: Maureen Martin

Product Manager: Beth Paquin

Production Editor: Daphne Barbas

Editorial Assistant: Jennifer Smith

Marketing Manager: Karen Seitz

Senior Manufacturing Coordinator: Laura Burns

Copy Editor: Harold Johnson

Cover Design: Laura Rickenbach

Compositor: Cadmus Professional Communications

Proofreader: Christine Clark

For product information and technology assistance, contact us at **Cengage Learning Customer & Sales Support, 1-800-354-9706**

For permission to use material from this text or product, submit all requests online at **www.cengage.com/permissions**
Further permissions questions can be emailed to **permissionrequest@cengage.com**

ISBN-13: 978-0-619-21627-6

ISBN-10: 0-619-21627-1

Course Technology
5191 Natorp Boulevard
Mason, OH 45040
USA

Cengage Learning is a leading provider of customized learning solutions with office locations around the globe, including Singapore, the United Kingdom, Australia, Mexico, Brazil, and Japan. Locate your local office at **international.cengage.com/region**

Cengage Learning products are represented in Canada by Nelson Education, Ltd.

To learn more about Course Technology, visit **www.cengage.com/coursetechnology**

Purchase any of our products at your local college store or at our preferred online store **www.ichapters.com**

Printed in the United States of America
4 5 6 7 8   16 15 14 13 12

FD249

To Rhonda, Rachel, Alex and Meghan,
Thank you for your loving support.

—*MEW*

Thanks to my family for your support
and understanding.

—*HJM*

CONTENTS

PREFACE

The need for information security education is self-evident. Education is one of the recognized needs to combat the threats facing information security. These readings provide students with a depth of content and analytical perspective not found in other textbooks. The fundamental tenet of *Readings and Cases in the Management of Information Security* is that information security in the modern organization is a problem for management and not a problem of technology—a problem that has important economic consequences and for which management will be held accountable. It is a further observation that the subject of information security is not presently widely included in the body of knowledge presented to most students enrolled in schools of business. This is true even within areas of concentration such as technology management and IT management. This textbook is suitable for course offerings to complement programs that adopt any one of the existing Course Technology textbooks. *Readings and Cases in the Management of Information Security* can be used to support *Principles of Information Security*, Second Edition, or *Management of Information Security* to further provide educational support for these markets.

PURPOSE AND INTENDED AUDIENCE

This readings text provides materials that give additional detail and depth on the management overview of information security to information security instructors and lecturers. These readings and cases can support a senior undergraduate or graduate information security class, or information technology class that requires additional depth in the area of information security. The cases can be used to enable individual or team projects, or used to support classroom discussion or writing assignments. This readings text can be used to support course delivery for both information security-driven programs targeted at Information Technology students and also IT management and technology management curricula aimed at business or technical management students.

SCOPE

Note that the title denotes support for the management of an information security program or organization. Current information security literature now acknowledges the dominant need to protect information, including the protection of the systems that transport, store and process it, whether those systems are technology- or human-based. The scope of the readings in the text covers fundamental areas of management of information security. The authors and many of the contributors are Certified Information Systems Security Professionals (CISSP).

FEATURES

- Designed for use with other information security textbook offerings, this text adds current research, informed opinion and fictional scenarios to your classroom.
- Prepares students for situations in the information security industry with articles, best practices, and cases relating to today's security issues.
- Creates an interactive classroom by using the readings as discussion starters and using the scripted questions when provided in several of the cases.

OVERVIEW OF THE TEXT

In addition to being an introduction to the text, we expect this section will also serve as a guidepost, directing students to relevant readings and cases.

Part One: Readings in the Management of Information Security

Reading 1. Mobile Device Security Management, Benjamin J. Halpert
Mobile devices, including Personal Digital Assistants (PDAs), mobile phones, laptops, smart phones, and removable media, can expose organizational data if not properly protected. This reading will cover different device types, areas of concern, and proposed solutions to mitigate the risks when using a mobile device.

Reading 2. Linking Business Objectives and Security Directives, Donald L. Pipkin
Security reduces a business's financial risk by enabling the organization to enter new markets and by increasing reliability. The foundation of information security must be firmly grounded in the objectives of the organization. Security decisions affect technology and people; however, security decisions must be based on business needs. Many companies suffer from not aligning the security plan to the business plan. This often leads to a security program which does not fit company culture.

Reading 3. Managing Incident Response, David M. Shackleford
Incident response, rather than being solely a technical discipline, is more a methodology concerned with the coordination of several technical and non-technical components. This discussion of incident response will cover the response methodology espoused by the National Institute of Standards and Technology (NIST) Special Publication 800-61. Each stage of the system will be covered at a high level, with techniques and methods commonly employed. The management of such a system will be evaluated, as well, with a discussion of the ISO 17799 components involved in assessing an organization's incident handling and response capabilities. Finally, sample incident types will be covered, as well as an open-source incident response management system currently being developed.

Reading 4. Zen and the Art of Information Security—A Philosophical, Spiritual and Mystical Approach to Protecting Information, Michael E. Whitman; Herbert J. Mattord
In this reading, the authors take a tongue-in-cheek approach to examining some important issues in information security. By relating key security topics to recognized "philosophical, spiritual, and mystical" allusions, they are better able to present these important messages in a format that promises to increase the awareness and retention of the readers.

Here the intellectual musings on the subject of information security include references to Sun Tzu, Socrates, Nietzsche, Winston Churchill, and others.

Reading 5. The Role of Information Security and Its Relationship to Information Technology Risk Management, Chrisan Herrod
Information Security is considered a risk management strategy and as such forms the foundation of an IT risk management program. This reading documents the evolution of information security as an IT risk management best practice; compares and contrasts risk management methodologies and strategies with an emphasis on developing return-on-investment; and documents IT risk management and information security's key role in managing compliance and meeting legislative requirements.

Reading 6. Architecting and Managing Secure Biometric Systems, Kameswara Raonamudur; Savitha S. Kadiyala
The field of biometrics, which involves life measurement, is perceived by many as overly intrusive. The challenge arises when designing a biometric solution that balances the needs of the system with the privacy issues of the individuals and the intrusiveness. In this reading, the authors provide an

overview of the biometric technologies currently in use. They also detail the implementation and management challenges associated with building and administration of example technologies. These challenges include capturing, processing, and generating new signatures and user records. While standards are emerging for these new technologies, most are so new that there are few recommendations for implementing biometrics. The authors also address the challenges with performance measures, including the reliability and confidentiality of the systems.

Reading 7. Integration and Ethical Perspectives for Information Systems Management, Ernest A. Capozzoli; Robert D. Winsor; Sheb L. True
The current business environment can be described as turbulent, full of uncertainty, and highly competitive. The demand for robust, highly integrated systems that are capable of crossing organizational lines, and corporate boundaries, as well as national boundaries, requires extra vigilance on the part of organizations to ensure ethical development and compliance. Ensuring that ethical considerations are thoroughly incorporated into business strategies that are in turn fully supported by Information Technology (IT) or Information Systems (IS) strategies is a daunting task. As such, the purpose of this reading is to provide a discussion of key issues associated with the process of linking and aligning business strategies, IS strategies, and ethical concerns for multiple stakeholders.

Reading 8. Security Education, Training, and Awareness from a Human Performance Technology Point of View, Melissa J. Dark
This reading focuses on the role of security education, training, and awareness (SETA) in an organization's overall information security strategy. Information security is about more than technology; it includes people and process as well as technology. In fact, the "people" piece of the security puzzle is perhaps the most critical for several reasons. Information technology is becoming more sophisticated and complex, yet in order to market products to lay users, vendors are creating applications that are seemingly easy to use. The ease of use often masks security issues and concerns. The lack of understanding of security issues coupled with the pervasive and growing use of computers by the general population makes people a critical factor in the information security equation.

Reading 9. The Provision of Defenses Against Internet-Based Attacks, Li-Chiou Chen; Thomas A. Longstaff; Kathleen M. Carley
This reading investigates the technological factors and economic factors in providing defenses against DDOS attacks, asking how Internet Service Providers (ISPs) can provide DDOS defenses to their subscribers. Many defenses that mitigate the effect of ongoing DDOS attacks have been proposed, but none of them have been widely deployed on the Internet

infrastructure at this point because of a lack of understanding in the trade-offs inherent in the complex system of attacks and defenses. The reading provides recommendations for subscribers, ISPs, and policy makers in making decisions about deploying DDOS defenses. This reading aims to increase the reader's understanding of these tradeoffs and to derive insights that will enable a more secure infrastructure.

Reading 10. **Trust, Controls, and Information Security**, Irene Woon; Atreyi Kankanhalli

From the employee point of view, higher levels of trust can lead to higher levels of job satisfaction and organizational commitment and consequently to lower levels of organizational crime, i.e., trust may have a positive effect on security. In order to tease out the apparently contradictory effects of trust on information security effectiveness, a study was designed to examine the relationships between managers' trust in employees, controls exercised on employees, and information security effectiveness. Although trust has been studied in a variety of contexts, it has not been investigated in the context of security controls and information security effectiveness. This reading provides a review of related literature, then a description and test of a model to explain the role of trust and controls in information security, followed by future trends and implications.

Reading 11. **Hierarchical Model of Organizational Work in the Sphere of Information Security**, Alexander Anisimov

The major perspective of this reading is to present the overview of the most important aspects of organizational work in the sphere of information security. It should support clear understanding of the fact that managerial work in information security may be performed at different organizational levels and may have different aims. At the same time, all the directions of this work are more or less closely connected and require consistent methodological and managerial support. The purpose of this reading is to develop and present the overall hierarchical model of organizational work in the sphere of information security that could reflect all the major levels and situations at which organizational issues are usually important. Practical importance of this model and the perspectives of its further development and usage are also considered.

Reading 12. **Transparency in Information Security System Design**, Herbert J. Mattord; Michael E. Whitman

Those who are trusted to protect the common good are faced with the temptation of abusing their positions for personal gain. In the information-driven age of the 21st century, control of information systems and their contents is already one of the most powerful and valuable roles in society. The challenge that faces the designers of such information systems is to make sure that the resulting systems perform as designed while also meeting security and transparency needs. This means that systems should provide essential confidentiality, integrity and availability as indicated by organizational policy. They should be resistant to unauthorized uses, and that they also do not have the unintended consequences of misuse by those seeking to gain or retain power at the expense of the privacy rights of the various constituencies that may use the systems.

Part Two: Cases in the Management of Information Security

Case A. Computer Gaming Technologies—CGT, Inc., Michael E. Whitman; Herbert J. Mattord

This case is meant to provide the student with an opportunity to prepare a bid response to a request for a comprehensive security review. Sufficient detail is provided to enable the student, working independently or in a team, to prepare a suitably detailed response.

Case B. Assessing and Mitigating the Risks to a Hypothetical Computer System, National Institute of Standards and Technology (NIST); Technology Administration; U.S. Department of Commerce

This case illustrates how a hypothetical government agency (HGA) deals with computer security issues in its operating environment. It follows the evolution of HGA's initiation of an assessment of the threats to its computer security system all the way through to HGA's recommendations for mitigating those risks.

Case C. Random Widget Works, Michael E. Whitman; Herbert J. Mattord

This case is drawn from *Management of Information Security,* a Course Technology textbook (©2004, ISBN 0-619-21515-1). This version of the case has been lightly edited.

Case D. Sequential Label Supply, Herbert J. Mattord; Michael E. Whitman

This case is drawn from the second edition of *Principles of Information Security,* a Course Technology textbook (©2005, ISBN 0-619-21625-5). This version of the case has been lightly edited.

Case E. Brightington Academy, Michael E. Whitman; Herbert J. Mattord

This case provides a different perspective on the need for information security, taking the form of an educational institution. While private industry has more control over its computing resources, academic institutions typically desire to sponsor academic freedom and the creative pursuits of scholarly work. As such there are typically fewer restrictions on faculty, staff, and student computer uses.

Case F. The 9/11 Commission Report, Herbert J. Mattord; Michael E. Whitman

A defining event in the political and cultural landscape of the 21st century occurred on September 11, 2001. The terrorist attack on that date has served not only as an alarm about national security in general but also to underscore several issues in the realm of information security, specifically the critical role of the incident response plan. This case addresses those sections of the report from the 9/11 Commission that are concerned with that end. Each excerpt is introduced with a short description in italics and followed with suggestions for classroom discussion and/or short writing assignments.

ACKNOWLEDGEMENTS AND THANKS

The authors would like to thank the following individuals for their assistance in making this text a reality.

- From Mike Whitman: To my loving family for their unwavering support during the writing of this work. Thanks to all others who have had a hand in this effort.

- From Herb Mattord: I would not be able to make the commitment of the time it takes to write without the support of my family. Thanks for your understanding.

- To the hard working, dedicated development team at Course Technology: thanks for your patience and tolerance in the development of this endeavor.

- All the students in the Information Security and Assurance Certificate courses at Kennesaw State University for their assistance in testing, debugging and suffering through the various writing projects undertaken by the authors.

- Special thanks to the authors and their reviewers who contributed these works.

Readings in the Management of Information Security

Objective

This collection of twelve readings is intended to provide a student in the field of information security management with opportunities to gain insight into several of the many aspects of the field. Some of the readings in this section are very theoretical, prepared with an academic treatment of the material, meant to pique the reader's interest into more specialized areas of the discipline. Others are very practical, meant to convey the best practices used by practitioners in the field to the future Information Security Officer (ISO). Some of the readings provide a mixture of the two extremes, offering good advice about management practices that are founded on solid theoretical structure.

Mobile Device Security Management

BENJAMIN J. HALPERT
Lockheed Martin

Benjamin Halpert currently works at Lockheed Martin where he specializes in information security. During his tenure with Lockheed Martin, he has worked on a multitude of significant projects. Mr. Halpert's areas of specialization within the information security field include emerging technology research, mobile and wireless technologies, and privacy protection. He was a contributing editor to the Wireless Network Security: 802.11, Bluetooth, and Handheld Devices Special Publication for the National Institute of Standards and Technology (NIST).

Additionally, he serves as an adjunct instructor for the Internet Safety Program on behalf of the Georgia Bureau of Investigation (GBI).

Mr. Halpert is also a frequent presenter at Lockheed Martin sponsored events and industry conferences including the RSA Conference and the Vanguard Enterprise Security Expo.

His memberships in the information security field include The Open Group Security Forum, the Information Systems Security Association (ISSA), the International Information Systems Forensics Association (IISFA), and InfraGard.

Mr. Halpert is currently pursuing a PhD in Information Systems from Nova Southeastern University. He earned his Master's degree in Management with a concentration in Technology from Rensselaer Polytechnic Institute. He graduated Cum Laude with a Bachelors of Business Administration in Management Information Systems (MIS) from the University of Georgia. Mr. Halpert holds several certifications, including Certified Information Systems Security Professional (CISSP) and Certified Wireless Network Administrator (CWNA).

Overview

With the dramatic explosion in the popularity of mobile devices, securing the data associated with these small, portable devices has become an increasingly difficult challenge. This paper provides an overview of the issues specifically associated with the security of these devices with recommendations on methods of mitigating risks unique to mobile technology.

As the author states: "Mobile devices can expose organizational data if not properly protected." Mobile devices come in many form factors.

The majority of devices that are classified as mobile include Personal Information Managers (PIMs), Personal Digital Assistants (PDAs), mobile phones, smart phones, camera phones, laptops, tablet personal computers (PCs), and removable storage media. To make the challenge more difficult to manage, many of these devices use proprietary or non-standard operating systems. In addition, many of these devices have removable media which further distribute the risk, and thus should not be overlooked.

Since these devices are so popular and so small, the author emphasizes that they have "become a target for individuals and groups involved in government espionage, corporate espionage, hacking, and device theft. As of the last report to Congress, there are 75 known countries, both allies and enemies of the United States, that are actively pursuing U.S. technologies. From a device theft standpoint, mobile phones were targeted in roughly 28 percent of all robberies." Add to this the loss from employee carelessness and damage from misuse, and the risk of lost, stolen, or unavailable information increases exponentially.

Before considering mitigation strategies, the organization must also realize that most of these devices (approximately 97 percent) are personal properties and thus not under direct control of the organization. In this reading, the author provides a number of discrete recommendations that will assist the organization and their employees in managing this increasingly diverse and vulnerable class of technology.

Introduction

Mobile device security is a major concern for organizations. Because of their small size, memory capability, and the ease with which information can be downloaded and removed from a facility, mobile devices pose a risk to organizations when used and transported outside physical boundaries. Mobile devices, including Personal Digital Assistants (PDAs), mobile phones, laptops, smart phones, and removable media, can expose organizational data if not properly protected. Subsequent sections will cover different device types, areas of concern, and proposed solutions to mitigate the risks when using a mobile device. Wireless security issues are an integral part of assessing an organization's mobile device risk posture. However, discussion of wireless security is out of scope for this discussion.

Mobile Device Types

The issue of security for mobile devices is based on a concern for securing data once it leaves the physical boundaries of an organization. Maintaining the confidentiality, integrity, and availability of sensitive or proprietary data is paramount. Mobile devices come in many form factors. The majority of devices that are classified as mobile include Personal Information Managers (PIMs), Personal Digital Assistants (PDAs), mobile phones, smart phones, camera phones, laptops, tablet personal computers (PCs), and removable storage media.

PIMs, PDAs, smart phones, and camera phones utilize operating systems such as Palm OS, Windows CE, Pocket PC, Smartphone 2002, Symbian,

EPOC, and Linux. Laptop and Tablet PCs typically run more resource demanding operating systems to include Windows XP Professional, Mac OS X, and numerous Linux variants. Mobile devices are morphing into new form factors not traditionally associated with PDAs. For example, Fossil has a product line called TECH. The TECH line has Wrist PDAs running the full PalmOne operating system[i] and Wrist Net products from Microsoft.[ii]

Removable media are also classified as mobile devices. Some examples of high density removable media include CompactFlash (CF), Secure Digital (SD), Memory Sticks, and removable USB drives, among others. The risk associated with portable MP3 (music) and MPEG (video) players should also be addressed by organizations. MP3 and MPEG players are essentially portable hard drives. Additionally, protection of data on traditional media including floppy disks, CDs, and DVDs should not be overlooked when developing mobile device protection and management strategies.

One aspect that all mobile device types share is that they all lack adequate security mechanisms. Although many mobile devices have some security functionality built-in, it is always optional and for the most part, designed poorly.[iii] As a result, third party security products will need to be evaluated and utilized to mitigate some of the risks of using mobile devices. The security ramifications of this fact will be explored further in subsequent sections.

Areas of Concern

Organizations are concerned about employee use of mobile device technologies for a multitude of reasons. First, the devices themselves are compact and have ever expanding internal memory capabilities. Beyond the device memory capabilities, most mobile devices can accommodate removable media that can store data, currently up to 1 Gigabyte, on SD cards that are roughly the size of a postage stamp. Both the combination of the portable device size, and the additional removable memory capacity, create opportunities for sensitive, export-controlled, and proprietary data to be removed from a facility and stored in an insecure fashion.

Mobile devices have become a target for individuals and groups involved in government espionage, corporate espionage, hacking, and device theft. As of the last report to Congress, there are 75 known countries, both allies and enemies of the United States, that are actively pursuing U.S. technologies.[iv] From a device theft standpoint, mobile phones were targeted in roughly 28 percent of all robberies.[v]

Not only do organizations need to be aware of espionage and theft related activities, but employee forgetfulness and oversight must also be addressed. Hurried travelers left 62,000 mobile phones, 2,900 laptops, and 1,300 PDAs in London taxi cabs over a six month period. That is an average of three phones per taxi.[vi]

Risk Mitigation Strategies

When analyzing risk mitigation techniques, organizations need to realize that 97 percent of the more than 3 million handheld devices deployed in the United States and used by employees are personally owned devices.[vii]

The ramifications of this fact are far reaching. Not only does an organization need to establish the proper processes, technologies, and awareness programs for the "approved" or "standard" device types, but they also must address the other 97 percent of devices that may be used within the organization. All risk mitigation strategies should be based on a risk assessment and subsequently detailed in policy.

GENERAL PROTECTION STRATEGIES

All mobile devices that may store, process, or transmit sensitive or proprietary data should utilize protection mechanisms that are commensurate with the mobile device capabilities. The data at rest on the device and the transmission of data to and from the device must be protected. As previously mentioned, do not rely solely on built-in security features of mobile devices. Many vulnerabilities have been discovered that limit the trustworthiness of such mechanisms.

The following is a non-exhaustive listing of risk mitigation strategies organizations should take to protect sensitive data on mobile devices:

- Utilize strong passwords consisting of alpha-numeric characters that are at least eight characters long and are unique.
- Install third party software protection mechanisms that can encrypt the contents of the mobile device, lock the device after a pre-specified time frame has passed, and wipe all the data from the device if the wrong password is entered more than the preset limit. Additional features to look for include the ability to disable Bluetooth, Infrared, Wi-Fi, and microphone functionality.
- Encrypt the device transmissions, while using appropriate n-factor security mechanisms. A two-factor example would be a password with an authentication token.
- Install and update virus protection on all mobile devices. Many vendors produce anti-virus products for Tablet and Laptop PCs. The market for mobile anti-virus solutions is beginning to emerge. The most important aspect of mobile device anti-virus capability is to have the product do on-access scanning. Many of the current products only provide on-demand scanning, which is insufficient.[viii,ix]
- If a mobile device has wired or wireless network access capabilities, utilize a mobile firewall.
- To ensure both personal and organizational-provided mobile devices are protected when storing or transmitting sensitive data, device management capabilities should be employed. This would include auto-discovery of devices upon connecting to the organization's network.
- Ensure that your organization has a mobile device policy that employees are familiar with.
- Create an awareness campaign to spread the word about mobile device security weakness and what employees can do to secure organizational, as well as personal, data on a mobile device. Utilize current communication channels to raise awareness. Some suggestions include holding Lunch and Learn sessions and presenting at organization events whenever possible.

CAMERA PHONE PROTECTION STRATEGIES

In addition to the general risk mitigation techniques as described earlier, camera phones pose additional risks to organizational data and individual privacy. Many companies, including BMW, DaimlerChrysler, and Samsung, prohibit camera phones from being brought onto company premises for fear that proprietary manufacturing methods and documentation may be photographed and removed from a facility. Additionally, many schools and health clubs have banned camera phones from locker rooms due to personal privacy issues.[x] Organizations will soon be hard pressed to procure mobile phones, smart phones, and PDAs that do not have integrated digital cameras.

USB MEMORY DEVICE PROTECTION STRATEGIES

USB memory devices come in many form factors. Some look like normal writing pens while others fit on a key chain. Data can be removed easily from a facility if USB devices are allowed to be used. Even if prohibited, it may be hard to control the devices entering and exiting a facility.

Some techniques an organization can utilize to limit USB use are:

- Disable USB ports on servers and other systems containing sensitive data.
- Disable auto-mounting features.
- Prevent auto-installation of necessary drivers.
- Restrict user access to existing devices.

For securely transmitting data on a USB memory device, PGP can be used to encrypt the device contents. Alternatively, a secure USB product, such as the Memory Experts International ClipDriveBio and the SONY Puppy, which provide data security via AES encryption and two-factor user authentication, password and finger-print biometric, can be utilized.[xi,xii,xiii]

Conclusion

Mobile device security is a major concern for organizations. Because of their small size, memory capability, and the ease with which information can be downloaded and removed from a facility, mobile devices pose a risk to organizations when used and transported outside physical boundaries. Familiarity with the different device types, areas of concern, and proposed solutions to mitigate the risks when using a mobile device are important for an organization to grasp prior to rolling out mobile devices to employees. Management of mobile devices must be coordinated in order to ensure sensitive, export-controlled, and proprietary data remains protected, no matter the device utilized.

References

[i]*Palm: Wrist PDA*. Retrieved September 24, 2004, from *http://www.fossil.com/ jump.jsp?iMainCat=447&itemType=CATEGORY&itemID=448*

[ii]Microsoft. *Wrist net*. Retrieved from September 24, 2004, from http://www.fossil. com/jump.jsp?iMainCat=450&itemType=CATEGORY&itemID=451

[iii]Ayers, R., & Jansen, W. (2004, August). Draft NIST Special Publication 800-72, Guidelines on PDA forensics. Retrieved August 24, 2004, from http://csrc.nist. gov/publications/drafts/draft-SP800-72.pdf

[iv]Annual Report to Congress on Foreign Economic Collection and Industrial Espionage—2002. (2003, February). Retrieved February 23, 2004, from *http://www.ncix. gov/news/2003/may/Annual_Economic_Report_Version.pdf*

[v]Mobile phone crime prompts UK gov't to call for help. (2002, January 8). *IT World*. Retrieved February 23, 2004, from *http://www.itworld.com/Tech/2987/IDG020108phonetheft/pfindex.html*

[vi]Taxis a haven for forgotten goodies. (2001, August 30). *BBC News*. Retrieved February 23, 2004, from *http://news.bbc.co.uk/1/hi/uk/1518105.stm*

[vii]Walking disasters. (200, April 24). *Computer World*. Retrieved February 23, 2004, from *http://www.computerworld.com/news/2000/story/0,11280,46867,00.html*

[viii]*F-Secure Anti-Virus*™ *for Pocket PC*. Retrieved September 24, 2004, from *http://www.f-secure.com/wireless/pocketpc/pocketpc-av.shtml*

[ix]*Trend Micro PC-cillin for Wireless*. Retrieved September 24, 2004, from *http://www.trendmicro.com/en/products/desktop/pcc-wireless/evaluate/overview.htm*

[x]*Camera phones don't click at work*. (2004, January 12). Retrieved September 24, 2004, from *http://www.usatoday.com/money/workplace/2004-01-12-phones_x.htm*

[xi]PGP Corporation. Retrieved September 24, 2004, from *http://www.pgp.com*

[xii]*Memory experts international ClipDrive Bio*. Retrieved September 24, 2004, from *http://www.clip-drive.com/product_clipdrive_bio.htm*

[xiii]Sony Electronics, Inc. Retrieved September 24, 2004, from *http://bssc.sel.sony. com/Professional/puppy/products.htm*

Linking Business Objectives and Security Directives

DONALD L. PIPKIN
Halting the Hacker, LLC

Donald L. Pipkin, CISSP, CISM, is an information security architect with over 20 years of experience in the industry. He is an internationally renowned security expert and a frequent speaker on security. He is the author of Halting the Hacker: A Practical Guide to Computer Security, *and* Information Security: Protecting the Global Enterprise, *as well as numerous articles on information security.*

As a Certified Information Systems Security Professional and a Certified Information Security Manager, he is versed in all aspects of security, including policy and procedures, and has hands-on experience with computer intrusions. He has made presentations on security at various conferences from a regional to an international level.

In his business, Halting the Hacker, LLC, he works to improve security through understanding by consulting on development of policies and procedures, offering security awareness programs and developing and delivering education and training on security technologies and products.

Overview

In this paper, renowned information security professional Donald Pipkin addresses the critical area of linking information security to the organization's business objectives. It is a well-known fact that when information security and business collide, security loses. In order to avoid this conflict, and more closely align the information security effort to support the organization's mission and operations, the information security executive planning team must begin by understanding the mission, vision, and strategy of the organization, and then seeking to determine how the security directives can best support each. As strategy is translated into tactical and operational planning, the specifics of integrating information security functions into the organization's core business efforts become more critical. As the author states: "As a business process, security directives must align with business objectives. Close alignment improves both the ability to integrate security into the processes and the level of acceptance of security when it is seen as part of the business process. An enterprise's culture has many aspects, which may include business objectives, principles, policies, management processes, and people's beliefs and practices. The degree of security needed depends on the culture and the people."

In order to make this alignment work, the information security executive planning committee must have support from top management. "A security program's success is dependent on being widely accepted, and to be well-accepted the security program needs to fit the organization." As this chapter illustrates, without this acceptance and support, the program will inevitably collide with the business, and be ineffective.

Introduction

Security reduces a business's financial risk by enabling the organization to enter new markets and by increasing reliability. The foundation of information security must be firmly grounded in the objectives of the organization. Security decisions affect technology and people; however, security decisions must be based on business needs. Many companies suffer from not aligning the security plan to the business plan. This often leads to a security program which does not fit company culture.

Business Objectives

Business objectives provide a complete picture of the goals of the organization, starting at the top with broad-based long term goals. At subsequent levels they provide more specific and measurable goals.

VISION

An organization's vision is a statement of its core values. They are the fundamental ideas in which the organization believes. An organization's vision sets the mood for the entire organization, defining the corporate culture. This is what makes one company feel like a family-run business, while another feels like a big corporation. It defines the openness of the organization, how easy it is to approach management, and the value of individual initiative.

The vision should be a guide to action. It should provide a guidepost for the members of the organization to endeavor to put into practice. It should not change unless there is a fundamental change in the company.

A clear and well-articulated vision attracts people whose personal values are in harmony with the company. This creates compatibility among the organization's members. The vision should guide your organization's members in performing their work. It should challenge and inspire the group to achieve its mission.

MISSION

A mission statement defines the organization's reason for being, its purpose. It should clearly state what the organization seeks to accomplish. It should be realistic and credible, well-articulated and easily understood, appropriate and ambitious.

Great companies not only exist to create a financial return to their investors, they exist to perform a greater good. They have a desire to, in some way, improve the human condition—a mission. Missions do not have to be grandiose. They can be simple and specific as in the case of one dentist: "to give everyone a smile they are proud to share."

A mission is ongoing, and not completely attainable. It always leaves something to strive for. Yet, it should be in some way achievable so that the work which is accomplished is obviously moving the organization toward its mission, with the knowledge that there is always more to do.

Organizations with a clear unwavering focus on their mission often crystallize their business around it. It becomes an enduring tag line, which is synonymous with the company.

STRATEGY

An organization's strategy defines how it plans to accomplish its mission. It defines the activities or programs the organization chooses in order to pursue its purpose. It assigns targets or goals, which are what needs to be accomplished to be considered successful.

Business strategies cannot be created in a vacuum, they must be built on an understanding of what the organization can provide, which is not currently being adequately provided. This requires an understanding of the market or industry as a whole and the other players in the market—the competition.

- **Market analysis** is the process of identifying the market of which the organization is part and determining what market factors provide opportunities to the organization. It should determine if these changes create opportunities for the organization.
- **Competitive analysis** is the process of identifying the other organizations in the market; determining the part they play in the market; and identifying gaps or shortcomings, which could be opportunities. This analysis is used to determine what sets the organization apart from the competition. Are there things which it does differently? Better? Will the customer perceive these differences as improvements?
- **Product analysis** is the process of evaluating the other products or services in the market to determine how well they address the customer's needs. This analysis will also highlight any missing or inadequate features, which could be an opportunity for the organization.

Strategies are considered long-term goals. However, they may need to be changed in response to changes in the market, competition, or products.

TACTICS

Tactics define how the organization is going to use the opportunities that it has identified to be successful in the market—how to implement the strategy. Tactics have short-term goals, which can be measured and evaluated as to their level of success so that the tactics can be adjusted to better meet their goals. Tactics identify the goals of how to position products or services, where to sell them, and who the target customers are.

Tactics are managed locally, possibly at a regional area. This smaller scope and shorter time frame allow tactics to be adjusted and tuned to local needs addressing issues of local importance, while still following the strategic direction.

OPERATIONS

Operations are the day-to-day working of the organization. Operations are concerned with the ability to effectively perform the work efficiently and sustainably. Well run organizations evaluate the costs of operations, looking for optimal methods that can be repeated to produce consistent results.

Operations are concerned with a high level of customer satisfaction and retention to maintain the lower costs of repeat business, and are focused on controlling costs and expenses to maintain an appropriate level of profitability.

Security Directives

Security is a business process. Security directives define how safety and security integrate into the business process. Selecting the right level and type of security should be based on a clear understanding of the business assets and processes, their values, the business impact if they are compromised, and the concerns of the organizations. Security must enhance the organization's profitability and productivity and provide stability in its operation.

As a business process, security directives must align with business objectives. Close alignment improves both the ability to integrate security into the processes and the level of acceptance of security when it is seen as part of the business process. An enterprise's culture has many aspects, which may include business objectives, principles, policies, management processes, and people's beliefs and practices. The degree of security needed depends on the culture and the people.

PHILOSOPHIES

An organization's security philosophy is a high-level executive position statement that gives direction and relative importance to the areas addressed. The language used in a security vision will be similar to that used in the organization's vision and mission. The high-level security vision statements of many organizations will look very similar. However, as the vision is expanded, statements that appear similar can have very different implications for different organizations.

Security philosophies reflect the culture of the organization. Some organizations provide a great deal of independence and freedom so that each individual can decide on the best way they can contribute to the organization. Other organizations are very rigid in the manner each individual is to perform the duties that are required. Most organizations are somewhere between these two extremes, giving the individual a certain level of independence within guidelines and specific limits.

A security philosophy will provide a foundation for easy-to-use, business-enabling information services that allow appropriate and secure access to information while ensuring protection against unauthorized access. It will define if access is to be freely granted or if it will require extensive validation. It will describe if authorizations will be broadly managed or tightly controlled, and if these controls will be widely distributed or tightly maintained by a limited few. An information security philosophy encompasses broad concepts of trust and protection.

- **Trust** is the level of confidence needed in the individuals, applications, equipment, transactions, and business functions that utilize the information. Trust determines who gets what authorizations, what processes have what privileges, who administers the systems, and who monitors which security services.
- **Protection** is the level of control, integrity, and auditing in your business and security practices. Protection determines the level of integrity checking required for transactions and information, the level of access controls, and the use of encryption and cryptography.

Security is often seen as a balancing act between the level of trust an organization puts in its employees and the level of controls it implements to monitor its employees. The correct balance for an organization is determined by its culture, what the organization is doing, and the criticalness of the resources with which the organization is working. These environments are often described as open or closed. An open environment is one where anything is permitted unless it is specifically denied, and a closed environment is one where everything is prohibited unless it is specifically allowed. Implementing security in a completely open or completely closed environment is simple. However, few organizations are completely open or completely closed, which make the issues with implementing security more difficult—defining what is allowed and what is denied.

PRINCIPLES

Principles take the philosophy and refine it into specific terms. They are the standards by which an organization conducts itself. They are the moral grounding—the conscience of the organization. They define corporate integrity. They are a reflection of the organization's culture and environment and must be created and promoted by management. They are often built directly on the beliefs of the founder of the organization. They create the standards to which all policies must adhere and define the structure in which policies are developed. They are often located in the statement of business conduct.

Security principles build the security architecture, which addresses broad topics and serves to ensure a common level of understanding and a common framework for design and implementation. A security architecture is usually defined as a blueprint showing the building blocks of a structure. The information security architecture covers the processes and conceptual aspects of information security, as well as technology, infrastructure, and services. A successful architecture must consider the company culture and the people, in addition to security technology and infrastructure. The culture and people are the supporting foundation of the security program and are almost always the determining factor of program success.

A security architecture is a definition of the basic principles with which a security implementation can be built. It is needed to achieve consistent and complete security infrastructure and to reduce fragmented and inconsistent efforts while working to meet security objectives that can be qualified and quantified, establish a formal baseline for future audits, and establish duties, responsibilities, and communication paths.

The security strategy is the approach that is taken to express the management's desire in a coherent manner. A security strategy is built with rules and guidelines.

- **Rules** define specific bounds in which the system must operate. They relate to an entire information systems structure and anyone with access—employees, family members, contractors, clients, vendors, partners, customers, etc.
- **Guidelines** assist in effectively securing the systems. The nature of guidelines, however, immediately recognizes that systems vary considerably, and imposition of standards is not always achievable, appropriate, or cost-effective. For example, an organizational guideline may be used to help develop system-specific standard procedures. Guidelines are often used to help ensure that specific security measures are not overlooked, although they can be implemented, and correctly so, in more than one way.

A good architecture will make security easier for people to use, and will empower the business. It improves credibility and visibility for information system initiatives, avoids disputes, and reduces internal political struggles.

The information security architecture should be independent of any specific technologies. It should support a heterogeneous, multi-vendor environment.

POLICIES

Policies are technology-independent descriptions of the security precautions that are required for different types of information and access. Quite often security policies apply to more than just information; they apply to all corporate resources. They should change only rarely and then only with the endorsement of management.

Policies are the primary building blocks for every information security design, defining the responsibilities of the organization, the individual, and management.

Policies specify what must or must not be done to fulfill the principles. Policies protect information, people, property, and reputation. They should be short, precise, and easy to understand.

Creating information security policies and procedures is no small task. It requires evaluation of information and systems, assignment of ownership and responsibilities and, most importantly, it requires support from the top of the company down. It is more important that the CEO of a company support and follow the information security procedures than anyone else in the company. This is both because it shows the importance of the policies, and because the CEO has access to the most valuable information in the company.

It is only through the close alignment of business objectives with sound strategy that a set of policies can be developed to truly enhance the abilities of your organization.

Security strategy defines how to implement the vision in accordance with the architecture given the technological constraints. A strategy is a documented high-level plan for organization-wide computer and information security. It will define standards to which the security implementation should adhere. Standards should not address specific technologies—this has a tendency to stifle creativity. Rather, they should employ general technologies and concepts.

Standards define the level of security required for each environment. If a system is unable to implement a standard, an explanation should be required as to why this system should be exempt from the standard or how the system is going to reduce the risk without implementing the standard. Standards provide a framework for making specific decisions, such as which defense mechanisms to use and how to configure services, and are the basis for developing secure programming guidelines and procedures for users and system administrators to follow. Because a security policy is a long-term document, the contents avoid technology-specific issues.

- **Resource policies** define the security requirements for specific resources. Special handling policies should be limited to those resources which are particularly valuable, difficult to replace, or hazardous if improperly handled. Appropriate resource classification can streamline the assignment of resource policies to classes of resources with similar security and safety requirements.
- **Behavioral policies** define how individuals are to act with other individuals when this action would reflect on the organization. Most of these policies are found in the human resources employee documentation and define inappropriate or unacceptable behavior. They also address issues of misconduct and disciplinary actions for anyone who violates the behavioral procedures.
- **Process policies** define the security requirements in the performance of specific processes. Many processes will require specific security steps to maintain accountability, verify integrity, or provide safety. These security processes are necessary to ensure that security is preserved.

PROCEDURES

Procedures are definitions of how to implement the policies to a specific technology. They will change when the technology to which they pertain changes. Procedures will also identify those technologies that are unable to implement a policy and where variances are acceptable.

Procedures are the detailed instructions on how to meet the criteria defined in policies. They are essentially an instruction manual to give your user community the confidence to implement your controls successfully—they clearly explain the duties and responsibilities within the security design.

Procedures determine how standards should be implemented. Generally, they are written to apply to a class of systems that have similar attributes or security issues. Procedures must take into account the limitations of both the systems that are implementing them and current technology. Procedures are specific steps to follow that are based on the corporate security policy. They should be reviewed periodically to encompass new technologies.

- **Standards** are basic security requirements. They define an acceptable level of security to which every system must adhere.

* **Exceptions** are definitions of specific instances where the standards will not be implemented. This may be because of limitations of the information systems themselves or other factors. The exception must define how the security issues, addressed by the standard which was not implemented, will be addressed.

PRACTICES

Practices are the actual day-to-day operations that implement the procedures. They must take into account the business environment, the capabilities, and the resources of the organization, as well as the budgetary, social, and logistical pressures on the organization. However, they must maintain their consistency to create a uniform level of security throughout the enterprise.

Practices may be specific to a specific system. They are likely to be different for different locations and different types of systems. They identify tasks, individuals, and schedules. They create the basic job definition for the operators.

Security practices must be reviewed and updated often to reflect changes that influence the specific systems to which the practice applies, and they must be tested to assure that they work. These reviews should lead to constant improvement in quality.

System administration practices play a key role in network security. Checklists and general advice on good security practices are readily available.

* **Responsibilities** define who will be performing the actions indicated in the specific practice. They assign accountability to help assure that the work is done. They include who is responsible for performing the work, who is responsible for assuring the work is done, and who is responsible for verifying that the work was done correctly.
* **Schedules** indicate when the activities are to be done. This can be used to define when an activity is past due and should be considered delinquent. Schedules can be time-based, in which an activity has to be done on a regular schedule, or event-based, in which it has to be done in anticipation of or in response to another event.

Practices are found in the operational manuals used to train new employees and referenced by experienced workers. They must provide enough details so that any operational questions which arise are answered.

Bringing It Together

A security program requires support throughout the organization. Everyone from the top down has a role to play in making a security program work. It is important that everyone understands their role and is comfortable with it. Close alignment of business objectives and security directives helps ensure that the right level of detail is provided to the correct level of management in the organization.

The top-level management, who solidifies the business vision, is also responsible for endorsing the security philosophies. It is this endorsement which empowers the security program to implement and enforce the security directives.

Security principles, just like the business mission, set the direction for the organization. They define how things should be. They provide direction and limits to guide the development of detailed decisions. The organization's board of directors or steering committee is responsible for setting the direction of the organization.

An organization's long-term goals are expressed in its business strategies and security policies. They are applicable across the organization and rarely need to be changed. Long-term strategic goals illustrate the organization's risk tolerance. The security policies have to define the appropriate level of security to provide the level of comfort the organization needs.

Security procedures define how things are to be done. Like tactics, they can be molded to meet needs of specific situations. They must support the policies and provide actual hands-on processes. They require continuous measurement and monitoring to determine how well they are moving the organization toward its goals.

Practices and operations document the actual manner in which the procedures or tactics are implemented. They include the specific details needed so that the processes can be performed in a repeatable manner. They are how the organization works.

A security program's success is dependent on being widely accepted, and to be well-accepted the security program needs to fit the organization. This takes a close alignment between the organization's business objectives and its security directives as well as the proper level of support throughout the organization. Support is best found by involving the right level of management in developing the business objectives and security directives. Organizations survive on a common vision shared by everyone, moving together toward common goals and a common understanding of what risks and safeguards must be taken to be successful.

Managing Incident Response

DAVID M. SHACKLEFORD, CISSP, GSEC, GCIH, G7799, MCSE, MCIWA
Norfolk Southern

Dave M. Shackleford has been involved in Information Technology, particularly the arenas of networking and security, for over nine years. Dave has worked as a security architect and manager for a number of large companies, and has also run his own consulting practice for several years. His areas of specialty include incident-handling and response, intrusion detection and traffic analysis, and vulnerability assessment (penetration testing). He is an authorized grader, question writer, and editor for the SANS Institute, where he works with the GIAC certification division and proctors technical bootcamp sessions. Dave holds CISSP, GSEC, GCIH, G7799, MCSE, and MCIWA certifications, and is working on an MBA.

Overview

A key component of any organization's information security posture is the ability to detect and react to intrusions to the organization's systems and networks. In this reading, the author examines the field of incident response from both a technical and a non-technical standpoint.

Understanding events and incidents is important to understand the threats facing an organization's information and the defenses the organization can employ to protect against those threats. "An event is any occurrence in a system or network that we can observe. Not all events are destructive or malicious in nature. For instance, a batch job kicking off to store data to tape backups is an event. An incident is an event, or multiple events, that had some adverse impact on a network or system; the threat of this occurring can also be considered an incident in some cases. Often, incidents are comprised of multiple events, not all of which are negative."

In this reading, the author focuses on the "response methodology espoused by the National Institute of Standards and Technology (NIST) Special Publication 800-61... [and] ISO 17799 components involved in assessing an organization's incident-handling and response capabilities." The reading also examines sample incident types, reviewing options available to the organization, specifically focusing on open-source solutions.

Introduction

Incident response, rather than being solely a technical discipline, is more a methodology concerned with the coordination of several technical and non-technical components. Several phases of a response effort are typically included in any standard operating procedures, ranging from the pre-incident preparation to the post-incident discussions that will lead to process improvement. In between are elements of risk analysis, systems analysis, management coordination, and a variety of technical tasks including systems hardening, bit-level disk duplication, vulnerability testing, etc.

This discussion of incident response will cover the response methodology espoused by the National Institute of Standards and Technology (NIST) Special Publication 800-61.[1] Each stage of the system will be covered at a high level, with techniques and methods commonly employed. The management of such a system will be evaluated, as well, with a discussion of the ISO 17799 components involved in assessing an organization's incident-handling and response capabilities. Finally, sample incident types will be covered, as well as an open-source incident response management system currently being developed.

Risk Management

The management of information security is primarily a field of risk management; unless your organization is in the business of information security itself (by selling products or services), then information security is solely a function that costs the organization money most of the time...right? This is very obviously a leading question, and the answer will vary significantly depending on the person answering it. Often, senior management is of the opinion that information security is more an expense than an asset. One of the simplest ways to change senior management's minds is through the proper management and documentation of an organization's incident-handling function.

In its own right, the previous statement is somewhat of an oxymoron. If incident response is truly effective, then management will never actually experience any major downtime or loss of business function. However, in order to appreciate information security, management must be familiar with the consequences firsthand when information security fails. How, then, should information security managers best "sell" the information security aspect of an organization so that its true value is known and appreciated by upper management?

In the case of major, widespread incidents such as the SQL Slammer worm, Code Red and Nimda, new IIS exploits, and others, the impact in terms of financial loss and other factors is often made available very rapidly. Through Web sites such as the SANS Internet Storm Center (*http://www.incidents.org*), systems administrators, information security professionals, and incident handlers share information about attacks that are occurring and their impact. Many organizations are more willing than ever before to disclose the impact, using some quantitative metrics, of such major attacks. The successful information security manager will use this information to justify a properly organized incident-handling program in his/her organization. Many people tend to forget that information security is *supposed* to be uneventful. If chaos breaks out, usually something has gone wrong.

Events Lead to Incidents

It is important to understand the concepts of events and incidents. An event is any occurrence in a system or network that we can observe. Not all events are destructive or malicious in nature. For instance, a batch job kicking off to store data to tape backups is an event. An incident is an event, or multiple events, that had some adverse impact on a network or system; the threat of this occurring can also be considered an incident in some cases. Often, incidents are comprised of multiple events, not all of which are negative. Say, for instance, that a server application or service contains a flaw for which a patch has been released. Within a day or so, malicious code exploiting this flaw is published on the Internet, and systems are being compromised fairly rapidly. If your systems are not patched, but they need to be patched quickly, this is an incident. Regardless of whether the systems have been compromised or not, the need to coordinate personnel, evaluate systems, install software, possibly create firewall rules or intrusion detection signatures, update antivirus applications, and notify users is certainly a number of events that have possible adverse effects on systems or networks.

In evaluating each situation to determine whether it is an event or an incident, it is essential to fully examine its context. For instance, your organization's Virtual Private Network (VPN) server crashes at 3 a.m. What does this mean? It is certainly an event, but other factors and information are important, too. For instance, you might ask the following questions:

- What caused the system to crash?
- Who, if anyone, was connected to the system when it crashed?
- Does the server have a history of being unstable?
- Have any changes been made to the server or surrounding environment?
- Was there any strange network traffic prior to the crash?
- Etc. . .

Answering these types of questions will assist an experienced incident handler in determining whether an incident should be declared at all.

There are a number of sites on the Internet that can assist incident responders and information security personnel in evaluating whether events may indicate a current or future incident. One excellent resource is the SANS Internet Storm Center. At the time of this writing, the URL for this site was *http://isc.sans.org*. This site receives input from network and systems administrators, as well as security professionals, around the world. The incident handlers on duty correlate the input they receive and create trends and charts showing what security events are happening around the world. For example, if you suddenly notice that port 24689 is receiving huge quantities of connection attempts from all sorts of IP ranges, you may wonder what is going on. By gathering input rapidly from a wide variety of sources, the folks at the ISC may be able to provide you with some insight. The site keeps up-to-the-minute reports of port access attempts, top source IP's for access attempts and attacks, and other information related to worldwide incidents. Another site that typically maintains relevant incident data is the CERT Coordination Center (CERT/CC) at Carnegie Mellon University, available at *http://www.cert.org*.

Organizing the Response Team

There are several different models commonly used for organizing incident-handling and response teams. The first is the centralized team. This type of team is typically best in smaller organizations, or organizations with one main geographic location. This can be a very good model for several reasons. First, people who work together closely on a day-to-day basis tend to be more familiar with each other's work methods and habits, and understand how to interact well to get the job done. Second, availability of personnel is less of an issue here. If one incident handler is not available, the chances are good that another qualified team member will be. Finally, this is the simplest model to coordinate during an incident.

Another team model is the distributed Incident Response team. This model splits a central team into smaller teams that are located in different areas. This can work well in organizations that are very large or spread out. Typically, at least one person per location will be designated as a Lead Handler or Technical Lead to be a primary liaison for the rest of the group. The disadvantage to this model is that the Lead Handler can become a single point of failure very quickly. If the other members of the distributed teams are not up-to-speed on the incident-handling process, there may be a significant amount of confusion or initial lag time when an incident occurs. This model relies on a stringent protocol of communication, both inter- and intra-team.

The last major model of an Incident Response team is the coordinating team. In this model, an experienced team acts as a "guidance counsel" over another team or several smaller teams without actually having any authority over them. This model is better than the standard distributed model for many large organizations. In most large organizations, the majority of experienced IT workers are in a central location such as Headquarters, with other small teams spread out in other locations. Having the central Incident Response team coordinate with the others, providing guidance (even when they are not involved in the current incident), can really increase the efficiency and effectiveness of the outlying IR teams. This is a sort of "mentoring" situation; if companies are willing to expend the resources for this model to work, the rewards are usually worth it.

Staffing the Response Team

Each organization must decide the types of staff they wish to use in forming IR teams. Often, the majority of full-time employees lack the specific knowledge needed to act as a qualified incident handler. Contractors are often hired to "fill the gaps" in an organization's information security group; most teams are comprised of both employees and contractors. Another option that many organizations are pursuing is the partially outsourced option. For devices that required 24x7 monitoring, such as firewalls and Intrusion Detection System sensors, external companies can provide monitoring services, incident-handling, and support for less than it costs to maintain onsite staff in many cases. Finally, some organizations may choose a fully outsourced scenario, where the entire security function in an organization is handled by onsite contractors. This is usually implemented when the organization is severely lacking in in-house technical knowledge.

There are a number of factors related to staff that should be considered in developing an IR team. This will: 1) be a mission-critical function of the organization, and the incident-handling team will be on call 24 hours a day, 7 days a week; 2) over time lead to employee morale degradation and "burnout;" and 3) vary from organization to organization, depending on the number and intensity of incidents, as well as the people. Full-time incident handlers should be given extra time to rest, more training, and other small benefits that can help to circumvent burnout. Part-time incident handlers may not be as prone to morale problems. Other issues related to creating and managing incident-handling personnel include costs, expertise, and organizational structure. Obviously, the costs and expertise have a positive relationship. As one goes up, so does the other. Organizational structure, too, can play a major part in how personnel are managed. For instance, some companies are more prone to hire contractors than others. Depending on where an organization is located geographically, the talent pool for security professionals with incident-handling skills may be extensive or very dry. This will dictate costs, too, obviously.

Response Methodology

Incident response methodology has several distinct phases. In order, these are: Preparation, Identification, Containment, Eradication, Recovery, and Lessons Learned. The National Institute of Standards and Technology (NIST) has documented this basic method in Special Publication 800-61, "Computer Security Incident Handling Guide." This is the de facto standard in use today in many organizations, and will serve as the basis for discussion of the individual phases.

PREPARATION

The Preparation phase should be in effect year-round. This phase, while not technically performed during the actual incident, should be a component of an organization's Standard Operating Procedure (SOP), and various checks should be done continually to ensure readiness for incidents. This phase is really the most important step in Incident Response methodology, for several reasons. First, by thinking proactively, an organization will prepare for more possible contingencies. Second, the better an organization's preparation is, the more rapidly it will be able to respond in the case of an actual incident; this initial response often determines the overall severity of the incident as a whole.

The first area where preparation is very important is that of policy. All organizations should have some sort of established policies on acceptable use, privacy, and other topics related to information security. Smaller organizations may have one large policy with multiple sections, whereas larger organizations may have a number of distinct policies that explain the organization's stance on various issues in some detail. When incidents occur, these policies will serve as guideposts for handling issues that come up, and all incident handlers should be familiar with the security policies at all times. Depending on the organization, there may actually be an incident-handling policy, with several key elements. These may include the default action to take with regard to notifying law enforcement, whether to contain hackers in a "honeypot" environment or immediately eradicate the attack, etc. Another important area of policy is the warning banner. All computer systems should present a banner to users stating that the system is owned by the organization, certain policies will apply, and the user is expected to abide by the rules. The actual policies may be spelled out here in detail, or the user may be given a brief statement or two and referred to a more comprehensive document or set of documents.

An organization should determine, as part of its Preparation stage of incident response, whether law enforcement will be involved in incidents as a matter of course. There are positive and negative aspects of this to consider, and management will have to decide what is best based on a number of factors including the business the organization is in, the size of the organization, how cooperative law enforcement is, the costs involved, etc. In most instances, any threat to public health or safety *must* be reported to law enforcement, period. This is done for the common good of society, primarily, but also reduces the possibility of later legal liabilities the organization may encounter from not informing authorities of a possible threat. Other reasons to involve law enforcement include helping other companies avoid threats, legal requirements, or enforcement based on industry (for example, the FAA mandates certain actions involving law enforcement whenever a security threat to an airplane is found), and attempting to pursue criminal damages against an attacker or other party. There are also many good reasons *not* to involve law enforcement. Once law enforcement gets involved, there tends to be an added element of "red tape." Although your goal may be to resume normal business functions as quickly as possible, law enforcement may not be able to move as quickly to resolve issues as management would like. Depending on the incident, many companies may also want to maintain a low profile and avoid any publicity or media involvement. Many times, especially for larger incidents or situations, involving the authorities can bring unwanted attention as well.

For companies that *do* want to entertain involving law enforcement at some point, there are a number of simple steps to take in the Preparation phase that will make things flow more smoothly once an actual incident has been declared. First, liaisons to law enforcement within the organization should be established. Then, law enforcement should be contacted to discuss how the organizational liaisons should go about maintaining communications going forward. Having names, contact information, and possibly a fair working relationship ahead of time can significantly aid in soliciting law enforcement's aid during an incident.

Another type of notification that can be addressed in the Preparation phase is that of other companies and organizations. Management should define clear guidelines regarding communication to external business partners, full-time contracting agencies, etc. This will help to alleviate any ambiguity when an incident occurs; particularly close attention should be paid to defining the communication necessary when the incident originates from one of these entities.

One of the most crucial activities to perform during the Preparation phase is building a cross-functional team with representatives from critical areas of the enterprise. For instance, it is important to have employees from information security, operations, the legal department, human resources, and other various divisions of IT involved in planning and strategizing the organization's incident-handling methodology. By involving various departments, the information security management will be more likely to get solid management buy-in from other areas of the organization. The next step is to identify team roles, such as Lead Incident Handler and Assistant Handlers, and assign these to involved parties. Each of these roles will need a very specific list of duties associated with it, and all Incident Response team members should understand the duties and what is expected in a given role. Depending on the team's organization (i.e., distributed versus centralized, etc.), these roles will vary widely from one organization to the next.

Once team roles have been established, a very important step to accomplish is gaining approval for accessing key systems whenever possible. It should be understood by all parties in the organization that security team members will have separate, unique accounts that will only be used for emergency access; these can be audited stringently. The political atmosphere in an organization will determine how difficult this is to accomplish, and it will likely be a continuous struggle in many companies. However, the amount of time wasted at the beginning of an incident from trying to contact people and gain access can be the single factor that causes irreparable damage. In keeping with this, however, it can not be emphasized enough that up-to-date "call trees" and contact lists be maintained by the incident-handling team. The call trees should clearly show who is contacted first, and then the contact information for escalation up the chain of command should be designated, as well. This information should be available at all times as the cornerstone of an emergency communications plan.

Another point to consider for the Preparation phase is the creation of a "war room," a secured area that security and the incident-handling team can use for storing sensitive data and forensic evidence, as well as meet and coordinate efforts during incidents. This area can also store the "Jump Kit," which is comprised of the tools and resources the incident-handling team will need when an incident is declared. This kit will typically contain the following types of items: a dual-boot (or multi-boot) laptop, backup software and media, all manner of security software (forensic, scanning/assessment, etc.), floppies/CDs with clean binaries, Ethernet RJ-45 cables and crossover cables, a hub, contact lists, cell phones with extra batteries, incident-handling forms and documentation, plastic bags for storing evidence, a flashlight, screwdrivers and other tools, etc. This is by no means an exhaustive list, as there are many tools and items that a team may find useful for handling an incident.

IDENTIFICATION

The second phase of the incident-handling process is the Identification phase. In this phase, the incident-handling team is alerted to something, and must determine whether an incident is really occurring at all. Typically, the most senior and experienced handlers will be the ones who make this call, and then the process will continue from there. One of the best ways to ensure success in the incident-handling process is to train various auxiliary staff in the organization to alert the team earlier versus later. One of the best areas to focus alerting training efforts is the corporate Help Desk. Many times, the Help Desk is the first line of defense in an organization, and training the Help Desk staff to contact security personnel quickly is considered a best practice. Once the Help Desk has contacted the incident-handling team, the team should make initial contact with other management, system administrators, and any additional personnel where it's appropriate. It is important to make sure that everyone is in the loop at this point. There are many indications that an incident is underway. Some of these include failed logon attempts, gaps in log files or suspicious logs, unexplained user accounts or files, Intrusion Detection alarms, interfaces in promiscuous mode (indicating the possible presence of a "sniffer"), strange access times, etc. The environment will dictate what is classified as out-of-the-ordinary.

Identification typically occurs at one of three levels in the organization: the perimeter, the host perimeter/internal network, or the host system itself. Examples of perimeter identification include firewall detection or dropped packets/connections, dropped packets from a router, or a perimeter IDS sensor sending alerts. The perimeter is the ideal segment on which to identify potential problems, as the threat can likely be contained before actually entering the organization. The next level at which identification can occur is the host perimeter. This level may consist of host-based firewalls, internal Intrusion Detection engines, etc. Detection at this level indicates that a threat has entered the network, but may possibly be contained. Finally, host system detection is often accomplished with tools like system integrity monitors and antivirus software. Detection at this level may indicate a more serious incident, and detection may not be enough to prevent system compromise. Typically, host-level detection includes some type of automated response action, such as the quarantine function in antivirus software.

Another factor to consider at the host (system) level is the user population in an organization. Depending on the organization's culture and adequacy of security awareness training, users can be an excellent first line of defense in alerting incident-handling teams to a potential problem. Usually, these alerts will be channeled through the help desk or similar IT function. Regardless of the initial alerting method, the security team, specifically the incident handlers, are informed of an event or multiple events that warrant investigation. At this point, someone should be declared the Lead Handler, and the event(s) should be probed. The results of this investigation will lead to the determination of whether an incident should be declared or not.

If an incident is declared, this phase will be concluded by asking some pertinent questions and establishing a chain of custody. The questions an incident-handling team might need answers to include:

- How widespread is the affected platform or application?
- What sort of effect does the vulnerability have on the platform or application?
- For computer system vulnerabilities, is an exploit publicly available?
- Is there a solution, workaround, patch, etc.?
- Is the event/incident occurring elsewhere? Are we a specific target?

After the initial questions have been answered, or information is pending, it is very important to establish a formal chain of custody. This simply dictates who handles any pieces of evidence gathered during the remainder of the investigation. If an organization is currently in good communication with law enforcement, they can provide some best practices on how to approach chain of custody. Otherwise, it is prudent to limit the handling of evidence to a select few individuals who are members of the incident-handling and information security teams. Designated locations for storage, preferably a war room of some sort, should be discussed as well.

CONTAINMENT

The third stage of an incident response is the Containment phase. In this phase, the incident-handling team will actually perform some modifications to the system(s) in question. The first item of business in this phase is coordination with any external Internet Service Providers (ISPs) if necessary. It is important to do this early so that any help the ISP can offer is put to use quickly. Frequently, this type of coordination is done by the information security manager or other management while the technical team performs other duties. Once the technical staff at the ISP is informed of what is going on, then the two teams can begin to cooperate. The incident-handling manager should also work with the team and other management to secure the area surrounding the problem, if possible. This can be as straightforward as restricting access to a particular rack of servers in a datacenter for a period of time.

The next step in the Containment phase is to make backups of affected systems. This may warrant pulling systems from the network. When to remove systems from the network should be outlined clearly in an incident-handling policy or guideline. This is also an area where management really needs to coordinate with other business units and associates, especially in larger organizations where political silos are often formed in various groups and departments. Building positive relationships before an incident occurs will go a long way to getting these types of actions handled quickly. If the systems involved in the incident are considered mission-critical, management may be reluctant to take them off-line. However, most large organizations will have some sort of failover or disaster-recovery backup in place for any systems of this level of importance, and this is the time to make use of these duplicate systems.

Once the system is in the possession of the incident-handling team, at least two bit-level copies of the system's hard drive should be made. One will be used for forensic analysis that may be necessary. The other will be available to put back into production if that's required before the situation can be resolved. The original copy becomes evidence, and should be bagged, tagged, and safely stored in a secured area. Once disk copies have been made, the incident-handling team should then assess the machines that are in the near proximity of the affected system or systems. Depending on the situation, the incident-handling team may want to perform vulnerability assessments and other evaluation of the systems in question. If sniffer software is found, or any device interfaces are found to be running in promiscuous mode without authorization, much more stringent investigation is warranted. The incident-handling team may want to change system passwords at this point, as well. Any changes of this type must be evaluated in the context of an organization's incident-handling policy. For example, if the standard for handling a server compromise is to "watch and learn" versus eradicating the threat immediately, an incident-handling team will *not* want to make any changes that could alert the attacker to their presence.

ERADICATION

The fourth step in the incident-handling plan is Eradication—actually removing the threat. This can be very difficult, depending on how pervasive the attack is, and how long it has been in existence. During this phase, the Incident Response team tries to determine the root cause, as well as the overall symptoms, of the attack or attacks. Again, this can be a very difficult proposition, especially in the case of a malicious code (virus, worm, etc.) attack that involved "zero-day" code; in other words, a brand new worm or virus for which no antivirus signatures yet exist. In this situation, observing network traffic patterns and/or observing system behavior is the only way of tracking the threat, and this is a situation where deep technical expertise truly comes in handy. Knowing how to quickly use tools such as router ACLs, Intrusion Detection and Prevention Systems, firewalls, and others can help to corral the threat and minimize damages.

For many organizations, the seemingly obvious way to proceed at this point would be to restore from backups and keep the business functioning. This is true, with one caveat. How can you be sure that the backups aren't compromised? It is important to inspect the backups before actually putting them into production. At this point, the incident team should be wary, and possibly know what to look for, so this job will be more routine than anything else. In the event that the incident team finds evidence of a rootkit, however, the only foolproof way to restore a system is to completely rebuild the operating system from scratch. Rootkits can actually modify system programs and embed commands into the operating system, so incident handlers can never be certain that the threat has been completely removed. During the Eradication phase, any number of other defense measures should also be applied. Some of these may include applying firewall or router rules, changing system names or IP addresses, changing DNS records, applying patches and hardening measures to systems, etc. At the conclusion of this phase, the information security team should perform a vulnerability analysis to determine the general state of the network, using port/vulnerability scanners and other tools.

RECOVERY

The Recovery phase is next. In this phase, the goal is simple: resume normal operations. To do this, any affected systems should be validated using standard organizational testing plans and procedures as well as baseline data. At this stage, once the incident-handling team and information security management has approved the system(s), it is a business decision to return the system(s) into production. Once in production, any systems should be monitored for abnormal behavior or traffic. One important task related to this is log monitoring.

LESSONS LEARNED

Finally, the incident is over. What now? Phase Six—Lessons Learned. In many organizations, information security professionals do not pay enough attention to this phase, which is really a mistake. This phase should begin with a detailed follow-up report from the incident-handling team and information security management. This may take a while, as it's important to gain consensus from those involved. Once the report is finished, a meeting should be held between information security staff and business decision makers to discuss what could have been done better, what was done well, what resources are lacking, vulnerabilities that may need to be addressed, etc. This is really an opportunity for a well-organized incident-handling team to demonstrate its worth to the organization, and gain support from decision makers.

MANAGEMENT'S ROLE IN INCIDENT RESPONSE

Overall, management's role in the information response process should be primarily concerned with communication, acting as a trusted liaison with other individuals and groups, keeping people informed of what's happening, and making decisions about the way the incident is affecting the business or organization. This falls into the category of standard operating procedure (SOP) for management, daily operational tasks. What about the big picture, though? One demonstration of the "big picture" for information security management is in the implementation of ISO 17799, an international security standard that incorporates controls representing information security "best practices" in many areas. There are a number of sites on the Internet devoted to overviews of ISO 17799, so that will not be covered here. Instead, there are several controls in the ISO 17799 standard that deal specifically with incident response.

ISO 17799—RESPONDING

The primary area of ISO 17799 concerned with incident response is section 6.3 of the standard, entitled "Responding to security incidents and malfunctions." The first area of this is section 6.3.1, "Reporting security incidents." This control is concerned with the existence of a formal reporting process that is established to allow management to report and escalate security incidents through the appropriate channels quickly. This section corresponds primarily with the Preparation phase of the NIST incident-handling process. The creation of call trees, incident-handling policies, and contact methods all satisfy this control.

ISO 17799—REPORTING

The next control in this group, 6.3.2, deals with "Reporting security weaknesses." This control deals with the way that weaknesses, or events, get reported. This control relies on several other components. First, users must be aware of abnormal behavior or observed threats to systems. Second, a means to report any threats, events, or incidents must exist. This control relates to the Preparation and Identification phases of incident-handling. The Preparation phase should address security awareness, both to the general user population and "front-line" responders like the IT Help Desk. These groups should then have some process in place that can be followed to report any suspected events or incidents. This would correspond to the Identification phase, where the incident-handling team is notified by the Help Desk or another individual or group that something is possibly awry. Control 6.3.3, "Reporting software malfunctions," is very similar to this one, but is concerned solely with specific software. This would be applicable if a user's work duties are impaired due to a specific piece of software malfunctioning, which would then be reported.

ISO 17799—LEARNING

Control 6.3.4, "Learning from incidents," specifically refers to mechanisms that are in place to monitor and report on the number, types, and costs of incidents that occur. This is primarily dealt with in the Lessons Learned phase of incident-handling. This control is primarily addressed with good documentation processes; an example of this might be standard, detailed incident-handling forms for each phase that are filled out and used as input for the final report. The final control in section 6.3 is 6.3.5, "Disciplinary process." Although not specifically addressed in the NIST incident-handling guidelines, several other areas of an organization's information security program are directly applicable. A detailed information security awareness program that discusses organizational policies and the punishment for violating them would aid in satisfying this control. Explicit, unambiguous security policies that explain the disciplinary ramifications of violation are really the primary input to this section of ISO 17799, however.

ISO 17799—PROCEDURES

Another major section of the ISO 17799 standard that addresses incident response is standard 8.1.3, "Incident management procedures." This multi-faceted control addresses several areas:

- Whether incident response/management procedures exist
- Whether the procedures address different types of incidents such as Denial-of-Service (DoS), breaches of confidentiality, unauthorized access, etc.
- Whether the procedures outline specific areas of responsibility, and how these different responsibilities will provide fast and efficient incident response
- Whether the incident-management procedures address the documentation of incident events, including the maintenance of log files and other audit controls

This section touches almost every phase of the incident-handling methodology, and also relates to a number of other ISO 17799 controls, including those pertaining to security awareness and policies, auditing and authorized use of systems, etc.

Classifying Incidents

There are a fairly large number of different incident types and classifications. The NIST incident-handling guidelines cover several, including Denial-of-Service attacks (DoS), malicious code incidents, unauthorized access, inappropriate usage, and incidents comprised of multiple components. Other specific types include insider threats and espionage. Espionage is a special type of incident that must be handled very discreetly. A small team of incident handlers is usually best, and as few people as possible should be involved in order to maintain secrecy. The most common type of espionage is theft of information, and a few signs that this is occurring include strange system access times and frequent access violations revealed by audits. Espionage is an excellent example of a type of incident where law enforcement assistance can really come in handy. In most of these cases, the affected organization will want to prosecute, and law enforcement will need to be involved regardless.

Unauthorized access is a common incident. In these types of incidents, the handler must often determine whether the access is accidental or malicious. If resources are not adequately protected, employees may "stumble" onto them innocently, without intending to create any problems. Although this can go too far if curiosity gets the better of the parties involved, this type of situation is typically worthy of a minor reprimand. Actual malicious trespassing is an entirely different situation, however. Stealing passwords, using social engineering, or any other method used to gain illicit access to restricted resources is a malicious incident, and should be handled appropriately. It is important to have clearly defined policies in place that outline how these violations will be dealt with; there are actually documented cases where organizations tried to prosecute former employees for unauthorized access, but no policies were in place to enforce this! Unauthorized access may be detected by strange login times or sources, hacking tools or exploit code found on systems, sniffer programs or promiscuous interfaces, keystroke loggers collecting data, etc. Intrusion-detection systems or file integrity monitors on systems can aid in detection of these types of incidents.

Unauthorized use of systems and resources is a common problem in many organizations. With the advent of the Internet as a business tool, many employees are prone to accidental breaches of organizational authorized use policies. For example, pop-up ads on legitimate sites may contain unauthorized content or other prohibited material. Other means of abusing organizational resources include inappropriate e-mail use, disseminating information with a sensitive or private data classification label, or using the organization's assets for purposes other than business. There are a number of ways to detect this, including e-mail filtering software, Web filtering software, Web server and e-mail server logs, firewall and proxy logs, etc. One other way, observed quite often, is end user reporting of these incidents. An employee will notice something on another's computer screen, or receive an offensive e-mail forwarded as a "joke," etc. The context of these events and incidents must be taken into consideration, as well, due to the large number of accidental and unintentional occurrences.

Denial-of-service (DoS) attacks are becoming more prevalent today. There are a number of varieties of this attack; some are directly launched at a target, some are "bounced" off innocent victims (making them appear to be the attackers), some are launched from multiple locations simultaneously (known as Distributed Denial-of-Service, or DDoS attacks), etc. Regardless of the particular type, there are a number of key steps that can help in responding to these attacks. First, preparation is the key here. Coordinating with an ISP beforehand to determine what kind of reactive measures can be taken will prevent delays when an incident occurs. For example, having an ISP implement simple router and firewall filters can be an effective way to block these attacks, with one or several phone calls being the only work necessary. Local detection of these DoS attacks can be done in a number of ways. Some include reports of system unavailability and connections dropping, intrusion detection alerts (both host- and network-based), firewall and router logs, and obviously spoofed packets being sent. Very often, effectively tracing these attacks back to the perpetrators is difficult, making prosecution unlikely.

The last incident type to be mentioned here is one that is rapidly becoming the most prevalent for security teams globally: the malicious code incident. Depending on the particular code involved in an incident, these incidents may easily overlap with other incident types such as unauthorized access and Denial-of-Service. The management of these incidents is primarily concerned with their prevention altogether. Preventing malicious code falls into many other areas of information security, including an effective antivirus software strategy, eliminating operating system and application vulnerabilities that are often exploited, and enforcing strong browser security. Blocking the transmission of certain file types and extensions is also very important. Unfortunately, new variations are constantly being released; most antivirus software relies on definition files, or signatures that match the malicious code, to recognize the threat. This creates a "lag time" from the release of the new code to the time when antivirus software vendors create a definition file to recognize it, and release this definition to customers. Centrally managed antivirus software is essential in large organizations, and can help to limit the spread of malicious code during an incident. Once a vendor's definition file has been released, it is critical to get this file to all clients as quickly as possible. This is done most effectively through the use of a central console managed by the information security team. E-mail servers and other ingress points into the network should be configured to block particular code types, as well; and the use of intrusion detection/prevention filters can also help to alert and prevent infected packets. Information security management will often have to engage in politics during malicious code incidents, as senior management often tends to have less restrictive computing policies applied to them, and thus are often more prone to contamination from malicious code. On the same note, however, malicious code incidents are often some of the most visible in the organization, and successful management of a widespread malicious code incident can garner significant support for the information security efforts underway. Any deficiencies in the incident-handling capabilities can also be noted, and management may be more likely to listen to budgetary requirements during the Lessons Learned phase.

Coordination and Communication

One point that can be noted regarding incident-handling and its management is that it is largely a manual process. Like any process or procedure in an organization, the more coordinated the individual pieces and parts, the more effective and efficient the process will be. For incident-handling, one factor that is essential to consider is that of communication. Better communication, as well as overall preparation and experience, can make the difference between a catastrophic incident and a relatively simple analysis and clean-up. Particularly in organizations using Distributed and Coordinated incident-handling team models, managing the communication between team members and other related parties can dramatically affect the outcome of the incident. One way to do this is by implementing a workflow system. Many different varieties of electronic workflow systems are currently available, ranging from content management systems that allow distributed teams to work together on documents and Web pages, to project management software that is centrally hosted and allows project teams and participants to update resources and time allocation.

One new open-source tool that has become available to aid in coordinating incident response is RTIR, or Request Tracker for Incident Response, from Best Practical Solutions, LLC (available at *http://www.bestpractical.com/rtir/*). Based on the Request Tracker software that has been in production for some time, RTIR is a specialized ticketing system that can create Incident Reports from e-mails that users send in to the incident-handling team. After investigation during the Identification phase, the incident-handling team can update an Incident Report to an actual Incident, and then allow multiple team members to update the Incident as needed. Contacts and machine IP addresses can be managed through the workflow system, and external parties can be contacted and updated on events and status information as needed. External parties can also be queried for information through the system, and responses can automatically update a particular Incident. For a manager trying to coordinate incident-response efforts in a geographically distributed organization, a central workflow system that keeps team members up to date in near real-time could be a major driver for productivity and efficiency increases.

Summary

Overall, the building and managing of an Incident Response team requires a significant investment in time and resources. In-depth knowledge of the organization, including political influence throughout the tiers of management, will be absolutely essential for an incident-handling team to be effective. As an organization's Incident Response team gets more comfortable working together, and effective preparation is done based on past experience, significant risks to an organization can be mitigated. As stated in this beginning of this reading, the paradox of effective incident-handling management is that management tends not to notice until something is awry. This implies that the incident is not being handled well, or that certain controls are not in place to effectively mitigate risk in the organization. Getting the proper attention for budget and support has long been the bane of most information security managers. However, with the almost daily increase in high-profile information security attacks and incidents, the process of incident-handling management may get a good deal more attention in the near future.

References

[1]Grance, T., et al. (2004, January). Computer security incident handling guide—recommendations of the National Institute of Standards and Technology. *NIST Special Publication 800-61*. Available from *http://www.google.com/url?sa=U&start=1&q=http://www.csrc.nist.gov/publications/nistpubs/800-61/sp800-61.pdf&e=8093*

Zen and the Art of Information Security—A Philosophical, Spiritual and Mystical Approach to Protecting Information

MICHAEL E. WHITMAN AND HERBERT J. MATTORD

Kennesaw State University

Michael Whitman, PhD, CISSP, is a Professor of Information Systems in the Computer Science and Information Systems Department at Kennesaw State University, Kennesaw, Georgia, where he is also the Director of the Master of Science in Information Systems and the Director of the KSU Center for Information Security Education (infosec.kennesaw.edu). Dr. Whitman is an active researcher in Information Security Curriculum Development and Policy and Ethics. He currently teaches graduate and undergraduate courses in Information Security, Local Area Networking, and Data Communications. Dr. Whitman is also the co-author of Management of Information Security, Readings and Cases in the Management of Information Security, *and* The Hands-On Information Security Lab Manual, *all published by Course Technology. Prior to his career in academia, Dr. Whitman was an armored cavalry officer in the United States Army.*

Herbert Mattord, MBA, CISSP, is an Instructor of Information Systems in the Computer Science and Information Systems Department at Kennesaw State University, Kennesaw, Georgia. Professor Mattord completed 24 years of IT industry experience prior to moving to academia. During his career as an IT practitioner, he served as adjunct professor at numerous institutions. Professor Mattord is also the Operations Manager of the KSU Center for Information Security Education and Awareness (infosec.kennesaw.edu), as well as the coordinator for the KSU Certificate in Information Security and Assurance. He currently teaches undergraduate courses in Information Security, Data Communications, Database, Project Management, Systems Analysis & Design, and Information Resources Management and Policy. He was formerly the Manager of Corporate Information Technology Security at Georgia-Pacific Corporation, where much of the practical knowledge found in this textbook was acquired. Professor Mattord is also the co-author of Management of Information Security, Readings and Cases in the Management of Information Security, *and* The Hands-On Information Security Lab Manual, *all published by Course Technology.*

Overview

In this chapter, the authors take a tongue-in-cheek approach to examining some important issues in information security. By relating key security topics to recognized "philosophical, spiritual, and mystical" allusions, they are better able to present these important messages in a format that promises to increase the awareness and retention of the readers.

Here the intellectual musings on the subject of information security include references to Sun Tzu, Socrates, Nietzsche, Winston Churchill, and others.

Introduction

When faced with the somewhat daunting task of organizing and managing the information security function, even the most stalwart Chief Information Security Officer may find himself or herself in need of inspiration. After all, the weight of the responsibility for the protection of an organization's life blood—its information—rests squarely on the CISO's shoulders. Day after day, the threats to information security continually attack, over and over and over again. No defense can withstand the constant bombardment from such a variety of assaults, both from outside the organization, and from inside, by human and non-human agents, by act of error and failure (by accident) or through intentional malice. Organizations' leadership push constantly for an expansion of the technology perimeter, pushing to integrate customers, and suppliers, providing goods and services worldwide, 24/7, 365 days a year. This level of exposure means the company's infrastructure is open to attack from agents from China, the former Soviet Union, the Pacific Rim, the Middle East, and yes from within the United States. While the CISO sleeps, the attackers move, striking without provocation, without remorse, constituting a clear and present danger to the security of the information contained within the thin walls of the organization's systems. In the words of a terrorist, "We only have to be lucky once, you have to be lucky all the time." It becomes obvious when faced with this awesome responsibility, and constant stress and strain, that the CISO does need words of inspiration and guidance. Words that motivate, inspire, advise, and instill confidence and wisdom.

You won't find those words here.

What you will find is a unique approach to understanding the management of information security, or specific tasks contained within the job of the CISO, combined with a twist of mysticism and philosophical sage. There are many anecdotes, sayings, and idioms that can be used to illustrate key management points in information security. The use of such parallels may aid in the remembrance of these valuable lessons. This first such prophetic statement is derived from an ancient Chinese general's treatise on warfare.

The Art of Information Security

"If you know the enemy and know yourself, you need not fear the result of a hundred battles. If you know yourself but not the enemy, for every victory gained you will also suffer a defeat. If you know neither the enemy nor yourself, you will succumb in every battle."

—Sun Tzu

The parallels between this quote and the management of information security are numerous and many. First and foremost is the realization that information security is a war. It is a war in which the defenders are fighting on a daily basis to protect the security of the organization's information. What's worse is that it's a defensive campaign in which the defenders cannot go on the offense, and they cannot win. The defenders can successfully defend their systems and the information contained within during an individual skirmish, or battle, but within a very short time, another attack will occur from a different direction or venue. Continually the enemy probes the defensive perimeter, looking for a weakness, until they discover a chink in the castle walls. They then push through the outer defenses seeking to gain access to the command and control function, or through to the intelligence section, to subvert, steal, modify, damage, or destroy and then disappear without a trace (or so they think). Security managers are not allowed to implement the "best defense is a good offense" strategy, as the law looks dimly on vigilante hacking. Even though some companies offer "back hack" or trap-and-trace software allowing a manager to seek to gain the true identity of an individual attempting to illegally access an organization's systems, that doesn't mean they should or can legally use them. In fact, these applications come with specific warnings about the use of the tools outside the confines of the organization's perimeter.

The next parallel is the understanding of the self and enemy. Once the security manager realizes that this is a war, with clearly defined sides (us and them), the next task is to understand both the offensive and defensive forces. Knowing one's self is the process of identifying, categorizing, prioritizing, and understanding the information of value to the organization and the systems that use, store, and protect it. These systems include the software, hardware, networking, people, data, and procedures involved with this information.

You must also know the enemy. Who is the enemy? To make sound decisions about information security, create policies, and enforce them, management must be informed of the various kinds of threats (a.k.a., the enemy) facing the organization, its people, applications, data, and information systems. A threat is an object, person, or other entity that represents a constant danger to an asset. To understand the wide range of threats that pervade the interconnected world, researchers have interviewed practicing information security personnel and examined information security literature on threats. While the categorization of threats may vary, threats are relatively well researched and consequently fairly well understood. There are 12 categories of threats, as illustrated in Table 4-1.

Thus only by knowing ourselves and the enemy can we be victorious in the battle to protect information. In the security managers' eyes victory can only be defined as closing the day the same as it opened, with the information securely stored and its confidentiality, integrity, and availability intact.

This method of knowing one's self and one's enemy can also be incorporated into an overall risk management strategy. Effective risk management begins with identifying and prioritizing the risks to information (knowing the enemy), then identifying and prioritizing the organization's information assets (knowing the self). You can then create a matrix with these two

TABLE 4-1   **Threats to Information Security**[i]

Categories of Threat	Examples
1. Acts of human error or failure	Accidents, employee mistakes
2. Compromises to intellectual property	Piracy, copyright infringement
3. Deliberate acts of espionage or trespass	Unauthorized access and/or data collection
4. Deliberate acts of information extortion	Blackmail or information disclosure
5. Deliberate acts of sabotage or vandalism	Destruction of systems or information
6. Deliberate acts of theft	Illegal confiscation of equipment or information
7. Deliberate software attacks	Viruses, worms, macros, denial-of-service
8. Forces of nature	Fire, flood, earthquake, lightning
9. Deviations in quality of service	ISP, power, or WAN service issues from service providers
10. Technical hardware failures or errors	Equipment failure
11. Technical software failures or errors	Bugs, code problems, unknown loopholes
12. Technological obsolescence	Antiquated or outdated technologies

[i]Whitman, M. (2003, August). Enemy at the gates: Threats to information security. *Communications of the ACM, 46* (8), 91–96.

lists on opposing axes. In each threat/asset cell, one records the vulnerabilities that exist (if any). The next step is to record the organizational controls (again if any) that have been applied to the threat/vulnerability/asset (TVA) triples. By examining the resulting data, one can quickly determine if any assets are exposed to attack by a particular threat. One can also create a list of priority for work by weighting the work from the upper-left corner (where the highest priority assets and threats exist) to the lower-right corner. Figure 4-1 illustrates the framework for this activity.

This allows the security manager not only to understand his/her responsibilities in managing information security, but also to formulate a positive strategy in dealing with the threats facing the organization's information.

The Unexamined Life

"An unexamined life is not worth living."

—SOCRATES (469 BC–399 BC), GREEK PHILOSOPHER

As noted earlier, Sun Tzu observed it is important to understand both ourselves and our enemies. The next logical step in this process is to examine ourselves critically from two perspectives. First we must examine ourselves from the perspective of knowing ourselves, examining information and systems from the inside out. Systems and security administrators build

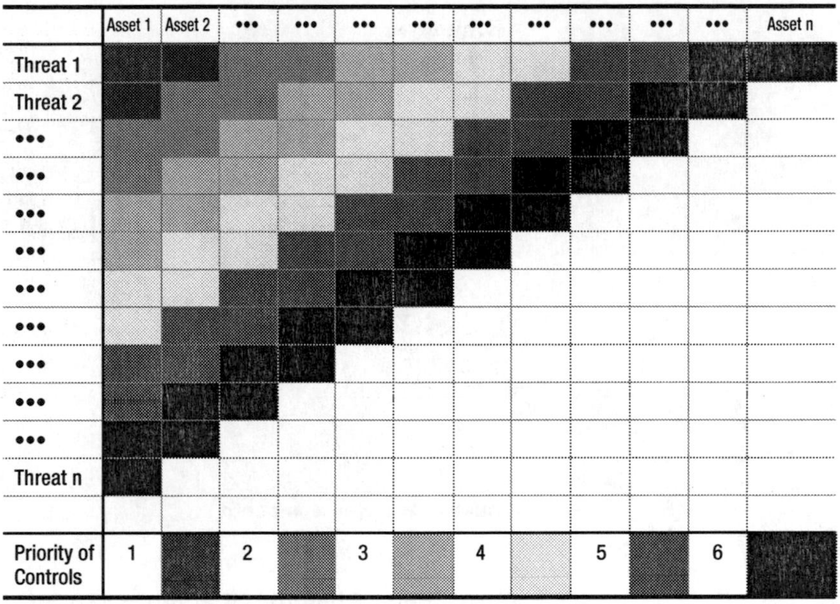

	Asset 1	Asset 2	•••	•••	•••	•••	•••	•••	•••	•••	•••	Asset n
Threat 1												
Threat 2												
•••												
•••												
•••												
•••												
•••												
•••												
•••												
•••												
Threat n												
Priority of Controls	1		2		3		4		5		6	

These bands of controls should be continued through all threat: asset pairs.

FIGURE 4-1 Bands of control

and maintain systems to store, use, and transmit systems and thus are in a position to best understand the strengths and weaknesses of these systems. It is also a well-known fact that if the enemy gets past the external defenses (i.e., the firewall) the level of protection drops dramatically. Unfortunately many organizations restrict their defenses to the perimeter/firewall level. The fundamental premise of defense-in-depth requires the organization to have multiple levels of defense, so that the information is protected even when the threats succeed in their attacks, initially. As shown in Figure 4-2, in order to access information from outside the organization, the external ne'er-do-wells must go though the Internet, into the organization's networks, and finally through the systems housing the information.

Unfortunately those within the organization's perimeter don't have the same potential for controls between them and the information. As a result, the largest threat by far to information security is the human factor. Almost all threats are perpetrated by humans, wittingly or by accident. Viruses are written by miscreants, hackers are malicious individuals with little redeeming social value. Even our best-intending employees make mistakes and damage or destroy information.

The second perspective focuses on looking at our systems from the "eyes of the enemy." It has long been a tradition in the Army, for the commander of a unit about to go into battle, to walk the battlefield the night before a big engagement, especially in the defensive, and look at his own position so as to see it as the enemy would. This shift in perspective sometimes allows the security administrators to see something they might otherwise overlook. How does the security administrator do this? By using the tools

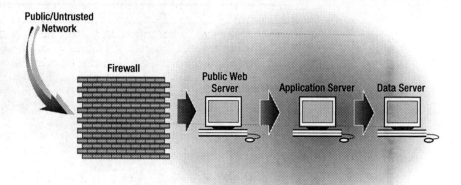

FIGURE 4-2 Defense-in-depth

and techniques that the electronic miscreants do, from outside the insecurity of the company firewall. These tools are readily available, and can be easily installed and used on laptops or external servers. It is then up to the security manager to decide whether or not to notify their own systems administrators that such an examination is in process. This could provide the 'acid test' of the systems administrators' abilities to react to an unauthorized investigation. Intrusion detection is the process of preventing, detecting, reacting to, and recovering from intrusions and attacks on the organization's information. A key part of any intrusion detection (and also disaster recovery) plans is the need to record events as they occur, and document the overall process. The appointment of a scribe in the early stages of an incident ensures that the actions taken by the incident response team (or disaster recovery team) will be documented for assessment later in the process. The final stage of the process involves the After Action Review (AAR). An AAR is a detailed analysis of the events that have transpired, with each team member relating the event from their perspective. This information, along with the official transcript, allows the team to dissect the event, examining what when wrong, what the root cause was, and how the team performed in the identification and control of the situation. It is this examination of performance that allows the team to review what they did well, isolate what they could have done better, and revise their policies and procedures for dealing with the event, to improve their performance in the next incident (or disaster). It is the continuous improvement through self-examination that allows the team to grow stronger.

That Which Does Not Kill Us

"That which does not kill us makes us stronger."

—FRIEDRICH NIETZSCHE (1844–1900), GERMAN PHILOSOPHER

As bad as it is to be constantly bombarded by attacks (both internally and externally), at least practice makes perfect. As stated earlier, the miscreants only have to be lucky once, the defenders must be ever vigilant. The incident response process of growth through self-examination of performance described in the previous section alludes to the need for continuous improvement. In order to perform well in response to actual events, the team must be prepared. Preparation comes from training and rehearsal. As the military states, "we sweat in training, so we don't bleed in battle" or "train as you fight, and fight as you train." If an organization has an effective plan, the plan may be ineffective unless it has been practiced. The levels of plan testing and rehearsal strategies can vary. Five testing strategies are presented here.

1. Checklist: Copies of the plan are distributed to each individual with a role during an actual incident. Each individual reviews the plan and creates a checklist of correct and incorrect components. While not a true test, it is an important step in reviewing the document before it is actually needed.

2. Structured walk-through: In a walk-through, each involved individual practices the steps he or she will take during an actual event. This can consist of an "on-the-ground" walk-through, in which everyone discusses their actions at each particular location and juncture, or it can be more of a "talk-through," in which all involved individuals sit around a conference table and discuss in turn how they would act as the incident unfolded.

3. Simulation: The next step up is a simulation of an incident. Here each involved individual works individually, rather than in conference, simulating the performance of each task required to react to and recover from a simulated incident. The simulation stops short of the actual physical tasks required, such as installing the backup, or disconnecting a communications circuit. The major difference between a walk-through and a simulation is the independence of the individual performers in a simulation, as they work on their own tasks and assume responsibility for identifying the faults in their own procedures.

4. Parallel: Yet another rehearsal method, larger in scope and intensity, is the parallel test. In the parallel test, individuals act as if an actual incident occurred, performing their required tasks and executing the necessary procedures. The difference is that the normal operations of the business do not stop. The business continues to function, even though the team acts to contain the test incident. Great care must be taken to ensure that the procedures performed do not halt the operations of the business functions, creating an actual incident.

5. Full interruption: The final, most comprehensive and realistic test is to react to an incident as if it were real. In a full interruption, the individuals follow each and every procedure, including the interruption of service, restoration of data from backups, and notification of appropriate individuals as discussed in subsequent sections. This is often performed after normal business hours in organizations that cannot afford to disrupt or simulate the disruption of business functions for the purposes of the test. This is the best practice the team can get, but is unfortunately too risky for most businesses.

Even with a well rehearsed plan, there is no substitution for experience. As terrible as it may sound, until the troops are "battle hardened" they won't know how they will respond when faced with a genuine incident. But the good news is that even a successful attack may not be catastrophic as you might think. The majority of attacks can be the results of "script-kiddes," "packet monkeys," or other hacker "wanna-be's" with a suite of tools but no real skills. Other attackers may simply be snooping employees, or honest hard-working employees who make mistakes. Preparing for such occurrences can assist in the recovery, not if—but when—they occur.

Zen—Nothingness

"It is of the highest importance in the art of detection to be able to recognize out of a number of facts which are incidental and which are vital.... I would call your attention to the curious incident of the dog in the night-time."

"The dog did nothing in the night-time."

"That was the curious incident."

—Sir Arthur Conan Doyle (1859–1930), British author
Sherlock Holmes talking to Inspector Gregory, in *The Memoirs of Sherlock Holmes*, "Silver Blaze," (1893)

One of the fundamental tenets of the Zen philosophy is the attainment of a state of *nothingness*. Translating this to the realm of information security, the very best information security programs work so completely in alignment with the objectives of the organization that they do not seem to exist, except for those who would violate their boundaries.

In information security the concept of nothingness represents the ideal goal, the ultimate position. A popular network security commercial describes a scenario where a *soi-disant* self-protecting server sits quietly in a room, while nearby a team of systems administrators work calmly performing routine tasks. Across town a group of hackers are also doing nothing, but are very frustrated since they are unable to penetrate the new server. If information security works as desired, then nothing happens. If user's data is protected, then they don't know. If the organization is not blackmailed by credit card thieves, then it is business as usual. The point is that the ultimate goal of information security is to obtain nothingness, a state of nirvana where information is in the location is it expected to be, in the form expected, and is only viewed by those authorized. Users don't notice the security measures, nor do they detect an impact on their work functions. They are able to focus exclusively on doing their jobs, effectively and efficiently, with little concern with the systems working behind the scenes to protect the information, constantly dodging incoming attacks.

Information security in this regard should work like the earth's atmosphere. Daily millions of meteorites plummet toward the earth, the vast majority of which burn up harmlessly in the atmosphere. Occasionally one is found lying in a field or witnessed splashing into the ocean. Almost never is a meteorite seen actually harming life or property. Yet many fear the coming of the "planet-killer" a la *Deep Impact* or *Armageddon*. Again, we hope for nothing.

Harmony / Balance

"Invisible harmony is better than visible."

—HERACLITUS (C. 535–475 BC), GREEK PHILOSOPHER

Closely related to the Zen—Nothingness of Information Security described here is the desire for a state of harmony or *wa* (*chi* in Chinese). In ancient Japan, the *wa* of one's house was sacrosanct. To protect this harmony, the warriors would result to violence if needed. This concept of protecting the operations of an entity—the organization—while fending off attackers is at the core of information security.

The defenders of the *wa* must ensure the harmony of the organization is not interrupted, as the organization works toward success in its market sector, whether public or private. Anything that disrupts the harmony of the workplace slows or stalls the productivity of the worker. If the worker is oblivious to the constant battles raging at the organization's perimeter, then they are free to focus on the goals of the organization.

How does one obtain harmony in information security? After all, the seeking of information security objectives is often observed to be an intrusive force. Only in a perfect world would there be no attackers, no hackers, and no viruses. Imagine the capabilities of an information system if it needed no security at all. It would be like the often lamented days of yore when living in a neighborhood meant no one locked their doors, everyone trusted their neighbors, and all took turns looking out for each other. The designers of systems, instead of spending enormous amounts of time and resources on developing security functions, debugging potential exploits and vulnerabilities, could focus instead on making the system meet the two holy grails of systems development—ease of use and usefulness. The systems would be extremely easy to use, with simple yet powerful interfaces, devoid of the pesky username/password login screens. Programs would provide information instantaneously, in the form, format, fashion, and location desired.

Dorothy, wake up! Unfortunately in this reality, there are threats to information security, and as such the information security function must strike a careful balance between security and access. Interestingly enough, the more security you place into a system, the less useful it is. This may seen contrary to logic, yet the more layers of security you place between a user and their data, the longer it takes them to gain access to that data, and the more difficult it becomes. Longer usernames and passwords, created from randomized characters, with multiple biometric authentication methods all slow down the login process. Each time the user needs to access data, the system re-authenticates. Each time the user needs to access a different system, network or communications circuit, the system re-authenticates. All data is encrypted using powerful algorithms, increasing processing time and storage requirements. All of this very powerful security will greatly increase the delay between user and data, and similarly increase the amount of processing needed in the user's system. And the users won't tolerate it. When business and security collide, security loses. When the layers of security begin to prevent the user from doing their job in an efficient and effective manner, security will be bypassed, officially or subversively.

Water seeks the path of least resistance, and so do workers. One of the "Peter's principles" is "don't let the rules get in the way of doing the job." A worker's livelihood may be directly correlated to the speed and efficiency in doing their job. When security threatens their productivity or even their job status, they will find a way to get around it. As a result, the security team should seek that balance between access and security, to re-establish the level of security that ensures the data is there when the users need it, yet does not overly restrict their access. Security is in effect establishing harmony—*wa*—in reassuring the users that all is well in the house and that they can do their jobs, while security stands quietly in the background.

The Value of Persistence

"Never give in, never give in, never, never, never, never—in nothing, great or small, large or petty—never give in except to convictions of honour and good sense."

—WINSTON CHURCHILL, PRIME MINISTER OF THE UNITED KINGDOM
SPEECH AT HARROW SCHOOL, HARROW, ENGLAND,
OCTOBER 29, 1941

"Never give up! Never surrender!"

—COMMANDER PETER QUINCY TAGGART, FROM THE MOTION PICTURE
GALAXY QUEST, PLAYED BY TIM ALLEN

Security can be a *very* frustrating job. After all, it's like playing goalie for a hockey or soccer team. You are constantly bombarded with attacks, and you never get to counter-attack and score a victory for your team. Yet serving on a security team is very similar to serving in the military, fire department, or other public service organization. There is an inherent sense of satisfaction with defending one's turf. A job well done carries its own rewards.

It is interesting to note how so many individuals who have served in the military and law enforcement find themselves in a security field. A sense of duty, honor, and country are noble pursuits. As such these same individuals share a "never say die" mentality, necessary for the success of any information security function. You can't quit, you can't give up, even when you win, even when you lose, for tomorrow is another day, and another battle is on the horizon. Even if you lose the battle, don't lose the war. And after all is it a war. Not one of those 100 hour wars, as many may be most familiar with, but one of those WWI trench wars. We dig in deep, refusing to give an inch without severe bloodshed and personal cost. The viability of the organization depends upon it.

A commonly quoted statistic states that "40 percent of all organizations that close their doors for a week, never open them again." If information security gives up, and fails to protect the organization's data, that could very well be the case. Consider the case of Egghead.com. Egghead.com was a "clicks and mortar" computer technology store, that also had an online auction. In December 2000, the story broke that Egghead had been hacked. The problems didn't stop there. Egghead initially denied the breach. Over 3.7 million credit card holders' data was at risk. One of the authors was among those affected. He received a letter in the mail about the same time, indicating that the *rumors* of the breach were unsubstantiated, and that he should take no action. He did anyway, canceling the card he used in their online auction. He received a second letter approximately two weeks later, stating that a breach *may* have occurred, and that my data *may* be at risk, but again not to do anything until confirmed. The company claimed to have contacted law enforcement, but the FBI stated that it had never been contacted. In reality, all 3.7 million credit card numbers were reported (finally) stolen. This was the largest credit card number theft recorded up until that time. Egghead never figured out exactly what happened, perhaps due to insecure servers, a lack of auditing software, or other security-related failures. Tylenol survived a pill poisoning attack, through positive action and acceptance of responsibility. Egghead.com is no more, its bits and pieces sold off to companies like Amazon.com. Never, never, never give up, never surrender. Character is what you are in the dark (when no one is looking). Character saved Tylenol, it could have saved Egghead.

Security Aphorisms

We leave you with a few (tongue-in-cheek) words of wisdom, to summarize our perspective on existential philosophy of information security.

EVERYTHING I NEED TO KNOW ABOUT INFORMATION SECURITY I LEARNED IN KINDERGARTEN

This list was originally created as an end-user information security awareness poster (note that this is copyrighted material). It is designed to stimulate awareness and understanding of acceptable behavior with regard to the use and protection of information.

1. Play nice with others. When using information and the systems that store, process, and transmit it, realize: 1) you don't own it, and 2) others use it too. You are a member of an organizational society, and as such must comply with the rules for a polite society. Don't create a hostile work environment by viewing inappropriate materials, don't hog the bandwidth, etc.

2. Leave your toys at home. Computer games are a great pastime. They don't belong in the office. All personal software, including games, should not be brought to the office and installed on office equipment. The software could be laden with viruses, backdoors, or Trojan horses, and the organization cannot be responsible for managing the copyright. So leave them at home.

3. Don't take others' stuff. Theft of information or other intellectual property is just wrong. Don't do it.

4. Don't talk to strangers. One of the leading mechanisms for gaining unauthorized access to information is through social engineering, using trickery to gain the confidence of someone inside the organization, slowly gaining enough information to gain access. Contrary to popular belief, the social engineer won't try to simply ask for your username and password—"Hi! I'm Joe from IT, and I understand you have a problem with your system (who doesn't?). Give me your username and password and I'll fix it for you!" It just doesn't happen that openly. Social engineers collect a little at the time, so you never know who is

on the other end of a conversation, and how much information they already have. So don't discuss any specifics of the organization, its systems, its personnel, or anything with outsiders.

5. Don't accept gifts from strangers. Games are good, free games are better! Unfortunately free games are the most common mechanism by which backdoors, Trojan horses, and viruses are delivered. You don't know who wrote the software, and if you didn't buy it shrink-wrapped in a store, or from a reputable online dealer, there is a very real risk that it's a bomb waiting to go off and infect your system, or worse.

6. Don't goof off in class. It is a natural tendency to take a break, every now and then, and wander down the information superhighway. Use caution, as it is possible to contract a computer virus simply by viewing a Web page (if certain conditions exist). It is also possible to create a hostile work environment, if you visit sites that others determine to be objectionable.

7. Keep your desk clean, and put your toys away. A clean desk policy does not require a clean desk (as the author's office will attest). It requires the individual to secure all restricted documents at the end of the work day, to prevent unwanted eyes from viewing this information after hours.

8. Keep your shots up to date. Anti-virus software only works if you keep the signatures (inoculations) updated. Managed solutions are better as they don't require direct user intervention.

9. Keep your secrets secret. Don't share your passwords, usernames, or vital system information, etc., with anyone. If you must record this information to remember it, use encryption.

10. If you see something wrong, tell an adult. Report suspected violations of security policy, or suspected incidents to the organization's abuse hotline. This may be through the help-desk, or through an anonymous message system.

A PRAYER FOR SECURITY

Not to be sacrilegious, but every security manager worth their salt has asked for assistance from some higher power. The following prayer summarizes the hope an admin may seek from time to time (with apologies to Reinhold Niebuhr).

Grant me the ability
to accept the information I cannot protect;
courage to protect the information I can;
and wisdom to know the difference.

Protecting one system at a time;
Enjoying one moment at a time;
Accepting intrusions as the pathway to expertise;
Taking this hackerful world
  as it is, not as I would have it;
Trusting that all things will be made right
  if I comply with our policies and practice my craft expertly;
That I may be reasonably happy in this profession.
Amen.

The Role of Information Security and Its Relationship to Information Technology Risk Management

CHRISAN HERROD

Nova Southeastern University

Chrisan Herrod accepted her position with the Securities Exchange Commission as the Chief Security Officer in August 2004. She is responsible for information security and IT business continuity for the Commission. She is pursuing her PhD in Information Systems at NovaSoutheastern University.

Prior to the SEC, she was at the National Defense University, Information Resource Management College. She served as Department Chair of the Information Operations and Assurance Department where she was responsible for curriculum including information security, assurance, and operations and as a Professor of Information Security and Systems Management. The University provides graduate level education for the Department of Defense and United States federal departments and agencies.

Previously, she was the Director of Global IT Security at GlaxoSmithKline (GSK), one of the world's leading pharmaceutical companies. Prior to joining GSK, she was the Director of Information Security at Fannie Mae, a leading real estate, financial institution. While at Fannie Mae, she became involved in the White House-sponsored Partnership for Critical Infrastructure Security as the Information Sharing and Analysis Working Group Chair and is currently serving as a Special Advisor to the Health Care Industry Information Sharing and Analysis Center initiative.

From 1993 to 1998 she was a senior civilian with the Department of Defense's Information Security Program Office serving as Director of Plans, Policy and Resource Management and Director of IA Education, Training and Awareness. From 1988 to 1992, she was assigned to the White House Military Office, Office of Emergency Operations at the Defense Information Systems Agency. Ms. Herrod served as an active duty officer in the US Army and retired as a Major, USAF Reserve.

She is an adjunct professor teaching information security and leadership courses with both the University of Fairfax and the University of Phoenix. From 1999 to 2001, she taught information security graduate courses at George Washington University.

Overview

This research investigates the relationship between traditional IT security risk assessment and incorporation of that function into an IT risk

management framework that includes key risk areas such as security, priv-
acy, data retention, regulatory compliance, and business continuity. Devel-
oping and implementing an IT risk management focus enables organizations
to develop a holistic mitigation plan. Key to the development of a risk man-
agement framework is the ability of the organization to determine business
impact and develop a defensible return-on-investment strategy. Organiza-
tions in both the public and private sector are being required to implement
risk management programs in order to satisfy government regulations.

Introduction

The information security discipline is part of a larger and more complex
issue, that of Information Technology (IT) risk management. Information
Security is considered a risk management strategy and as such forms the
foundation of an IT risk management program. The purpose of this paper is
to document the evolution of information security as an IT risk management best practice; compare and contrast risk management methodologies
and strategies with an emphasis on developing return-on-investment; and
document IT risk management and information security's key role in
managing compliance and meeting legislative requirements.

Risk management has traditionally been included as an integral part of
an Information Security program. For example, it is a key objective in the
Certified Information System Security Professional (CISSP) certification
and is addressed as part of the Security Management Domain in the CISSP
review book.[1] It is assumed to be a critical job function of an information
security practitioner. The trend therefore is to view risk management as
strictly a security issue when in fact security should be viewed as an element of IT risk management and addressed as one of many key risk areas.
The difference is not subtle.

The key driver in this evolution is the cost of security and documenting
the rationale behind the need to purchase security technology and implement a security program. The emotional rationale for defending the need
to implement security—that of fear, uncertainty, and doubt—is not useful
in justifying resources. Soft claims cannot be quantified. Allegations that
security events will create a "loss of brand" or a "decrease in market
value" are perfectly valid but do not establish causation between financial
impact and an event.[2] These tactics were used in lieu of defensible return-
on-investment (ROI) strategies, however they are no longer acceptable in
the view of senior managers who must cost-justify IT investments across
the board. Credibility is often at stake. Defensible facts and data-driven
conclusions are required. The importance of translating information
security into a business-based language is the primary rationale for using a
sound risk management methodology.

Incorporation of information security as a key risk area within an IT risk
management program elevates the importance of information security and
ties its practice together with other key IT risks. Information security is a
business practice that supports and enables other business processes such
as privacy, data retention, and regulatory compliance. Information security
also provides the underpinning for the safe use of untrusted communication networks such as the Internet.

The most pressing corporate issue is assuring quality compliance to regulatory requirements. The Sarbanes-Oxley Act of 2002 was enacted on July 30, 2002 in response to a number of major corporate and accounting scandals involving some of the most prominent companies in the U.S. The Act requires publicly traded companies to explicitly evaluate and report to the public on the effectiveness of specified internal controls.[3] The linkage to IT risk management and information security's role is critical in that the Securities and Exchange Commission (SEC) requires that a formal risk assessment be performed to evaluate the internal and external factors that impact an organization's performance. The results of the risk assessment will determine the controls that need to be implemented.

Information Security's Relationship to Information Technology Risk Management

The Information Security discipline includes within it the concept of risk management. Most text books on Information Security have a chapter on risk management and performing risk assessments. Recent news articles discussing the role of information security professionals point out that the performance of risk assessments are a key component of good information security, specifically risk identification. Over time, performing risk assessments and managing risks have fallen into the "job jar" of the information security professional. Traditional physical security practices have always relied on risk assessments to determine threats and vulnerabilities. Threat and vulnerability identification are perceived to be the exclusive purview of security organizations; somehow the terms are mystically intertwined. Extending this linkage as part of the practice of information security can be attributed to much the same logic. Threat and vulnerability identification is not, however, the driving force for coupling risk management with information security practices. The latest trend and rationale for continuing to include risk management as part of security is to develop a return-on-security-investment (ROSI) strategy. The only disciplined way to derive a return on investment is to perform a process oriented, data-driven risk assessment.

In addition to ROSI, the other trend that is driving the linkage of the two practices is developing a culture of shared accountability for risk management. The reasoning is that security is supposed to educate the business leader about threats the organization faces, about the likelihood and consequences of those threats, about costs, and the effectiveness of possible remedies. The only way to effectively accomplish this is through process-oriented risk management so that business leaders can make the decisions on acceptable risk, squarely putting leadership at the heart of risk management accountability and decision-making. The complex nature of doing business in today's technical and legal environment increases the type of risks that organizations must address, which leads to broader considerations that a more comprehensive IT risk management program includes. Including the information security program as part of an IT risk management approach enables an organization to effectively perform enterprise-wide collaboration and strategic planning. Risk management then becomes much more than an information security problem, it becomes an issue that is corporate in nature and multi-dimensional.

The Case for Information Technology (IT) Risk Management

Risk is an uncertain event or condition that, if it occurs, may have a negative effect on activities being performed in the business. Risk management is the systematic process of identifying risk, assessing the likelihood of its occurring and the impact it may have, and taking the action necessary to ensure that the reward from the activities performed will be realized.[4]

Risk management is the balancing of risk and reward to ensure that rewards are maximized and risks are minimized to a degree acceptable to the business. It is the planned control of risk and involves monitoring, analyzing potential risks, and making decisions about what to do about potential risks.[5]

Operational IT risk management is a significant new function that will provide companies the capability to implement world-class IT enabled business processes. A comprehensive IT risk management program includes information security, privacy, regulatory compliance, IT business continuity, data management, and hardware and software project risks (see Figure 5-1). As pointed out in the introduction, integrating risk management functions aggregates the importance and helps establish the function on an equal footing with other more traditional key risk areas such as financial risk management and managing the risk posed to an organization's reputation.

The question for senior leadership in both the public and private sectors is what should IT risk management deliver? As the complexity of IT infrastructures increases and the requirement to comply with new laws grows, the risks also dramatically increase. Businesses continue to rely upon the Internet as the communication backbone for e-business, which also

- Regulatory compliance
- Business continuity
- Security and privacy
- Project management
- Acquisition (vendor viability)
- Human resources

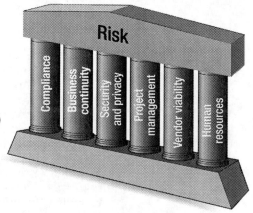

FIGURE 5-1 Risk-related programs

increases operational risks. For these reasons deciding upon and implementing a risk management process and methodology will greatly reduce the risks associated with the introduction of new technologies that support the mission of the business and with new legislation that dictates business behavior.

The inherent complexities of developing, deploying, and managing IT services on a global scale are obvious. Add to these the legislative and regulatory framework that govern business practices in many industries, and companies are faced with a situation where only constant vigilance can ensure they are operating safely and legally. Peril cannot be eliminated from the business life cycle, and failures can result in loss, injuries, and lawsuits. At the same time, IT is essential to the success of any business. Many opportunities arise from exploiting information technologies in ways that advance business and serve customers.[6]

The goal of an IT risk management organization should be to ensure potential risks are identified and assessed and, where the business considers it necessary, to implement controls that mitigate the potential impact of the risk. This is achieved by:

- Creating policy
- Making process improvements
- Defining procedures or standards
- Instituting controls through management practices
- Following guidelines
- Building contracts
- Using groups in the organisation
- Outsourcing where necessary
- Insuring against the consequences

Whenever a business introduces change, a dynamic that affects risk is also introduced. Change has the potential for increasing or decreasing risk. Most change has an associated reward, which is why a business is willing to confront risks that might be incurred. Risk management starts with the monitoring of projects and programs and other external and internal factors that may create risk. A business change will often generate multiple potential risks. Each risk may affect multiple business units or functional areas. Corporations tend to respond to risks in one of four ways (see Table 5-1).

TABLE 5-1 **Responses to Risk**

Response	Description
Mitigate a risk	Steps are taken to reduce the probability of a risk maturing (occurring), or reduce the impact or loss should that risk mature.
Avoid a risk	The decision is made to avoid taking the risk. Typically, this means the reward/benefit to the company cannot be acquired.
Transfer a risk	The anticipated loss of the maturing risk is transferred to another party. Typically, this would be a third party (e.g., insurance against lawsuit).
Accept a risk	No steps are taken to mitigate, avoid, or transfer the risk. Basically, in accepting a risk, the company has chosen to accept the consequences should the risk mature.

The purpose of IT risk management is to determine the appropriate response and to ensure that key stakeholders are involved in the process of risk management. The operating principle, regardless of the response, is that the risk is evaluated using a consistent process. IT risk management is dependent upon a consistently used methodology that is applied across the key risk areas. Given that this is a generally accepted axiom, the next section documents the state of risk management methodologies and processes and compares and contrasts the methodologies.

The IT Risk Management Framework

The decision to respond to risk should be based on the use of a standard risk management methodology or framework. Decisions about the way risk is managed should not be made in isolation and definitely not be made without some due diligence. The issue of due diligence is increasing in importance due to Sarbanes-Oxley, and other industry specific legislation that sets legal requirements for protecting data such as the Health Insurance Portability and Accountability Act (HIPAA), which protects patients medical records, and Gramm-Leach-Bliley (GLB), which regulates the financial services industry. These laws will be discussed in detail in later sections.

A risk management framework provides a process which, if followed, results in a logical basis for making decisions about risk. Facts and data are collected and presented in a rational manner. There are many risk management methodologies in use both in the public and private sector. There are differences among them, but there is an overarching commonality, which is illustrated in the framework shown in Figure 5-2.

The methodology shown in Figure 5-2 is a composite of best practices from industry and government models, most notably the National Institute of Standards and Technology (NIST Management), the Information Systems Audit Control Association (ISACA), and ISO standard 17799.

Risk is an art and a science, and there is literally no correct way of performing the function. But there are generally accepted steps, and they can

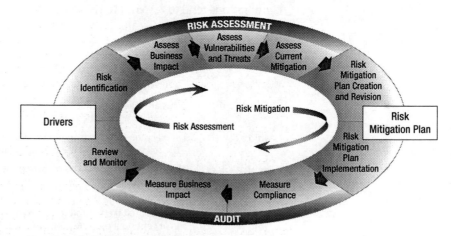

FIGURE 5-2 Generic risk management framework

and should be adapted to fit the environment and/or the culture of the organization. Typically a risk management framework is guided by key principles:

  ▓ Risk and its impact should be viewed holistically—that is, from the perspective of the entire business. Assessing the impact of risk from a more narrow perspective poses risks in its own right since business needs may outweigh a negative IT impact.

  ▓ Risks are only significant if they have a business impact or quantifiable loss.

  ▓ The framework must provide a basis for the evaluation of all kinds of risk, from minor security incidents to potentially catastrophic events.

  ▓ It may sometimes be necessary to handle incidents before studying the driver that causes them to occur—treating risks holistically doesn't mean the business collapses before fixing the problem!

The key to success is not the framework but whether it works for an organization. A standard methodology that all business units use to assess risk will provide the key ingredient for a successful program. Some key concepts embodied within the risk management process model are worth noting:

  ▓ Risk is seldom eliminated; it is merely mitigated or controlled. As such, the risk management model is an endless loop. A risk, once mitigated, should be periodically reviewed, and controls should be tested for compliance at regular intervals.

  ▓ The essential process steps, Risk Assessment and Risk Mitigation, successively gather information that supports the key steps in the overall process.

The following paragraphs discuss the risk management model shown in Figure 5-2, and define and explain the steps in the process.

RISK IDENTIFICATION

A key step in any risk management technique is to identify the perspective of interest (i.e., from whose perspective should the risk scenario be analyzed—essentially who will suffer which losses and gain which rewards?). For some risk scenarios, it may be important to analyze the same situation from more than one perspective (e.g., different business units or functional areas within the company may each have a different perspective on the same risk) in order to acquire the full corporate perspective.

Identification of scope is another key critical aspect of risk management. When conducting the risk identification process, a clear understanding of the boundaries of the analysis and the topics to be covered within the analysis should be agreed. What is inclusive and what is exclusive? This is particularly important when calculating the amount of loss or reward, as these will be directly affected by the amount and size of items in the scope. The scope may include technology, organizational, geographical, or functional boundaries.

Based on an understanding of the perspective and the scope, identify the potential risks to the company. These risks may be ongoing risks that have already been addressed or may be new risks. Outline both IT and business risks. When the risks have been defined, a cursory review should be completed to determine which risks currently have been addressed and have had controls implemented through prior efforts, and which risks are new and have not been formally reviewed in the past. Risks can be categorized as follows (see Table 5-2).

From a business perspective it is useful to classify risks according to business functions. This aligns the IT risk management function with the business and makes it easier to relate the issues to the business stakeholders. This becomes extremely important when an organization is trying to implement a risk management culture that includes joint accountability for risk management.

A sample list of business functions is below:

- Product development and safety
- Product quality and availability
- IT systems
- Information management
- Safeguarding key assets, resources, and processes
- Sales and marketing practices
- Financial controls
- Legal

BUSINESS IMPACT ANALYSIS

Defining the business impact and quantifying the risk is the most difficult and frustrating step in any risk management methodology. It is not precise but it will yield an estimate. A standard approach to risk quantification is shown below. This standard is based on two considerations:

- The expected value or financial impact ($ Impact) if the risk were to occur; this is always viewed from a business perspective not a technology perspective
- The probability (P), or likelihood, that a risk will occur

The formula for calculating risk is Risk ($) = P × ($ Impact).

Risk quantification requires knowledge of the expected value of the business impact if the event occurs, which means that the business has to be involved in estimating the impact to the business. It is not possible for an IT risk manager to know what the business owner knows about the importance of an application or a function to the overall mission of the organization.

TABLE 5-2   **Risk Categories**

Risk	Description
Major business risks	Mergers, acquisitions, introduction of new e-business sites and opportunities, legislation, legal issues.
Key IT risks	Introduction of new technologies supporting business processes whether internal or external
Project risks	Risks to business continuity introduced by a project or Risks to the benefits realization of a project (risks to achieving benefits of project) or Risk to successful project delivery
Individual risks & incidents	Inherent in work and practices involving use and practice of IT

THREATS AND VULNERABILITIES

This step in the assessment process identifies all the components that may contribute to the actualization of the potential risk. These components are referred to as vulnerabilities and threats. In most cases, there will be several vulnerabilities and threats for each potential risk to the business.

Typically, different vulnerabilities and threats will exist within different areas, all contributing to the risk(s) under review. Those working in IT have a tendency to make judgments from a technology perspective. Often, though, it is not the technology itself that is at issue, but rather, how the technology is managed, or human factors affecting the use of technology. To understand vulnerability, the assessment process needs to determine what is putting a component at risk.

Threats and vulnerabilities are related to either technology, people and process. The relationship of a threat to vulnerability is shown in Figure 5-3. Vendors, legislation, business partners, infrastructure systems, facilities, the environment, financials, and social and organizational considerations can all be viewed as vulnerabilities. The point is to determine the most likely threats relating to the company's defined vulnerabilities. Vulnerabilities are established based on past experiences, the nature of the business, the competition, the physical location, the extent to which the business relies on technology, geographical and political considerations, etc.

MITIGATION STRATEGIES

The next step is to assess the mitigation strategies that are currently in place and determine what additional mitigation strategies need to be used in order to effectively manage the risks. Controls may include those that form a part of the hierarchy of controls, or they may be the result of transfer of the risk.

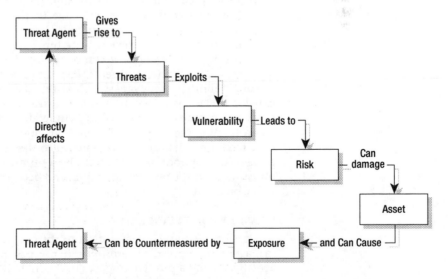

FIGURE 5-3 Threat relationship

Typically, different vulnerabilities and threats will exist within different areas, all contributing to the risks under review. Where appropriate, the assessment of current mitigation may be undertaken by different business areas. For example mitigating risks associated with access controls is in fact a shared responsibility between IT, business managers, and human resources. The risk cannot be isolated and mitigated simply by introducing new software. A process, agreed to by all parties, must be developed and adhered to in order to ensure, for example, that accesses are terminated when an individual leaves the company.

Identify the processes that are currently being used to mitigate the vulnerability or threat. Mitigation categories refer to types of controls. The most common controls are:

- Policy
- Process
- Management practice
- Guidelines
- Standard operating procedures (SOPs)

Other types include:

- Technical standard
- Contracts
- Organisation/councils
- Training
- Regulation
- Software tools

The assessment of current controls should review four key areas:

- Are there controls in place for this vulnerability or threat—i.e., do they exist?
- Are these controls properly implemented—i.e., are they implemented everywhere they are required? Are they implemented consistently?
- Are the controls effective in managing the vulnerability or threat? Have the controls been effective in the past at addressing similar potential risks? Have the potential risks been realized in the past—i.e., have the risks previously matured?
- Are there safeguards or compensating controls in place to mitigate this vulnerability or threat? Have these been effective in the past?

Based on the effectiveness of existing controls and in light of the detailed review of vulnerabilities and threats, make recommendations on what else can be done to mitigate vulnerabilities and threats. Additional controls, new processes, and/or new technology may be necessary. The final recommendations incorporated into the risk mitigation plan should present the options felt to offer the optimal "value-added" return on investment for the resources required and hence deliver the greatest impact to the business.

MEASURE COMPLIANCE

Measuring compliance is critical to the overall success of the entire risk management process. Determining if the risk management methods are actually having a positive impact and being able to measure the extent to which the mitigation controls are in fact being used is the last step. Clearly compliance measurement is somewhat onerous; however, successful implementations depend on how easy the process is and the perception that the process is useful, and will not have a negative impact. Typically auditors are brought in at this point in the process. The key here is to ensure that the auditors are on-board with the process and their findings will not be used against the organizations being audited. Compliance monitoring should not be viewed as the penalty phase of risk management. This is why it is so important to have a separate risk management function that is a partner with the company's audit team.

Consider the following when planning compliance measurement tools:

- Scope of compliance measurement, i.e. who will be measured, where and when measurements are to be taken, and possibly by whom
- How to perform data capture, e.g., self-assessment questionnaires, Web-based tools, interviews, audit results, metrics returned from execution of routine processes (do not underestimate time required to capture data)
- How to solicit responses, e.g., how to ensure responses are made to questionnaires, how to ensure data is returned as requested
- Methods to collate and store the responses
- Methods to measure responses, i.e., determine how to use the data to measure compliance
- Follow-up actions that may be required

Other information may need to be gathered in this initial planning task, including:

- An inventory of what is currently under control
- The conflict resolution process and escalation process

From an IT risk management perspective the issue is whether there is a consistent, repeatable, and documented risk management process. The framework presented in this section embodies all these characteristics; it is not prescriptive but rather strategically oriented and can be tailored to meet any organization's needs. It represents the current philosophy of risk management.

Contemporary Risk Assessment Methodologies

IT risk management should deliver, at a minimum, an agreed-upon risk profile, an understanding of risk exposure, and an awareness of risk management priorities. Most contemporary risk management methods are designed to accomplish these requirements. Some are extremely complex, others very simple. The primary differences lie in the definitions used and the focus of methods. A standard risk management process is shown in Figure 5-4.

FEDERAL GOVERNMENT METHODOLOGIES

The federal government has two primary sources for risk assessment methodologies, the National Security Agency (NSA) and the National Institute for Standards and Technology (NIST). Given that NSA is culturally part of the Department of Defense and NIST culturally represents the civilian or non-DOD agencies, the use of these methodologies generally falls out

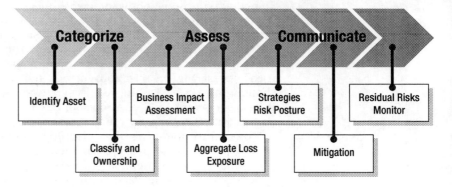

Without a well-defined and communicated process,
managing risks becomes a game of chance.

FIGURE 5-4 Risk management processes

according to affiliation. Recent events, however, are changing the way the federal government in general is viewing risk management. This is due in large measure to the Federal Information Security Management Act (FISMA) of 2002, Public Law 107-347 which gives NIST statutory responsibilities in the area of risk management but more importantly requires that federal departments and agencies perform risk assessments and annually report their departmental security posture to the Office of Personnel Management (OPM).

As stated there are two primary sources of risk management methodologies. The first is the National Security Agency's Information Assessment Methodology (IAM). The IAM is not a complex model and is used in part because of its ease of use and relatively unstructured reporting requirements. IAM is touted as being a "white hat" methodology designed to assist organizations in addressing their information security weaknesses before the Inspector General (IG) does.

The IAM's focus is on determining which information is critical to the organization, identification of systems that process, store, or transmit critical information, identification of potential vulnerabilities, and recommending solutions to mitigate or eliminate those vulnerabilities. There is no focus on developing a return on investment strategy or business impact. The methodology relies on evidence review from a documentation standpoint and is heavily dependent on interviews of key personal. The process is informal and is clearly targeted at assessing the current information security posture. The reporting requirements are minimal, and are limited to an out-briefing and a short (five-page) report. The methodology doesn't address several key aspects of the risk assessment process and is not useful for determining ROSI.

In contrast, NIST has taken a much more traditional view of the risk management process and has oriented its methodology on assessing the risk in IT systems. NIST's Risk Management Guide for Information Technology Systems is in draft. The document is very comprehensive and encompasses three processes: risk assessment, risk mitigation, and evaluation and assessment. Risk management is defined as the process that allows IT managers to balance the operational and economic costs of protective measures and achieve gains in mission capability by protecting IT systems and data that support their organizations' mission. The basis of NIST's risk management methodology is total integration into the system design life cycle. Risk management is viewed as an iterative process throughout all phases of the cycle from initiation to disposal, which is defined as the disposition of information, hardware, and software.

NIST also published the Federal IT Security Assessment Framework, which identifies five levels of IT security program effectiveness. The benefits of this framework include identifying a standard way of performing self-assessments and providing flexibility in assessments based on the size and complexity of the asset. Assessment in this case refers to the entire process of collecting and analyzing system data. This process is supported by a software tool, the Automated Security Self-Evaluation Tool (ASSET). ASSET is freely available at *http://csrc.nist.gov/asset* and facilitates the data collection and reporting steps of the process.

INDUSTRY RISK ASSESSMENT METHODOLOGIES

There are several well documented information security risk assessment methodologies. The most prominent are Operationally Critical Threat, Asset, and Vulnerability Evaluation (OCTAVE), and Qualitative Risk Assessment. Both are report-oriented and provide a myriad of tables and formats that are used in documenting the risks to an organization.

OCTAVE is a self-directed approach, which means that people from an organization manage and direct the information security risk evaluation from that organization. OCTAVE uses four major components: asset, threat, vulnerability, and impact. An information security risk evaluation must account for all components. OCTAVE is an asset-driven evaluation approach, framing the organizations' risks in the context of its assets. OCTAVE includes three phases: build asset-based threat profiles; identify infrastructure vulnerabilities; and develop security strategies and plans.[7]

Qualitative Risk Assessment is used to determine the level of protection required for applications, systems, facilities, and other enterprise assets. It is a systematic examination of assets, threats, and vulnerabilities that establishes the probability of the threats occurring, the cost of losses if they do occur, and the value of the safeguards or countermeasures designed to reduce the threats and vulnerabilities to an acceptable level. The qualitative approach attempts to prioritize the various risk elements in subjective terms.[8] The quantitative risk analysis approach attempts to assign numeric values to all risks and potential losses while the qualitative approach assigns a rating to each risk and countermeasure and is derived from a "gut feeling" or opinions of internal employees who are considered experts. There are several variations on the theme of Qualitative Risk Assessment (QRA) such as the Facilitated Risk Assessment Process (FRAP). It is QRA-lite and as such is designed as a vulnerability analysis that is normally conducted to determine the current level of conditions. It is not a risk management methodology.

As noted above, since quantitative risk analysis deals with numbers and monetary values, formulas are involved. This gets to the issue of calculating business impact if an asset was damaged by a specific threat. The goal of annualized loss expectancy (ALE) is to understand how much a company could logically spend to protect the asset from this threat. The issue is that this type of risk management methodology, while considered more useful, is much more difficult to achieve. Not only is it difficult to determine the financial business impact of a loss, but it is equally difficult to determine a meaningful ROI.

Return-on-Investment (ROI)

Traditional approaches to IT investment attempt to identify projects with the best profit potential. Proponents of the investment must "make the business case" to senior management. The heightened strategic importance of IT, however, has forced companies to think differently. They must now weigh the returns on individual investments against demands for organization-wide capabilities. They also must assess opportunities to leverage and improve existing capabilities and infrastructures in light of opportunities to create new capabilities and test new business models. The complex trade-offs are leading to new IT-investment patterns.[9]

Given that this is true for IT investments, what then is the impact on information security? Security is critical to IT strategies, including transformation, renewal, process improvement, and experiments or IT pilot programs. From an investment point of view security must be considered when developing an IT investment strategy to meet IT initiatives. These constitute the drivers that lead to the requirement to justify all IT costs and to develop a quantitative return-on-investment.

Using this simple definition of ROI puts clarity around the approach:

$$\text{ROI} = \frac{\text{(Change in Revenue)} + \text{(Cost Savings)}}{\text{(Investment)}}$$

Investment is the cost of the product plus administrative overhead plus effects on operations plus license renewals plus training and/or adding personnel. Change in Revenue equates to added benefits from the increase in functionality that the security implementation provides. Cost Savings is really about loss avoidance. This is the hard part because no one really knows how likely a company is to be exposed to a particular kind of security-related loss within a particular time period. The number of virus attacks per year can be estimated. How many cause losses and how massive are the losses are the unknowns. Worse, it is not abundantly clear whether security technologies prevent losses or whether they even defeat attacks.[10]

Transformation initiatives include ERP implementations, building data warehouses, implementing middleware to manage WEB environments, and standardizing desktop technologies. All of these initiatives have a critical dependence on security technologies and processes. Implementing ERP solutions such as PeopleSoft are inherently non-secure and, depending on the type of data processed, have privacy and security risks that must be assessed. A key part of the risk assessment process is developing the business impact and the ROI for secure implementation.

For example, access management for a PeopleSoft implementation could involve several layers of security and process development. Most PeopleSoft implementations are used for human resources, customer management, and financial management. The data in all probability will be personally identifiable data (PID) that is sensitive and must be protected. The business impact analysis will determine the cost to the company if the data is lost, stolen, or manipulated. That essential determination will factor into determining the ROI of implementing role-based access management versus implementing role-based access management with an additional layer of security such as public key infrastructure (PKI) or biometric technology.

The cost to implement role-based access controls will most likely be factored into the PeopleSoft implementation by the vendor, but the additional cost of adding security layers will require an ROI. The ROI in this case can be developed based on the number of employees, type of operating system and application interfaces, integration and testing, and required training for users and system administrators. If PKI is in the mix then the added costs of either owning or outsourcing the Certificate Authority (CA) and all of the overhead with maintaining and managing the CA must also be factored into the equation.

The cost differences between a basic security approach and a layered approach are weighed against the business impact analysis, and a risk determination is made. The decision process was based on an ROI and risk management strategy that considered two key risk issues, security and privacy. Two axioms are worth remembering, the cost data will never be precise, and the cost data will always be challenged. This is why the risk management process can be problematic and why so many attempts at ROI fail. If expectations are set at the beginning of the risk assessment process then the "precision factor" issue can be managed and mitigated.

Research shows that:

- Securely engineering software to proactively fix problems has a concrete value. The ROI for reviewing security in the design phase can be up to 21 percent, versus 15 percent in the implementation phase and 12 percent in the testing phase.
- Security can also create efficiencies that contribute to the top and bottom lines. Minimizing unnecessary functionality in an infrastructure can attain efficiency gains greater than 3 percent.[11]

IT Risk Management and Regulatory Compliance

The importance of IT risk management is growing because of the increase in regulations governing both the public and private sectors. IT security technologies can address regulatory compliance issues. Organizations must begin to focus on the IT security implications of various audit and regulatory requirements as documented below:

- The U.S. Public Company Accounting Reform and Investor Protection Act of 2002 (Sarbanes-Oxley) makes a public company's senior management and advisors individually accountable for the accuracy of its financial performance reporting. Section 404 specifies the presence of appropriate controls. The integrity of systems and applications that produce financial reports must be demonstrated.
- The Gramm-Leach-Bliley Financial Services Modernization Act of 1999 (GLB) requires that financial institutions ensure the

security and confidentiality of customer personal information against "reasonably foreseeable" internal or external threats.

* The U.S. Healthcare Information Portability and Accountability Act (HIPAA) specifies that healthcare and insurance organizations must have procedures to prevent, detect, contain, and correct security violations.

* The Federal Information Security Management Act (FISMA) requires federal agencies to develop, document, and implement agency-wide programs to secure data and information systems that support agency operations and assets, including those managed by other agencies or contractors.

* The European Union Data Protection Directive specifies that personal data must have appropriate security.

The regulations don't specify what companies must do to achieve compliance. Therefore to determine risk exposure, all aspects of IT risk management must be addressed. Managing vulnerabilities can only be achieved by first understanding the impact of risk across the business enterprise.[12]

Vendors are producing products to assist risk managers in defining the risk to corporations based on the requirements specified in the above legislation. Products such as Symantec's Enterprise Security Manager incorporate a module that automates government agencies' audits for compliance with FISMA.[13] Oracle and Aspect Communication Corporation developed a corporate controller application to help companies address Section 404 of Sarbanes-Oxley.

Conclusion

Legislative regulations impacting IT security, privacy, data retention, business continuity, and regulatory compliance issues pose many challenges to the public and private sectors. Implementing a risk management program that focuses on operational risks as described in this reading can help mitigate the impact of these legislative regulations.

There are a number of IT security risk management methodologies that are used by the private and public sectors. These methodologies can be used as baselines to develop a more inclusive risk management approach. The methodology is not as important as the implementation, and that will depend on the culture of the organization and the importance placed upon the process by senior management.

Documenting business impact and return-on-investment will be essential to get the resources needed to implement appropriate mitigation strategies. Risk management from an operational and IT perspective inclusive of IT security will assist organizations in meeting these growing and complex challenges.

References

[1]Myers, M., & Harris S. (2002). *CISSP passport* (pp. 10–11). New York: Osborne.

[2]Karofsky, E. (2001, Fall). Insight into return on security investment. *Secure Business Quarterly*, Cambridge, MA.

[3]The Sarbanes-Oxley Act of 2002. (2002). *Strategies for meeting new internal control reporting challenges: A white paper, PriceWaterhouseCoopers.* Retrieved February 2, 2004, from PriceWaterhouseCoopers: *http://ww.pwc.com*

[4]McNair, P. (2001). *Controlling risk, ACM computing surveys.* Retrieved March 1, 2004, from *ACM*: *http://www.acm.org/ubiquity/views/p_mcnair_1.html*

[5]McNair, P. (2001). *Controlling risk, ACM computing surveys.* Retrieved March 1, 2004, from *ACM*: *http://www.acm.org/ubiquity/views/p_mcnair_1.html*

[6]Herrod, C. (in press). *IT risk management, advise from IT security experts.* New York: Aurbauch.

[7]Alberts, C., & Dorofee, A. (2003). *The OCTAVE approach* (pp. 11–19). New York: Addison-Wesley.

[8]Peltier, T. (2001). *Information security risk analysis* (pp. 23, 53, 91). New York: Auerbach.

[9]Ross, J., & Beath, C. (2002, Winter). New approaches to IT investment. *MIT Sloan Management Review.*

[10]Blakley, B. (2001, Fall). An imprecise but necessary calculation. *Secure Business Quarterly.* Cambridge, MA.

[11]Karofsky, E. (2001, Fall). Insight into return on security investment. *Secure Business Quarterly*, Cambridge, MA.

[12]Nicolett, M. (2004). IT security technologies can address regulatory compliance. *Gartner Research Note COM-22-1253.* Boston: Gartner Group Publishing.

[13]FISMA. (2002). *Federal Information Security Management Act Title III—Information Security Sec 301.* Retrieved March 19, 2004, from U. S. Department of Homeland Security. Available from *http://www.fedcirc.gov/library/legislation/FISMA.html*

Architecting and Managing Secure Biometric Systems

KAMESWARA RAO NAMUDURI
Wichita State University

SAVITHA S. KADIYALA
Georgia State University

Kameswara Rao Namuduri is an Assistant Professor in the Department of Electrical and Computer Engineering at Wichita State University, Wichita, Kansas. His research interests include Information Security, Computer Forensics and Video Processing and Communication. He is leading the research and education activities in the area of Information Assurance and Security at Wichita State University through the Center for Information Security. His research has been published in premier journals such as IEEE Transactions on Signal Processing, Image Processing, and Circuits and Systems for Video Technology. He currently serves as the Associate Editor for Pattern Recognition Letters.

Savitha S. Kadiyala is a doctoral candidate in the Decision Sciences group of the Department of Managerial Sciences of the J. Mack Robinson College of Business, Georgia State University, Atlanta, Georgia. Her research interests include knowledge management, information systems outsourcing, knowledge discovery in databases and applications of data mining specifically, customer relationship management, and security. Prior to joining the doctoral program, she worked as a management consultant at the Center for Organization Development, Hyderabad, India, specializing in the areas of motivation and organizational culture.

Overview

Biometrics is gaining in favor as a method of providing strong authentication—authentication by more than one factor. Unfortunately the field of biometrics, which involves life measurement (hence the name), is perceived by many as overly intrusive. Other privacy advocates are concerned with the collection and possible theft of biometric information. Most security experts agree, however, that many biometrics provide a level of authentication desired in modern systems. The challenge arises when designing a biometric solution that balances the needs of the system with the privacy issues of the individuals and the intrusiveness. In this reading, the authors provide an overview of the biometric technologies currently in use. They also detail the implementation and management challenges associated with the building and administration of example technologies. These challenges include capturing, processing, and generating new signatures and user records. While standards are emerging for these new technologies, most are so new that there are few recommendations for implementing biometrics. The authors also address the challenges with performance measures, including the reliability and confidentiality of the systems.

Introduction

Biometric systems are increasingly being considered as better fool-proof methods of ensuring security in several areas ranging from national security to credit card processing, as opposed to traditional methods such as alphanumeric passwords and personal identification numbers (PINs).[1] Biometrics includes physical characteristics such as a fingerprint, hand geometry, voice, face, retina, and iris. Jain, Ross, and Prabhakar[2] noted that a biometric characteristic is a human physiological and/or behavioral characteristic that satisfies the requirements of universality, distinctiveness, permanence, and collectability. They defined a biometric system as essentially a . . .

> *". . .pattern recognition system that operates by acquiring biometric data from an individual, extracting a feature set from the acquired data, and comparing this feature set against the template set in the database."*[3]

Biometric systems have already been deployed in many places, and soon they will be used in variety of commercial and federal applications ranging from personnel detection in offices and online point of sale applications, to border patrol and law enforcement, among others. This reading presents the basic principles underlying the architecture, implementation, and management of secure biometric systems.

There are two types of biometric systems from their application perspective—identification and verification systems.[4] Identification systems are those that identify an unknown person based on his/her biometric signature. Verification systems are those that verify the biometric signature of a person in order to authorize him/her and provide access to the underlying application. In both applications the core functionality of the systems is the same.

The scope of biometric systems employed for certain applications such as law enforcement may extend to national and international.[5] The volume of data that is expected to be processed by a biometric system is usually very large. Given such a scope and volume of data that these systems are expected to process, it is clear that biometric systems tend to be large, scalable, and distributed in general.

The increasing popularity of biometric systems, because of the advantages that they provide as opposed to the traditional security systems, demands that standards be specified for developing interoperable products and applications. In this connection, the Biometric Consortium, in coordination with the National Institute for Standards and Technology (NIST), has been developing standards for biometric systems. Numerous organizations from private industry, federal and state government agencies, as well as academia participate as members in the Biometric Consortium. The intent of this consortium is to develop widely acceptable standards for the application level and device level interfaces that are independent of the operating systems and vendors, and to be able to support a variety of biometric applications. These efforts resulted in several standards such as the biometric application interface (BioAPI standard) for biometric-based personal identification and verification systems,[6] and the Common Biometric Exchange File Format (CBEFF)[7] to facilitate exchange and interoperability of biometric data. BioAPI Version 1.1 and its reference implementation for the Linux Operating System have already been developed and available for the public (*www.bioapi.org*). Several biometric data formats for fingerprint, facial scar mark and tattoo, signature, and hand geometry are at various stages of development.

Due to the sensitivity of information contained in biometric systems, it is expected that such systems will be attacked by intruders both from within and outside the country. Assurance and security mechanisms need to be provided for the information stored in the biometric systems both in stored and transit modes. It is important to understand the design principles underlying the architecture and management of biometric systems so that appropriate mechanisms can be used to secure such systems. Biometric signatures complement the existing non-biometric based information assurance and security mechanisms such as the public key infrastructure (PKI).

In order to maximize the level of security provided by biometric systems, multimodal systems are being considered as better alternatives to relying on a single biometric for identification and verification purposes.[8,9] Multimodal biometric systems utilize multiple signatures of the same individuals obtained from different sensors. Information (signatures) obtained from multiple sensors can be fused together to improve the performance of identification and verification systems and compensate for lack of sufficient features from the signature obtained from a single sensor. Information fusion[10] can take place while extracting features, while matching the scores obtained from different modalities, or while making decisions. Results obtained from information fusion suggest that the reliability of biometric systems can be significantly improved by combining two or more biometric signatures.[11-13]

For instance, a fingerprint, which is an input from a single sensor, might be combined with another biometric such as hand geometry to increase the accuracy or the confidence with which a biometric system identifies or verifies a person's identity. Multimodal systems also provide anti-spoofing measures by making it difficult for an intruder to duplicate a signature.[14-16]

Numerous applications of biometric systems are being developed in various industries including law enforcement, transportation, finance, and e-commerce. One such illustration is EyePass (EP-4), which has been implemented in Charlotte-Douglas International Airport in North Carolina to identify airport personnel. U.S. citizenship and Immigration Services (USCIS) makes use of fingerprint technology for performing background checks on immigrants.

Overview of Biometric Systems

Based on their functionality, biometric systems could be classified as identification systems and verification systems.[17,18] Identification systems recognize an individual by searching the signatures of all users available within the database for a match. In other words, one signature is matched against many records to establish the identity of the individual. An example of this system would be if an emergency unit in a hospital attempts to recognize an unconscious patient by taking his or her fingerprints and matching against fingerprints available on a state drivers' license database. On the other hand, verification systems validate a person's identity by comparing the captured biometric data with his or her own biometric signatures stored within the system. Here one signature is matched with only one signature from the database to verify the identity. An illustration of this system would be when an individual claims identity by giving some information such as an alphanumeric password, and then the system checks his or her biometric signature to verify the individual's claim.

Regardless of whether the system is used for identification or verification, the core functionality of a biometric system involves the following stages: capture, process, and compare. Biometric sensing devices such as optical cameras, fingerprint scanners, or iris scanners capture the physical and behavioral features of an individual in the form of a facial image, fingerprint, or iris scan. This raw image is processed to extract the unique signature corresponding to the individual.

Prior to identification or verification, enrollment or registration of valid individuals should take place in the biometric system. For instance, in verification system developed for authorizing users of a system, enrollment refers to storing the biometric signatures of individuals who are authorized to use the system. During the time of logon, the newly captured biometric signature is compared with the signatures already enrolled in the verification systems. This comparison results in the verification of the individual's identity.

A user record in a biometric system consists of the biometric signature of an individual along with his/her credentials or identifiers (such as passport number, Social Security number, driving license number, etc.). In access control systems, this user record also contains the role, rights, and access privileges associated with the role. User records need to be transported over wired and wireless channels in a distributed biometric system.

A biometric system designed for identification and verification applications contains a database of user records of all known individuals. Depending on the scope of the application, the database may be central or distributed spanning several platforms and operating systems. When an individual's signature is presented to the biometric system, search tools are utilized to compare the signature with those that are stored in the database. The response of a biometric system depends on the efficiency of the database system as well as the tools used for search and comparison operations. For confidentiality and privacy of the templates during storage as well as during transit, the user records need to be encrypted. During each user session with the biometric system, a session key is used along with the encryption mechanism to fully protect the information being transferred to and from the system. The security system can be integrated with the biometric system, or it can be independent, controlling each and every user access to the biometric system. Access policy and its administration play a central role in implementing the security kernel around the biometric system.

An example of a biometric system as adopted from Podio[19] is presented in Figure 6-1.

The common biometric exchange file format (CBEFF) defines a common format for exchanging the biometric signature between different components of a system or between different biometric systems. Figure 6-2 shows one instance (or record) within a CBEFF file. This structure contains three blocks of information. The first block is the standard biometric header, in which the processing information such as the identification of biometric type and information about the biometric data are described. This could be considered as a description of the biometric documented in the record. The second block, which is the biometric-specific memory block, holds the actual biometric data such as the image of an iris scan, or that of a fingerprint. The third block holds the signature used to authenticate the user data. Signature (also called biometric code or sample) plays an important role in biometric systems. A biometric signature is a compact code that uniquely identifies an individual from others. Voice, face, fingerprint, and iris codes are generated using signal processing and compression schemes that attempt to reduce the amount of data, while at the same time retaining their unique features that distinguish individuals. As noted in the introduction, a biometric signature is a personal code assigned to an individual. The importance of biometric codes stems from the fact that they cannot be lost, forgotten, or stolen as opposed to personal identification codes or passwords. The design of an efficient biometric signature for a given modality that withstands the variations caused due to physical conditions such as illumination, time of day, position of the camera, and pose of the person still remains a technical challenge to engineers and scientists, especially when the biometric systems are being simultaneously developed by several vendors.

CBEFF facilitates information exchange between biometric systems developed by different vendors, as shown in Figure 6-2, by allowing biometric data interchange. Additionally, CBEFF also supports security features such as digital signatures and encryption.

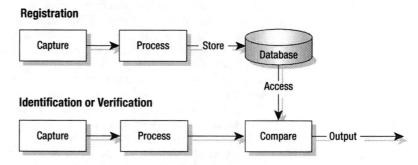

FIGURE 6-1 Core functionality of a biometric system (adapted from Podio[20])

FIGURE 6-2 Components of the common biometric exchange file format (CBEFF)

Standards for Biometric Systems

The International Committee for Information Technology Standards (INCITS) and International Organization for Standards (ISO) are two entities that work together to develop biometric standards. In the United States INCITS established a technical committee, M1, for national and international biometric standards and their approval.[21] M1 serves as the U.S. TAG (Technical Advisory Group) for the ISO/IEC JTC1/SC37 Biometrics subcommittee, established June 2002. The M1 program of work includes biometric standards for data interchange formats, common file formats, application program interfaces, biometric profiles, and performance testing and reporting. The M1 technical committee works towards accelerating the deployment of standards-based security solutions for homeland defense, prevention of identity theft, and other government and commercial applications based on biometric personal authentication. The tasks undertaken by M1 include finger minutiae format for data interchange, finger pattern-based interchange format, iris interchange format, finger image-based interchange format, face recognition format for data interchange, signature/sign image-based interchange format, and hand geometry interchange format. Some of these tasks and standards being developed are described in the following paragraphs.

Minutiae-Based Fingerprint Data Interchange Format: In this format, a fingerprint is represented in terms of the ridge endings and splits called minutiae. This standard contains precise definitions of minutiae data formats. The format is compact in size, extensible, and designed for interoperability.

Face Recognition Data Interchange Format: This format facilitates the use of face information in applications that have limited storage (e.g., passports, visas, driver licenses, etc.) and allows interoperability among facial recognition vendors. This format minimizes the amount of data necessary to store, improves system throughput, and ensures that enrolled images will meet a quality standard needed for both automated face recognition and human inspection of facial images.

Biometric Application Interface (BioAPI): This interface defines the standard for biometric software applications to interface with underlying biometric services and technologies. This API is an open-system standard developed by the biometric consortium consisting of vendors, integrators, and end-users.

Common Biometric Exchange File Format (CBEFF): This format defines a data structure for creating files of biometric data that supports interoperability between biometric components and systems. As discussed earlier, this file format consists of a standard header, a biometric-specific memory block, and an optional digital signature.

X9.84: This describes the controls and proper procedures for using biometrics as an identification and authentication mechanism for secure remote electronic access, or for local physical access control, for the financial services industry. It defines a data processing framework and mechanisms for cryptographically securing biometric data prior to transmission. Biometric signatures can be integrated with digital certificates, signatures, and smart cards to handle remote authentication. An X.509 certificate can store a biometric template as an information attribute within a fixed number of bytes.

Performance Measures

Performance measures of a biometric system depend on the type of application to which the system is associated. For example, in a law enforcement application for identifying suspects, the database consists of records of individuals with a criminal background (such as those released after serving time in prisons). According to the report[22] generated by the Department of Justice (DoJ) in 2002, 270,000 offenders accumulated 4.1 million arrests before the most recent imprisonment and another 744,000 arrests within 3 years of leaving prison. This report suggests that preserving biometric records helps the law enforcement agency to solve cases involving ex-criminals quickly.

The input to the law enforcement application consists of a user record (mug shot) of the suspect. Comparison of this record with existing records results in one or more hits or matches. This output corresponds to the list of the possible suspects (top matches) found in the system. It is expected that this list is short and the prime suspects appear in the top of this list. In verification and positive identification systems, the output is expected to be precise with the match resulting in proper verification of the user record presented to the system.

In general, the performance of a biometric system is characterized by the following four key metrics: false match rate (FMR), false non-match rate (FNMR), equal error rate (EER), and failure to enroll rate (FTER).[23,24]

FMR measures the ratio of incorrect matches over the total number of trials. A false match occurs when there is a high degree of similarity between two individuals' biometric signatures stored in the system.

FNMR measures the ratio of false rejections to the number of trials. False non-matches occur when there is not sufficient similarity between the individual's signature that is stored in the biometric system and the signature presented for identification or verification. FMR and FNMR are similar error measures that will have zero values in an ideal system.

A biometric system needs to be trained to meet the desired performance trade-off between the two error measures. EER is the threshold at which FMR and FNMR are equal. This metric can be used to describe the accuracy of biometric systems and compare their performance. In applications where the output is a list of possible matches, the rank or sequence number at which the correct hit appears might be a useful metric.

FTER measures user registration error or the probability that an individual will be unable to enroll in the system. This can be due to a number of reasons including insufficiently distinctive signature or sample. It could also be due to system design flaws making consistent registration difficult. A third failure to enroll could be due to the individual lacking the requisite biometric sample (i.e., false or missing body part).[25]

Biometric Systems Operations and Management

During the early stages of deploying a biometric system, capturing, processing, and generating new signatures and user records constitute major activities. In addition, the system needs to be trained to meet the desired performance criteria. After the system is fully trained and deployed, day-to-day operations of the system consist of processing queries and generating the corresponding outputs. A query consists of an input user record that needs to be compared with those that are present in the system. Matching and comparison operations need to be performed in real-time. Other operations such as the addition of new user records, deleting user records that are obsolete or modifying existing user records to reflect currency of the record, routine maintenance and troubleshooting take place during off-peak times. These activities are similar to those performed on any database management system and may be performed using both manual as well as automated methods. Capturing, processing and generating new signatures and user records will also take place infrequently after the system is deployed fully.

As is obvious from the prior discussion, the pressure on a biometric system could be enormous due to the high volume of transactions expected to be performed and due to the huge number of records held in its database. In order for the system to function smoothly, certain challenges to biometric systems in general are identified and discussed here. The challenges to biometric systems can be classified as system design-related and data-related. The system design-related challenges are with respect to making the system scalable, distributed, fault tolerant and flexible. The data-related challenges are with respect to ensuring reliability and confidentiality of data.

A biometric system processes a high volume of data and is expected to store a large number of records in its database. Additionally, with the gaining popularity of biometric systems, there may be sudden surges in the number of users that access the system from time to time either to enroll or to verify. According to the Webopedia dictionary, scalability of a system relates to the extent to which a system can adapt to the growing demands. For instance, as noted, a biometric system is expected to grow in terms of the number of transactions as well as number of users that access the system. In order to ensure that the system is able to withstand the transaction and user load placed on it, scalability of the system is an important design consideration.

The scope of biometric systems ranges from international to national to local units. Hence a biometric system is expected to have users at various locations and hence a distributed design of the system is preferred over a centralized system. A distributed design, however, comes with its challenges such as maintaining integrity of data that is available to the various units and the speed and accuracy with which new data is updated within a distributed system.

Fault tolerance of a system is related to the amount of downtime a system experiences when processing transactions. As is customary with information systems in general, having an adequate backup server or a mirror site will ensure that the system is fault tolerant. Although having backup sites is expensive, the cost of system down time might be far more expensive.

Biometric systems are a relatively new addition to the array of information systems.[26] As a result, a number of new algorithms are being developed constantly. Hence a biometric system is required to be flexible in order to accommodate new algorithms. In other words, the biometric system should be customizable to either replace old algorithms with newer ones or to add on new algorithms to the existing ones.

Next, the data-related challenges to biometrics are discussed. One of the key challenges for the data in a biometric system is reliability. It is imperative that the data in a biometric system is validated from multiple sources, and that several biometrics are used to identify a single person instead of relying on a single biometric. Validating biometrics plays a more important role when the system produces fuzzy results regarding the identity of the person. For instance, if a hair sample that is used to identify a person returns a match with 50% confidence, then matching the iris or fingerprints could increase the confidence with which the system identifies a person. This challenge for reliability of data residing in a biometric system stems from one of the possible threats to a biometric system, which is presenting false biometric data such as a fake finger, a face mask or a reused biometric sample.[27,28] The multibiometric systems referred to in this reading[29,30] are one of the several ways by which the reliability of data could be ensured.

The next challenge to the data in a biometric system is confidentiality. A biometric system is particularly vulnerable to abuse of important biometric data, thereby posing a potential invasion of a person's privacy. In particular, when combined with non-biometric information such as date of birth and Social Security number, the biometric data stored in several distributed systems could pose a potential threat to an individual's privacy. In order to ensure confidentiality of data, techniques such as cancelable biometrics are currently being developed, which would alleviate the privacy issues surrounding the use of biometric data.[31]

Applications of Biometrics

This section outlines some of the applications based on biometric signatures, which are at various stages of development and implementation.

REGISTERED TRAVELER PROGRAM

The Transportation Security Administration (TSA), an agency within the U.S. Department of Homeland Security, has launched the Registered Traveler[32] pilot program in partnership with selected airlines and airports across the country. This pilot program is designed to improve the security screening process by helping TSA align screeners and resources with potential risks. Approved travelers will be positively identified at the airport through biometric technology.

The TSA will collect personal information including name, address, phone number, and date of birth from volunteers along with biometric data, including a fingerprint and/or an iris scan. A security assessment that will include analysis of law enforcement and intelligence data sources and a check of outstanding wants and warrants will also be conducted.

SMART BORDER PROGRAM

The Smart Border program[33] facilitates the secure flow of people and goods through the borders. Canada and the United States have agreed to develop common standards for the biometrics and adopt interoperable and compatible technology to read the biometric signatures. Biometric cards that are capable of storing multiple biometrics will be used for this purpose.

At present, the Immigration and Naturalization Service (INS) and the State Department issue biometric border crossing cards (BCC), also known as laser cards, to Mexican citizens who wish to enter a limited border zone through a port of entry along the U.S./Mexico border. These cards include a photograph and machine-readable biometric information of the card-holder. The biometric data on the card will be matched to the individual crossing the border by the sensor and scanner placed at the check point.

US-VISIT

The Department of Homeland Security started the US-VISIT program as a part of a continuum of security measures that begins overseas, when a person applies for a visa to travel to the United States, and continues on through the entry and exit at U.S. air and seaports, and at land border cross-ings. The US-VISIT program enhances the security of U.S. citizens and visi-tors by verifying the identity of visitors with visas. At the same time, it facilitates legitimate travel and trade by leveraging technology and the evolving use of biometrics to expedite processing at our borders.

The Department of Homeland Security, Department of Justice, and National Institute of Standards and Technology have been working together with other agencies to set the standards for visa biometrics, initi-ate the process of modifying the U.S. visa to include the specified technolo-gical enhancements, and ensure interagency interoperability. These efforts will result in machine-readable, tamper-resistant visas and travel and entry documents that use biometric identifiers.

SMART CARDS

Smart cards with biometric signatures are being developed by various organizations for a variety of applications including access control to build-ings, computing systems, emergency medical services, and even as a possi-ble solution to national ID.[34] Smart cards can perform computations and run cryptographic algorithms with the help of a microprocessor placed on the card. Through appropriate access controls, it is possible to limit the amount of data any one official can access. For example, an ER doctor could view medical information and enter data about treatment (if the card's data storage device is read-write capable), but could not see security-related data (such as a traveler's flight history, or a non-citizen's visa status) that an airport or INS official might require.

DATA MINING FOR SECURITY AND INTELLIGENCE GATHERING

Data mining for homeland security is one of the high end applications that can be built upon a biometric system. A geographically distributed large scale biometric system containing records of voices, faces, fingerprints, and iris scans of people who have previously been involved in activities harm-ful to national security can be extremely useful for homeland security applications. Such a system can be even more powerful when linked to databases containing other types of data such as travel or financial records. However, accessing such information brings up privacy issues

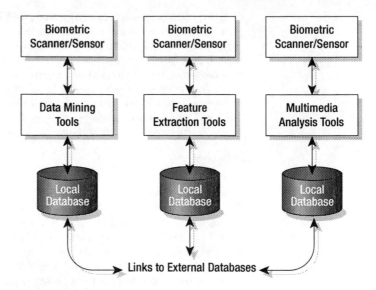

FIGURE 6-3 Data mining system architecture

which need to be addressed appropriately. Figure 6-3 illustrates the data mining system architecture, which could be customized for a homeland security application.

Individual databases contain only the data collected from one agency or organization including law enforcement and federal agencies, banks, and airlines. When data from disparate sources (from various federal agencies) are combined, it is difficult to identify records containing information related to the same individuals or groups of individuals—especially when the records are fraudulent. Data mining tools can be used in such situations to group related user records based on common characteristics they exhibit.

For homeland security applications, the scope of the biometric system needs to be at an international level with access to systems from other countries as well. In addition, databases from various federal agencies should be linked to the application system. The application system should be able to process images, video, audio, and text. Summarization tools for text documents, compact representation, and indexing for images, video, and audio should be integrated with the system.

When a suspicious activity takes place, information related to the event should be given as input to the above application. Relevant data mining tools, summarization methods, and search tools should be triggered based on the nature of the event to generate the output that might help the investigators to identify the perpetrators.

Summary

In this chapter, we defined several concepts and terms such as biometrics, biometric systems, and signatures, which are frequently used in biometric literature. We then introduced biometric systems by discussing in detail the two types of biometric systems—identification and verification systems. Next, we discussed the underlying architecture of a biometric system based on its functionality. The main functions of a biometric system are enrollment, template extraction, and matching. Additionally, the chapter presented the current work being done in relation to establishing standards for biometrics and developing performance measures of biometric systems. We identified several challenges to biometrics and illustrated several applications of biometric systems.

References

[1] Lawton, G. (1998). Biometrics: A new era in security. *IEEE Computer, 31,* 16–18.

[2] Jain, A. K., Ross, A., & Prabhakar, S. (2004). An introduction to biometric recognition. *IEEE Transactions on Circuits & Systems for Video Technology, 14,* 4–20.

[3] Jain, A. K., Ross, A., & Prabhakar, S. (2004). An introduction to biometric recognition. *IEEE Transactions on Circuits & Systems for Video Technology, 14,* 4.

[4] Phillips, P. J., Martin, A., Wilson, C. L., & Przybocki, M. (2000). An introduction evaluating biometric systems. *IEEE Computer, 33,* 56–63.

[5] Soutar, C. (2002). *Biometric system security.* Bioscrypt, Inc.

[6] BioAPI. (2001, March 16). *BioAPI specification version 1.1.* BioAPI Consortium.

[7] NIST. (2001). *Common biometric exchange file format, 2004.*

[8] Jain, A., & Ross, A. (2004). Multibiometric systems. *Communications of the ACM, 47,* 34–40.

[9] Frischholz, R. W., & Dieckmann, U. (2000). BioID: A multimodal biometric identification system. *IEEE Computer, 33,* 64–68.

[10] Jain, A., & Ross, A. (2004). Multibiometric systems. *Communications of the ACM, 47,* 34–40.

[11] Jain, A. K., Ross, A., & Prabhakar, S. (2004). An introduction to biometric recognition. *IEEE Transactions on Circuits & Systems for Video Technology, 14,* 4–20.

[12] Jain, A., & Ross, A. (2004). Multibiometric systems. *Communications of the ACM, 47,* 34–40.

[13] Ross, A., & Jain, A. (2003). Information fusion in biometrics. *Pattern Recognition Letters, 24,* 2115–2125.

[14] Jain, A. K., Ross, A., & Prabhakar, S. (2004). An introduction to biometric recognition. *IEEE Transactions on Circuits & Systems for Video Technology, 14,* 4–20.

[15] Jain, A., & Ross, A. (2004). Multibiometric systems. *Communications of the ACM, 47,* 34–40.

[16] Ross, A., & Jain, A. (2003). Information fusion in biometrics. *Pattern Recognition Letters, 24,* 2115–2125.

[17] Jain, A. K., Ross, A., & Prabhakar, S. (2004). An introduction to biometric recognition. *IEEE Transactions on Circuits & Systems for Video Technology, 14,* 4–20.

[18] Ratha, N. K., Connell, J. H., & Bolle, R. M. (2001). Enhancing security and privacy in biometrics-based authentication systems. *IBM Systems Journal, 40,* 614–634.

[19] Podio, F. L. (2001, May). Biometrics—Technologies for highly secure personal authentication. *National Institute of Standards and Technology, ITL Bulletin.*

[20] Podio, F. L. (2001, May). Biometrics—Technologies for highly secure personal authentication. *National Institute of Standards and Technology, ITL Bulletin.*

[21] INCITS. (2004). *M1-Biometrics 2004.*

[22]Greenfield, L. A. (2002, November). *Developing improved identification systems: Biometric systems for investigations and background checks*. Bureau of Justice Statistics.

[23]Jain, A. K., Ross, A., & Prabhakar, S. (2004). An introduction to biometric recognition. *IEEE Transactions on Circuits & Systems for Video Technology, 14*, 4–20.

[24]Rhodes, K. A. (2003, September 9). *Information security: Challenges using biometrics*. United States General Accounting Office.

[25]Committee on Transportation and Infrastructure. (2004, May 19). Subcommittee on aviation hearing on the use of biometrics to improve aviation security. Retrieved December 2, 2004 from: *http://www.findbiometrics.com/viewnews.php?id=1147*

[26]Lawton, G. (1998). Biometrics: A new era in security. *IEEE Computer, 31*, 16–18.

[27]Jain, A., & Ross, A. (2004). Multibiometric systems. *Communications of the ACM, 47*, 34–40.

[28]Bolle, R. M., Connell, J. H., & Ratha, N. K. (2002). Biometric perils and patches. *Pattern Recognition, 35*, 2727–2738.

[29]Jain, A., & Ross, A. (2004). Multibiometric systems. *Communications of the ACM, 47*, 34–40.

[30]Frischholz, R. W., & Dieckmann, U. (2000). BioID: A multimodal biometric identification system. *IEEE Computer, 33*, 64–68.

[31]Bolle, R. M., Connell, J. H., & Ratha, N. K. (2002). Biometric perils and patches. *Pattern Recognition, 35*, 2727–2738.

[32]TSA, (2004). *TSA announces start of registered traveller pilot program*. Minneapolis-St.Paul, MN: TSA press office.

[33]Ackleson, J. (2003). Securing through technology? Smart borders after September 11th. *Knowledge, Technology & Policy, 16*, 56–74.

[34]Tynan, D. (2002). Airport security for the 9/11 age. *Popular Science*.

Integration and Ethical Perspectives for Information Systems Management

ERNEST A. CAPOZZOLI
Kennesaw State University

ROBERT D. WINSOR
Loyola Marymount University

SHEB L. TRUE
Kennesaw State University

Ernest A. Capozzoli is an Assistant Professor in the Accounting Department in the Coles College of Business at Kennesaw State University. He has a PhD from the University of Mississippi in MIS and is a CPA. His research interests are in the e-business area, especially the impact of integrated systems on organizational structure and strategy and the ethical implications of information systems. Additionally, he has over 25 years of business experience and has participated in and managed large scale information systems projects for the Arabian American Oil Company, where he retired as an EDP Manager.

Robert D. Winsor, PhD, is a Professor of Marketing at Loyola Marymount University. He has experience in the wholesale and retail industries, and has formerly owned and managed a retail store in Los Angeles. Robert has been a business and marketing strategy consultant for a number of retail and international consumer-products businesses. Dr. Winsor has published over 65 articles in publications such as the Journal of Business Research, *the* Journal of Organizational Change Management, Competitiveness Review, Structural Equation Modeling, *the* Journal of Business and Behavioral Sciences, *and the* Journal of Consumer Marketing. *Professor Winsor has been twice named educator of the year for the College of Business Administration at LMU.*

Sheb L. True, PhD, is a member of the graduate faculty and a Professor of Marketing in the Department of Leadership and Professional Development at Kennesaw State University where he teaches exclusively in the Executive-MBA program. He is the Director of Business Ethics for the Corporate Governance Center, and serves on the steering committee for the RTM Institute for Ethics, Leadership and Character. He has co-edited two books on business ethics and is the editor of the Journal of Executive Education. *He has served as a marketing research and strategy consultant for a variety of organizations, and teaches seminars on business ethics, customer satisfaction and relationships, the role of culture in business, and why/how to conduct marketing research.*

Overview

Individuals and the legal system are increasingly holding organizations liable for their actions. Sarbanes-Oxley was one recent example of corporate misconduct resulting in a legal statute providing liability for executives' ethical performance. This reading looks at the big picture of organizational business strategy, information systems and information security strategies, and the necessary alignment and linkages that reflect the ethical and legal perspectives of executive management.

As the authors state: "Most information systems development problems are managerial, organizational, or behavioral in nature, rather than rooted in technical origins." This statement is equally applicable to the strategies that underlie the implementation of information security in the modern organization. The legal and ethical perspective and corresponding actions of the organization will reflect the beliefs and values of management. While great strides have been made in the healthcare and financial industries, due in no small part to legal requirements such as HIPAA and GLB, the rest of the private and public sector are only now realizing the need to provide due care and due diligence in the protection of information. By closely aligning ethical performance with strategy, the organization can demonstrate a forward thinking approach to the management and protection of information.

Introduction

The current business environment can be described as turbulent, full of uncertainty and highly competitive. Competitive forces and advances in technology impose changes upon an organization at accelerating rates. One significant change is an increase in systems integration activities across the organization. The demand for robust, highly integrated systems that are capable of crossing organizational lines, and corporate boundaries (which demarcate a multitude of external business partners), as well as national boundaries, requires extra vigilance on the part of organizations to ensure ethical development and compliance. Ensuring that ethical considerations are thoroughly incorporated into business strategies that are in turn fully supported by Information Technology (IT) or Information Systems (IS) strategies is a daunting task. As such, the purpose of this reading is to provide a discussion of key issues associated with the process of linking and aligning business strategies, IS strategies, and ethical concerns for multiple stakeholders.

Strategic Alignment

The alignment of business and IS strategies is not an event, but a process of continuous adaptation and change.[1,2] It is a dynamic, ongoing process that describes the level of interaction and extent to which the overall business strategy, mission, objectives, and plans are supported and complemented by IS strategies, mission, objectives, and plans. This alignment can enhance both IS success and organizational success;[3-5] and thus must, by consequence, relate to the fit between business strategy and IS strategy.[6-8] They must be concomitantly linked and aligned, and at their foundations, must incorporate ethical concerns that require consideration from the perspectives of multiple stakeholders. However, the difficulties surrounding strategy alignment and its attendant consequences can be understated, and the course an organization embarks upon to achieve alignment is often difficult and fraught with hazard.[9]

Although technology can create new or modified business practices at a rapid rate, successful adoption of new business practices must stand the acid test of free-market forces. Technology and the marketplace are continually reshaping business activities, and as a consequence, business strategies. An organization must continually work towards an alignment that fits into the organization's business strategy, IS strategy, and ethical advancement and compliance strategies. This alignment should improve the likelihood that IS initiatives are explicitly linked to areas that are critical to successful business performance, provide a source of competitive advantage, and ensure ethical compliance. The process of aligning strategies should heighten management's awareness and use of information systems to better support organizational goals, objectives, and ethical compliance. According to Hirschheim and Sabherwal, "Strategic alignment focuses on an organization's ongoing efforts to establish and maintain a series of interdependent relationships between business and IS strategies. These relationships involve the movement (i.e., change) of business strategy and/or IS strategy in such a way that the two are in alignment."

Efforts to achieve alignment between IS strategies and the business are not always successful and often go astray. A recent study by Hirschheim and Sabherwal in 2001 described three types of deviations from alignment efforts: paradoxical decisions (a decision that actually takes an organization out of alignment), excessive transformation, and uncertain turnarounds. Organizational inertia may explain some paradoxical decisions.[10] Once a pattern of alignment is established it may be difficult to change, because alignments will likely lead to structural and cultural inertia and conservatism.[11] Paradoxical decisions may also be explained by the differences in technical knowledge and the perspectives between executive and IS management as they pertain to their respective strategies and associated interactions of those strategies.[12,13] Strategy alignment may also become more problematic by virtue of the very nature of how IS projects are developed and implemented and their effects upon other organizational processes.

Most IS development problems are managerial, organizational, or behavioral in nature, rather than rooted in technical origins.[14–16] There is also often a problem in identifying critical success factors and in linking them to the stakeholders' business strategies and concerns.[17] Organizations must choose priorities carefully and then fully monitor and communicate any observed interactions or resultant drift. To redirect organizational energies, organizations must be certain of the requirements associated with aligning strategies. Furthermore, as a result of complex interactions, organizations cannot take a piecemeal approach to a strategic realignment because even small changes in one element are likely to have second or third order consequences for other parameters.

Systems Integration

The role of IS should be that of a strategic enabler for competitive success, rather than just an operational supporter.[18] As such, because strategic development cannot be conducted in isolation, systems integration is a mission critical activity, whereby integrative efforts must be holistic and encompass the entire strategy development process. Implicit in this holistic process is an understanding of current organizational practices and standards as compared to organizational goals or target positions.

Understanding where a company stands in terms of the relationship between its IS strategy and business strategy, versus where it wants to be based on internal goals and the external competitive environment, can be a difficult and chaotic process. To facilitate a better understanding of this perspective, business processes, IS technologies, and the level of systems integration required to support them can be plotted along a continuum depicting the extent to which an organization system's integration technologies are aligned with its overall business strategy.[19] See Figure 7-1.

Pressure to integrate systems is evidenced in almost all forms of business. Healthcare, finance, and government are examples of areas where systems integration requirements are increasing. The healthcare industry typifies the increasing operational requirements that sensitive patient information be collected, stored, and retrieved. Efforts are underway in this industry to make patient data available 24×7, from anywhere. By its very nature, patient data is highly sensitive and must be restricted in access to only the proper/approved individuals. In the healthcare environment, information technology is playing a key role in evidence-based medicine. Data on best practices and other research is being mined internally and accessed externally via the Internet from many sites.[20] Information technology enables management to gather data enterprise wide, analyze it, and feed it back to clinicians to help change processes and refine best practices. At Lifespan, a healthcare delivery system with five hospitals and 2,400 affiliated physicians, a long-term goal has been to provide information to clinicians wherever they may be and at any time, says Nancy Barrett, director of systems integration and development.[21]

As another example, one goal at Sarasota Memorial Health Care System (SMHCS) is to reduce its disparate information systems. According to Bruce H. Berg, MD, Chief Medical Information Officer at SMHCS, they are trying to get rid of systems that don't "talk" to each other by increasing connectivity and eliminating standalone systems. The trend in healthcare is towards integrated systems. Results from the Health Data Management

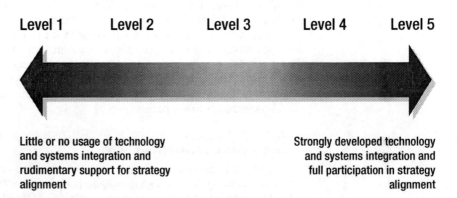

| Level 1 | Level 2 | Level 3 | Level 4 | Level 5 |

Little or no usage of technology and systems integration and rudimentary support for strategy alignment

Strongly developed technology and systems integration and full participation in strategy alignment

FIGURE 7-1 Continuum of strategy development and system integration

2004 CIO Survey show that two-thirds of the respondents—511 IT leaders at provider organizations—are spending at least 20% of their IT budgets on clinical information technology. Of those respondents, one-third have allocated more than half of their IT budgets.[22]

The government is also a driving force in healthcare system integration. Key elements of what Newt Gingrich calls a 21st century intelligent health system include:

- A secure, Web-based networking infrastructure.
- Physicians, hospitals, and medical personnel using interoperable electronic medical records.
- Web-based electronic medical records for every American, beginning with seniors enrolling in Medicare as of Jan. 1, 2005. Everyone would have a health record that they and their clinicians can access electronically from anywhere at any time.
- Medicare and financial incentives to encourage doctors to adopt clinical systems and prescribe electronically.
- Mandatory use of EMRs by physicians at some point during the next 10 years.
- Huge databases—starting with the data of people in federal health programs—that can be used for outcomes research, to identify participants for clinical trials, and to allow real-time reporting of medication problems and health problems to improve care and accelerate drug development, approval, and recalls.
- A virtual network for public health surveillance to safeguard against biological attacks. This would include a registry of active and retired physicians, nurses, pharmacists, veterinarians, and others with medical experience who could be contacted during a crisis.[23]

Ethical Dimensions

The integration of information systems affects ethics issues in a complex and interrelated fashion. When information system practices have not taken a holistic approach to incorporate ethical requirements into the development process, gaps in both strategy and execution may occur. As organizations move along the continuum and advance to the next higher level towards more systems integration (e.g., as more and more patient data is collected, stored, and accessed), the effect of these misalignments is the creation of "ethical stress points" on information sources and confidential/sensitive data (see Figure 7-2). The direction and intensity of these impacts can be difficult to predict. To more thoroughly address these potential points of stress, one must determine whether the data or records concern customer, client, or subject information, or whether the information is merely of an organizational nature.

ETHICAL CONCERNS REGARDING CONSUMER/
CLIENT/SUBJECT INFORMATION

In general, there are eight concerns related to ethics that must be addressed when information systems are designed, modified, or implemented—benefit, privacy/confidentiality, accuracy, property, accessibility, degree/depth of information use, system reliability, and categorization.[24] We address each

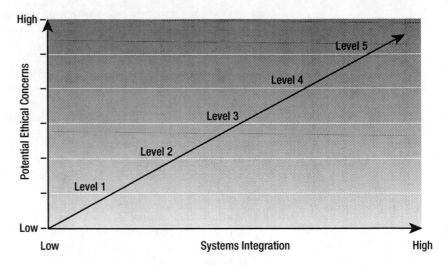

FIGURE 7-2 The relationship of ethical concerns and systems integration

of these issues, and discuss how increasing systems integration efforts may affect an organization's ability to establish and conform to ethical standards concerning these issues.

The first of these questions, and the one upon which many of the other issues hinges, is "for whose benefit is the information collected?" Typically, the benefits of information systems accrue primarily or solely to the organizations compiling and systematizing the information. In others, such as healthcare, the benefits of information systems are largely for the patients themselves, and although the information is used largely by health service professionals, the interests of the patients remain the paramount objective.

The second issue impacting the way in which ethical issues must be addressed is that of privacy/confidentiality. Consumer concerns about George Orwell's "Big Brother" and the misuse or improper disclosure of information are paramount in most debates about ethics and information systems. With some exceptions, increasing centralization and integration of information systems typically impacts individual concerns regarding privacy in a negative fashion. That is, increasing centralization generally results in less privacy and a higher risk to confidentiality.

The third issue concerns the accuracy of the information. Often, the impacts of inaccurate information bear upon both the organization using the information and also the subject of the information. As a result, issues of accuracy are complex and highly interrelated when examined from an ethical perspective. For example, if a person's name is incorrectly spelled when added to a "registered sex-offender database," the ethical impacts may be severe for an innocent person named, for the law enforcement organizations relying upon this information, and also for individual citizens residing within the community where the true (but concealed) offender lives.

Regarding information accuracy, increasing systems integration has both negative and positive effects upon an individual's or an organization's ability to advance and conform to specific ethical standards. Higher levels of integration often make it easier to detect errors within existing information databases, for example, because more people have access to the data. Similarly, when corrections need to be made, integration often makes this process far simpler. At the same time, it may be more difficult to initiate the correction of inaccuracies within highly integrated databases due to accessibility safeguards that have been established to manage privacy concerns. Additionally, centralization and integration tend to amplify any negative impacts that inaccurate information may have upon either organizations or individuals.

The fourth issue impacted by system integration is that of property. This issue relates to ownership of the information and rights regarding its use and distribution. Again, integration tends to amplify any potentially negative consequences regarding ownership disputes, and therefore this issue needs to be thoroughly addressed at the time integration is proposed.

The fifth issue is one of accessibility. Who has access to the data, and under what conditions? Most importantly, can the data be reviewed and amended by the subjects of the information? Generally, systems integration improves accessibility. Again, it is critically important to address these accessibility issues at the time system modifications are proposed.

The sixth issue is the degree of data usage. For what purposes is the information to be used? Although this issue relates to that of benefit (i.e., for whose benefit is the information being collected and utilized?), this aspect concerns more the "depth" of usage, rather than the "direction." In other words, using the information for the exclusive benefit of an organization, rather than the subject or individual on whom the information was collected, concerns the first issue (i.e., benefit), whereas the limitations regarding how extensively the information can be used concerns the sixth issue (i.e., degree of usage). For example, patient health information is collected for the explicit purposes of improving the organization's ability to implement patient care and treatment. The use of this data for the purposes of educating student doctors pushes this usage into another realm, but may still be viewed as consistent with the general interests of the patient. Another leap is made when this information is provided to public health officials to be used in controlling infectious diseases. Again a hurdle is passed when this information is used to enable pharmaceutical manufacturers to market directly or indirectly to patients.

Ethical matters demand that this issue of intensity of usage, and boundaries or limitations upon usage, be studied and addressed with utmost concern and care. Potential or actual conflicts of interest need to be addressed and resolved, if possible. System integration can again broaden and intensify any negative impacts or conflicts, and this potential should thus be carefully examined.

The seventh issue relates to system reliability. Will the information be reliably and consistently available when needed by the beneficiary? Again, if information provides a critical benefit, as it well might, what are the ethical implications when system failures make this data unavailable? System integration tends to have a mixed effect upon information reliability. In general, integration implies a narrowing of focus in systems hardware and software (at least in terms in compatibility), with a corresponding broadening of applications. Integration, when implemented correctly and prudently (i.e., with backup databases and parallel systems), can thus generally impact reliability in a positive fashion. Yet when poorly conceived or implemented, systems integration can have devastating impacts upon reliability.

The eighth and final issue related to ethics and systems integration is that of categorization. This issue relates to that of information accuracy, but is somewhat different in terms of diagnosing or fixing systematic problems, and in the impacts resulting from system integration. Virtually all databases rely upon one or more systems of classification. In general, any categorization process has the goal of minimizing variation within a single category, and maximizing variation between different categories. Occasionally, where binary or discrete categorical data naturally occurs, this is easy, as in the classification of gender (i.e., male or female), or political affiliation. More commonly, however, human descriptors are collected in areas that are "continuous" or without natural boundaries (e.g., attitudes, physical attractiveness, overall health, etc.). In addition, information that is typically discrete but occurs across a broad range of values is often re-classified in fewer categories (e.g., income). Finally, where categories have been formerly established, but where blurring may exist due to blending or simultaneous occurrences, categories might be imposed resulting in a poor fit (e.g., race). In the latter three instances (continuous, re-classified, or poorly fitted information), ethical issues can emerge regarding the manner in which classification occurs and the ultimate category into which subjects are placed. Impacts of these problems can range from simple displeasure on the part of the subjects to inaccuracies resulting in economic (e.g., the incorrect awarding of a scholarship) or physical (e.g., improper medical diagnosis or treatment) damages. In general, increases in system integration result in potentially greater ethical risks from errors of classification. This is because system integration often requires information standardization or "cleaning," and also because the impacts of errors are magnified and more difficult to fix when duplicated across the many facets of an integrated system.

ETHICAL CONCERNS REGARDING CORPORATE
OR INTER-ORGANIZATIONAL INFORMATION

Ethical concerns for corporate or inter-organizational information are often different from those involving individuals. In this section, we list three ethical issues that are likely to be impacted whenever system integration is increased.

The first issue is that of information consistency. Ethical issues often emerge whenever organizations attempt to maintain two differing databases of information. This "two-sets-of-books" dilemma is often resolved or reduced whenever system integration is implemented, due to the difficulty in designing large integrated systems capable of preserving the integrity of multiple, but differing, databases.

The second issue related to the interaction of system integration efforts and ethical issues concerns the intentional propagation of false or inaccurate information, or the illegal acquisition of information for potentially anti-competitive uses. Issues such as corporate espionage, strategic manipulation of competitors' data and databases, and the provision of false or misleading information to third-parties (e.g., the government or the media) are all within this issue. In general, systems integration can either negatively or positively impact efforts to maintain ethical practices in these areas, depending upon the specific nature of the information and the number and nature of the individuals and organizations that have the ability to collect, view, or modify the information.

The third issue is one of misleading or selective interpretations of information. Organizations all too often supply or highlight information that is beneficial to their strategies or goals, and withhold or creatively interpret information with potentially negative impacts. The targets of this information may be customers (e.g., product quality data), suppliers (e.g., credit or other financial information), distributors (e.g., product line sales figures), stockholders (e.g., profitability, sales, or financial information), or other stakeholders (e.g., the press or governmental agencies). Again, increased system integration generally improves the ability of all parties to implement and conform to ethical standards. The exception would be where system complexity encumbers efforts to view or understand information or information-gathering methodologies.

Conclusion

The need for integrated systems is evidenced by demands that information be available 24 × 7, that it be available from a variety of avenues such as local area networks, expanded intranets, or the Internet, and that it be reliable, as well as free from errors and protected from improper use.[25] These expectations are not only driven by internal strategic goals, but from the pressures to be leaders, or at least to stay current, in an increasingly competitive marketplace. However, in the rush towards providing better goods or services at competitive rates, ethical issues will arise in the systems development process and through systems use. The creation and use of complex, highly integrated systems containing large amounts of data of a business and personal nature will create ethical stress points.

An organization must be able to identify and address these stress points. Ideally these stress points should be identified in the development process and rectified to ensure that both technical and ethical requirements of a system are met. It is essential that technical standards and ethical systems development practices and processes be incorporated as a vital part of the strategy development process for the organization as a whole and for information systems development in particular. The balancing of operational requirements and ethical requirements by its nature will create a level of tension. Ensuring that the development processes incorporate an ethical perspective from the very beginning can reduce this tension. In the end, the process should be holistic in nature and designed to produce systems that operate in an effective and efficient manner, provide competitive advantage, and eliminate ethical stress points. Additionally, these systems should clearly describe the parties benefiting from the system and data collection efforts; be operated in a manner ensuring that the privacy/confidentiality and accuracy of information is maintained; establish clear property rights to the information;

properly control and monitor accessibility, and the degree/depth of information use; establish system reliability expectations; and properly classify/categorize information.

References

[1] Hirschheim, R., & Sabherwal, R. (2001). Detours in the path toward strategic information systems alignment. *California Management Review, 44* (1), 87–108.

[2] Henderson, J. C., & Venkatraman, N. (1993). Strategic alignment: Leveraging information technology for transforming organizations, *IBM Systems Journal, 32* (1), 4–16.

[3] Henderson, J. C., & Venkatraman, N. (1992). Strategic alignment: A model for organizational transformation through information technology. In T. A. Kochan & M. Useem (Eds.), *Transforming organizations*, New York: Oxford University Press (pp. 97–116).

[4] Chan, Y. E., Huff, S. L., Barclay, D. W., & Copeland, D. G. (1997). Business strategic orientation, information systems strategic orientation, and strategic alignment. *Information Systems Research, 812*, 125–150.

[5] Sabherwal, R., & Chan, Y. (2001). Alignment between business and IS strategies: A configurational approach. *Information Systems Research, 12* (11), 11–33.

[6] King, W. R. (1978). Strategic planning for management information systems. *MIS Quarterly, 2* (1), 27–37.

[7] Ein-Dor, P., & Segev, E. (1982, September). Organizational context and MIS structure: Some empirical evidence. *MIS Quarterly, 613*, 55–68.

[8] Henderson, J. C., & Venkatraman, N. (1993). Strategic alignment: Leveraging information technology for transforming organizations. *IBM Systems Journal, 32* (1), 4–16.

[9] Thompson, J. D. (1967). *Organizations in action*, Chicago: McGraw Hill.

[10] Tushman, M. L., & O'Reilly, C. A. (1996). Ambidextrous organizations: Managing evolutionary and revolutionary change. *California Management Review, 38* (4), 8–30.

[11] Hirschheim, R., & Sabherwal, R. (2001). Detours in the path toward strategic information systems alignment. *California Management Review, 44* (1), 87–108.

[12] Rockart, J. F. (1988). The line takes the leadership — IS management in a wired society. *Sloan Management Review, 29* (4), 57–64.

[13] Ward, J., & Peppard, J. (1996). Reconciling the IT/business relationship: A troubled marriage in need of guidance. *Journal of Strategic Information Systems, 5* (11), 37–65.

[14] Johnston, A. K., (1995). *A hacker's guide to project management*. Oxford: Butterworth-Heinemann.

[15] Martin, J. E. (1994). Revolution, risk, runaways: Three Rs of IS projects. *Proceedings of the Project Management Institute's 25th Annual Symposium*, Vancouver, Canada. Upper Darby, PA: PMI (pp. 266–272).

[16] Whitten, N. (1995). *Managing software development projects* (2nd ed.). New York: John Wiley & Sons.

[17] Hartman, F., & Ashrafi, R. A. (2002). Project Management in the information systems and information technologies industries. *Project Management Journal, 33* (3), 5–15.

[18] McFarlan, F. W., & McKenney, J. L. (1984). Information technology changes the way you compete. *Harvard Business Review, 62* (5), 98–103.

[19]Capozzoli, E. A., & True, S. L. (2001). An e-commerce systems integration frame-work. *Southern Business Review, 26* (2), 27–32.

[20]Briggs, B. (2004). Clinical systems move to the head of the IT class. *Health Data Management, 2* (6), 38–42.

[21]Briggs, B. (2004). Clinical systems move to the head of the IT class. *Health Data Management, 2* (6), 38–42.

[22]Briggs, B. (2004). Clinical systems move to the head of the IT class. *Health Data Management, 2* (6), 38–42.

[23]Chin, T. (2004, August 9). Gingrich's grand vision. *American Medical News, 47* (30), 13.

[24]Gordon. (2004). *Our discussion of the issues of privacy, accuracy, property, and accessibility is derived from the works of Mason (1986) and the ISO standard #17799.*

[25]Gulati, R., & Garino J. (2000, May–June). Get the right mix of bricks and clicks. *Harvard Business Review*, 108.

Security Education, Training, and Awareness from a Human Performance Technology Point of View

MELISSA J. DARK

Purdue University

Dr. Melissa Dark leads continuing education programs for the Center for Education and Research in Information Assurance and Security at Purdue University. This innovative program interfaces with business and industry, government, and higher education to meet the education and training needs of a variety of organizations and users. Dr. Dark teaches information security courses in the Technology Management Masters of Science degree program and has guest lectured to a variety of audiences, including college faculty, trustees, executives, and end users, on information security issues. Dr. Dark works with a variety of organizations such as the Indiana CPA Society, the Indiana State Police, the Indiana FBI, the U.S. Secret Service, and InfraGard to broker security education. Dr. Dark is currently involved in a nationwide curriculum initiative to determine core information security topics to be included in accredited information security programs at the undergraduate and graduate levels. She has conducted several needs assessments in security education, led an information security public awareness in Indiana, oversees the production of multimedia educational products, and serves on the editorial board of Information Systems Security Journal. *Her research interests include methods for effectively transferring new knowledge into educational systems and organizations, and the return on investment for doing so.*

Overview

One of the least costly and most effective information safeguards is the Security Education Training and Awareness (SETA) Program. While policy is the essential first step in the security program, it must be distributed to employees, and reinforced through constant education, training, and awareness efforts. With the increasing threat from accidental or intentional actions by internal employees, unless those employees know what the organizational policy is, what the consequences of their actions are, and the proper methods of handling information, the organization cannot expect to protect its information from those actions and mis-actions. This reading examines this human perspective of information security and the role of SETA programs in assisting the organization in managing its information risk. The author approaches this human perspective with an

*examination of human performance technology, including the founda-
tional principles and the analysis of human performance issues in information security.*

Introduction

This reading focuses on the role of security education, training, and
awareness (SETA) in an organization's overall information security strategy.
Information security is about more than technology; it includes people and
process as well as technology. In fact, the "people" piece of the security
puzzle is perhaps the most critical for several reasons.

Information security incidents continue to rise. More people are using
more information technology for more tasks, and this trend is expected to
continue. Information technology is becoming more sophisticated and
complex, yet in order to market products to lay users, vendors are creating
applications that are seemingly easy to use. The ease of use often masks
security issues and concerns. The lack of understanding of security issues
coupled with the pervasive and growing use of computers by the general
population makes people a critical factor in the information security equation. In most organizations, novice or lay information technology users
range from the receptionist to the CEO. These individuals are prime targets
for information security breaches because of their lack of understanding of
the technology and associated threats and vulnerabilities.

Organizations need security education, training, and awareness because
many times the first line of defense is the human line of defense. Human
beings are an essential part of the prevention, detection, and response
cycle. Knowledgeable human beings can better prevent information security breaches that occur due to negligence or accident as well as breaches
that stem from malicious activity. Knowledgeable human beings can detect
malicious activity of other human beings as well as anomalous behavior of
systems. Finally, knowledgeable human beings can efficiently and effectively respond to incidents by reporting, quarantining, and diagnosing and
treating problems correctly. Employees are a critical factor in the information security equation.

Given the acute need for people who are information security savvy and
the breadth of knowledge that is needed, it is no surprise that there are many
different types of SETA programs. For organizations looking to add information security education, training, and awareness, the issue of where to start
can be a daunting task. The cost of designing and developing new SETA programs can be high. However, the cost of acquiring SETA programs is also high.
And regardless of whether an organization elects to develop the program in
house, outsource development, or purchase an existing program, there is still
the cost of implementation that includes trainer fees, travel, and release time
for employees to attend training. No organization wants to invest in SETA
that does not actually improve its information security posture. So the critical
question becomes, how can an organization increase the likelihood that its
SETA program will provide a positive return on investment?

To help address this question, we turn to an overview of human performance technology with a focus on how human performance technology
can help assure that the information security SETA program is effective.

An Overview of Human Performance Technology

Human performance technology (HPT) is also referred to as 1) performance engineering and 2) the science of improving human performance. HPT is the field of work that uses an engineering approach to attain desired results from human beings. It draws on the science of learning, teaching, instructional design, organizational behavior, industrial engineering, and psychology. HPT is based on the application of scientific principles to practical ends. The practical end that HPT is focused on is human performance, and more specifically, how human performance within an organization contributes to the accomplishment of the business goals of the organization.

HPT PRINCIPLES

A major tenet of HPT is that human performance is necessary to accomplish organizational results; when human performance is systematically aligned with organizational goals, human performance can contribute to the achievement of organizational goals in meaningful and significant ways. In this way, HPT adds value to the organization.

Another tenet of HPT is that organizations are complex systems with multiple entities and functional interdependencies. That is, organizations are comprised of multiple functional units, such as finance, human resources, maintenance, administration/management, production, customer service, sales, information technology, and so on. In order for the organization to perform effectively, the business units need to perform effectively. And in order for the business units and the organization to perform effectively, the workforce needs to perform effectively. HPT focuses on identifying the gap between desired and current organizational, unit, and human performance, with a focus on how the improvement of human performance can lead to an improvement in unit and organizational performance. Therefore, to affect meaningful change in organizational performance, it is necessary to determine desired unit and workforce performance.

A third major tenet of HPT is a focus on results. Given a gap between current and desired human performance, unit performance, and organizational performance, the results of the intervention will be measured to determine change in human performance and the consequent impact on unit and organizational performance. Finally, the last tenet is that not only does HPT take a systems view, HPT is a system itself. The HPT process takes a systematic approach to 1) assessing performance gaps, 2) the reasons for those performance gaps, 3) finding interventions that address the known gaps, 4) implementing those interventions, and 5) evaluating the consequent results. Figure 8-1 provides an overview of the HPT process.

PERFORMANCE ANALYSIS

Performance analysis is conducted for the purpose of defining the performance need or opportunity. Performance analysis consists of two elements: 1) organizational analysis, and 2) workforce performance analysis. The purpose of organizational analysis is to revisit the organizational vision, mission, values, goals, and objectives with specific attention to factors that are detracting from the accomplishment of organizational goals.

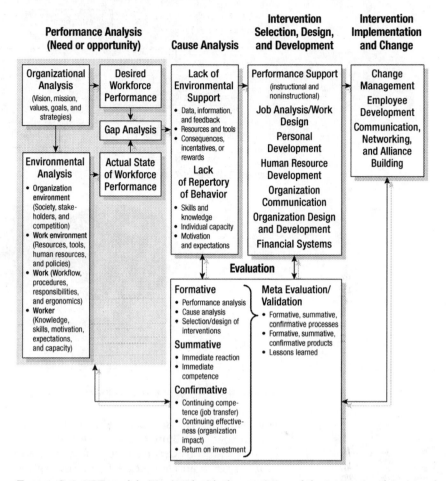

FIGURE 8-1 HPT model. *(Reprinted with the permission of the International Society of Performance Improvement)*

Organizational analysis consists of analyzing the 1) organizational environment to determine key stakeholders, competitors, etc., 2) work environment including tools, resources, policies, etc., 3) work to determine job task requirements, work flow, required efficiencies, etc., and 4) workforce to determine aptitude, knowledge skills, desire, and commitment.

HPT is focused on present and desired levels of human performance in the context of organizational performance. The purpose of workforce performance analysis then is to determine the gap between desired workforce performance and current workforce performance. Workforce performance analysis is more comprehensive than identifying the need for education, training, and awareness. SETA programs assume that a lack of knowledge is the primary cause of substandard human performance. HPT assumes that: 1) performance is a function of ability and motivation, 2) ability is a function of aptitude and education and 3) motivation is a function of desire

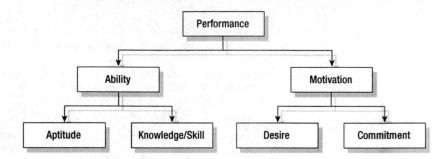

FIGURE 8-2 Performance model

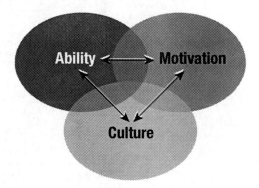

FIGURE 8-3 Ability, motivation, culture model

and commitment (see Figure 8-2). It therefore assumes that there are many factors that contribute to poor performance.

HPT also considers human performance in the context of the organization, its goals, and its culture. So HPT actually extends past the model of performance shown in Figure 8-1 by considering the dynamic influence of the organizational culture on human performance and conversely the influence of human performance on the organization (see Figure 8-3).

The process of conducting performance analysis can begin with the organizational analysis or with the workforce performance analysis. Often the two are done simultaneously or in rapid iterations. This is because they are mutually interdependent; workforce performance issues cannot be analyzed without analyzing the larger organizational environment and analysis of the organizational environment is meaningless without a focus on some aspect(s) of workforce performance.

CAUSE ANALYSIS

The next component of HPT is cause analysis. While gap analysis documents the gap between current and desired behavior, often the results of gap analysis are merely the identification of the gap. Cause analysis then is the diagnosis of why the gap exists. Cause analysis in HPT usually considers the influence of the following factors on performance: 1) consequences, incentives, and rewards for good performance; 2) data, information, and feedback used to set and reinforce expectations; 3) environmental support, resources, and/or tools needed to perform the job task; 4) individual capacity; 5) worker motives and expectations; and 6) worker knowledge and skills. By conducting cause analysis, the organization is more likely to implement solutions that address all root causes or at a minimum the most important root causes. The output of cause analysis is a detailed specification for selecting or designing/developing various types of interventions that are targeted at closing the gap. If the root cause has been identified as a lack of appropriate tools or resources to perform the job, then the recommended intervention will focus on making tools and other resources available. If the root cause has been identified as a lack of expectations and a lack of consequences or rewards/incentives, then the recommended solution will be methods to communicate expectations along with enforcement policies and incentive systems if appropriate. In practice, there are often several root causes; seldom is the recommended solution just one intervention. In addition to providing guidelines for selecting or designing/developing the intervention, the design blueprint is also used to develop valid measures that will indicate if the program is accomplishing its goals.

INTERVENTION SELECTION, DESIGN, AND DEVELOPMENT

The next component of HPT is intervention selection, design, and development. As shown in Figure 8-1, the types of interventions are many, e.g., performance support, job analysis/work design, organizational communication, training, and so on. The types of intervention that are appropriate are determined by the cause analysis. The design blueprint that is developed as a result of cause analysis is a list of all potential interventions. However, it is often the case that it is not possible or desirable to select or design/develop interventions for every cause that was identified. The main reason that it is not possible is resource constraints (limited time and money). Most organizations are looking to spend time and money on solutions that will produce high benefit or impact with limited investment. In order to determine those solutions that will have higher impact, yet cost less, a cause prioritization should be conducted.

Cause prioritization can be based on several factors. A few of the commonly used factors are 1) capability, 2) opportunity, 3) administrative access and control, and 4) cost. Capability refers to the collective knowledge and skills of individuals, departments, and the organization needed to execute the solution. A solution might be appropriate for the problem identified during cause analysis, but if the organization lacks the knowledge or skill needed to develop the solution or if the organization lacks the resources to outsource the solution to a vendor with the appropriate knowledge/skill, then that solution is not as viable as another. Opportunity refers to the level of organizational support and commitment. Organizational support and commitment are necessary from the highest levels within the organization. Thus, it is important to focus on solutions that have support at those levels. Administrative access and control refers to the levels of organizational structure the project requires; generally speaking there is a direct relationship between the number of functional areas involved and the time required to execute the project. A solution that requires less coordination across business units to execute is usually more desirable. Cost refers to the money required to acquire or design/develop the solution, as well as the implementation and evaluation of the solution. Cost should be considered not only in terms of the least expensive solution, but the potential for the solution to produce high impact results given the cost investment.

The design blueprint should be referred to several times throughout this phase to ensure the integrity of the solution. The output of intervention selection or design/development includes products, processes, systems, and/or technologies that address the performance gap(s) and root causes. Examples of products, processes, systems, and technologies include training, performance support tools, newsletters and other communication tools, a new incentive program, a re-engineered process, the deployment of a new technology, and so on. The type of intervention that is needed will also be considered when designing and developing an evaluation to determine if the workforce performance gap is being closed.

INTERVENTION IMPLEMENTATION AND CHANGE

The next component of HPT is intervention implementation and change. This phase of HPT includes deploying the solution and managing the change that is required within the organization to sustain the desired performance. Research has shown that performance interventions have a significant immediate impact on human performance, but without ongoing change management efforts, there is a diminishing return. For the most part, human beings like to know why change is necessary and are more likely to change if they know why it is necessary. When explaining why change is necessary, research shows that individuals are more likely to change when they understand 1) how change will help them individually, as well as 2) how the collective change will help the organization. Research also shows that if immediate change is recognized, reinforced, and rewarded, the change is more likely to continue over time. Therefore, the change management plan should include feedback strategies that communicate what level of change is occurring, reinforces the desired performance, and specifically rewards those who have changed as well as reiterates expectations and consequences for those who do not. The change strategy then should detail how the effort will be communicated and to whom, and exactly what will be communicated about the effort before, during, and after the intervention has occurred. Other items to consider in the change management plan include a project management plan with a rollout schedule, and contingency plans outlining what to do in case of resistance.

EVALUATION

The next component of HPT is evaluation. The output from the performance analysis feeds into cause analysis; and the output from both performance analysis and cause analysis feed into the design, development, and implementation of the evaluation. In other words, meaningful evaluation cannot be conducted if it is not based on performance and cause analysis.

There are three types of evaluation that are used in HPT: formative, summative, and confirmative evaluation. Each type is conducted for a different purpose. Formative evaluation is conducted for purposes of making improvements in the HPT program and is usually conducted during the design and development phases. Things that are typically evaluated during formative evaluation include the output of the performance analysis and cause analysis and the corresponding selection/design of the intervention. By comparing the emerging intervention with the performance and cause analysis, the human performance technologist is looking for ways to improve the program and ensure that it will meet its workforce performance and organizational impact goals. Summative evaluation is conducted for the purposes of determining immediate impact on workforce performance and is conducted immediately after the program. Generally speaking, during summative evaluation you are measuring what you did and the degree to which the solution produced the desired results. In addition, summative evaluation often includes measures of cost. Cost-benefit analysis combines benefits gained in light of costs incurred and is frequently a part of summative evaluation. Confirmative evaluation goes beyond summative evaluation to look at the longer term effects of the intervention. The time at which confirmative evaluation is conducted varies, but a reasonable range is 2–12 months after implementation of the intervention(s). Confirmative evaluation looks at continued competence on the job, continuing impact on organizational performance, and continuing return on investment.

Given this overview of HPT, we will now take a look at an extended case study where HPT was applied to information security management within an organization.

Information Security HPT Case Study

The material discussed so far has focused on describing the HPT tenets and model. The material that follows will be a detailed case study of an information security HPT program that was developed using the HPT model. This case study was performed for a Midwestern university with approximately 15,000 students and 5,000 faculty and staff. The case study is organized according to each major step of the HPT model. The results of each step and how the data were gathered are reported in detail. The hope is that by studying an extended example, you will be better able to utilize the HPT model to improve information security within your organization.

PERFORMANCE ANALYSIS

The first step was to conduct the performance analysis. This consisted of conducting both an organizational analysis as well as a workforce performance gap analysis. The goals of the performance analysis were to:

1. Define organizational mission, vision, and goals.
2. Define business need, target environment, and target performers.
3. Collect actual and desired organizational performance data.
4. Conduct environmental analysis.
5. Conduct workforce performance gap analysis.

Define Organizational Mission, Vision, and Goals

The mission of the university is to serve the citizens of the state, the United States, and the world in three areas: 1) research that expands the realm of knowledge, 2) teaching through dissemination and preservation of knowledge, and 3) service through exchange of knowledge. The vision of the university is to be prominent in research, teaching, and service. The goals of the university are to achieve and sustain prominence in research, teaching, and service.

Against the organizational backdrop, the mission of Information Technology department is to provide IT infrastructure in a cost effective manner that allows students, faculty, and staff to make maximum use of the appropriate information technology tools in the learning, teaching, research, outreach, administration, and support activities. The vision of the Information Technology department is to be the best in leveraging and expanding IT infrastructure in a manner that helps the institution achieve and sustain prominence. The goals of the IT department are to:

- Leverage technology to support research, teaching, and service.
- Find cost effective IT solutions.
- Explore emerging technologies that show potential for application in all mission areas.

Define Business Need, Target Environment, and Target Performers

The business need driving the performance analysis is the need for a secure IT infrastructure within the organization. The organization requesting the performance analysis is a university with slightly more than 20,000 users. Among the 20,000 users, approximately 15,000 of the users are students. The students use the computing network in the dormitories called StudentNet. The IT department is encountering excessive workload due to the insecure practices of students using StudentNet. Because of this excessive workload fighting to keep StudentNet secure, the IT department is unable to meet other performance goals for the business year. For example, the university is interested in a new payroll system as well as a new online library system. Neither of these projects will be possible given current demands in security. The university has decided that it needs to reduce the amount of staff time dedicated to securing StudentNet from 7 FTE to 4 FTE. One FTE is about 2,020 hours of work per year and roughly $84,500 in salary and fringe benefits. The reduction from 7 FTE to 4 FTE will provide a salary savings of almost $255,000 that can be reallocated to the new payroll system and the new online library system.

Collect Actual and Desired Organizational Performance Data

Table 8-1 shows the current and desired IT security performance data in several key areas. The difference between the current and desired performance is the gap that needs to be closed. In addition, Table 8-1 indicates how the data were collected.

It was determined that if the IT department could achieve the desired performance levels listed in Table 8-1, then it would be in a position to reallocate 3 FTE to the other IT projects thereby helping the IT department fulfill its mission, which in turn helps the university better fulfill its mission.

Conduct Environmental Analysis

The environmental analysis was conducted to provide information about the work environment, the work processes, and the target performers. For each of three performance issues listed in Table 8-1, tools and

TABLE 8-1   **Performance Analysis Results**

Performance Issue	Current Performance	Desired Performance	Data Collection Method
Machines compromised in any outbreak of vulnerability	28% of machines compromised	<5% of machines compromised	IT staff
E-mail spam	40% of e-mail messages are spam	<20% of e-mail messages are spam	IT staff
Mailhub viruses	Average of 2,000 machines infected during last 5 virus outbreaks	0 machines infected during next 5 virus outbreaks	IT staff

TABLE 8-2   **Environmental Analysis Results**

Tools/Resources	Work Processes	Knowledge/Skill/Motivation
Passwords	Creating strong passwords	Users know how to create strong passwords. Users choose to create strong passwords.
Security settings	Users changing security settings to the highest level	Users know how to change security settings. Users choose to change security settings.
Disabling or discarding cookies	Users disabling cookies or discarding them when a Web site is closed	Users know how to disable cookies and discard them when closing a Web site. Users choose to disable cookies and discard them when closing a Web site.
Safe downloading	Users not downloading unknown files or programs from the Internet	Users know how to check to see if the file/program is safe. Users elect not to download files/programs that cannot be guaranteed as safe.
Firewalls	Installing and configuring a firewall	Users know how to select, install, and configure a firewall. Users choose to select, install, and configure a firewall.
Anti-virus software	Installing, configuring, and updating anti-virus software	Users know how to select, install, configure, and update anti-virus software. Users choose to select, install, configure, and update anti-virus software.
Patches and system updates	Installing and testing patches and system updates	Users know how to apply and test patches and system updates. Users choose to apply and test patches and system updates.

resources required for accomplishing the desired state were identified and then the associated work processes/responsibilities and knowledge/skill and motivation levels were identified and documented. The results of the environmental analysis are in Table 8-2.

TABLE 8-3   **Cause Analysis Results**

Tool/Resource	Work Process	Knowledge/Skill Level	Performance Level
Passwords	Creating strong passwords	57% report they know how to create strong passwords.	8.1% report creating strong passwords.
Security settings	Users changing security settings to the highest level	48.2% report they know how to change security settings.	34.6% report they change security settings to the highest level.
Disabling or discarding cookies	Users disabling cookies or discarding them when a Web site is closed	59.5% report they know how to disable cookies or set them to be discarded.	44.2% disable cookies or set them to be discarded.
Safe downloading	Users not downloading unknown files or programs from the Internet	77% report they know how to determine if a file/program is safe to download.	66.1% choose not to download unknown files or programs.
Firewalls	Installing and configuring a firewall	54.8% report they know how to install and configure a firewall.	50.9% use a firewall.
Anti-virus software	Installing, configuring, and updating anti-virus software	76% report they know how to install, configure, and update anti-virus software.	73.1% use anti-virus software. 50.5% update anti-virus software once per week.
Patches and system updates	Installing and testing patches and system updates	71% report they know how to apply and test system updates and patches.	65% apply and test system updates and patches.

Conduct Workforce Performance Gap Analysis

Given these organizational performance gaps, the next step was to determine the workforce performance gaps. The workforce performance gap analysis sought to answer the following question: What are the actual and desired knowledge levels and performances of the students with regard to the tools/resources and work processes identified?

The data for the workforce performance gap analysis were collected via a survey. The results of the workforce performance gap analysis are reported in Table 8-3.

The data generated from the workforce performance gap analysis were then analyzed to determine more specific causes for the gaps in human performance, and also used to set performance goals and associated metrics for evaluating the HPT intervention. The more specific performance goals are shown in Table 8-4. The metrics are described in a later section.

CAUSE ANALYSIS

The next step was to analyze the human performance gaps to determine root causes for the gaps. By determining why a gap exists, solutions can be

TABLE 8-4 **Workforce Performance Gap Analysis**

Work Process	Knowledge Current	Knowledge Desired	Performance Current	Performance Desired
Users create strong passwords	57.0%	100%	8.1%	100%
Users change security settings to the highest level	48.2%	100%	34.6%	100%
Users disable cookies or discard them when a Web site is closed	59.5%	100%	44.2%	100%
Users do not download unknown files or programs from the Internet	77.0%	100%	66.1%	100%
Users install and configure firewalls	54.8%	100%	50.9%	100%
Users install, configure, and update anti-virus software	76.0%	100%	73.1% use 50.5% update	100%
Users install and test system updates and patches	71.0%	100%	65.0%	100%

TABLE 8-5 **Firewall Survey Questions and Root Cause Mapping**

Question	Root Cause Categories
I have not installed a firewall on my computer because:	
I didn't know I needed to.	Expectations and feedback
I don't know what a firewall is.	Knowledge and skills
I don't have the firewall hardware or software.	Tools and resources
I don't know how to install a firewall.	Knowledge and skills
I don't want to install a firewall.	Desire
I don't know how to get help.	Tools and resources
I don't think it is worth it.	Rewards and incentives

selected/designed that more effectively address the human performance gap. The data for the cause analysis were collected using the survey. Each content area on the survey (content areas include creating strong passwords, changing security settings, disabling cookies, etc.) had questions aimed at assessing users' knowledge and users' reasons for *not* taking the desired action. The latter was the data used for determining root cause. Table 8-5 shows sample questions items from the survey in the firewall content area and the corresponding coding to root cause categories.

Using the data from the survey, a summary of root causes was developed. Figure 8-4 shows the summary by cause category. Respondents were allowed to select as many reasons as applied.

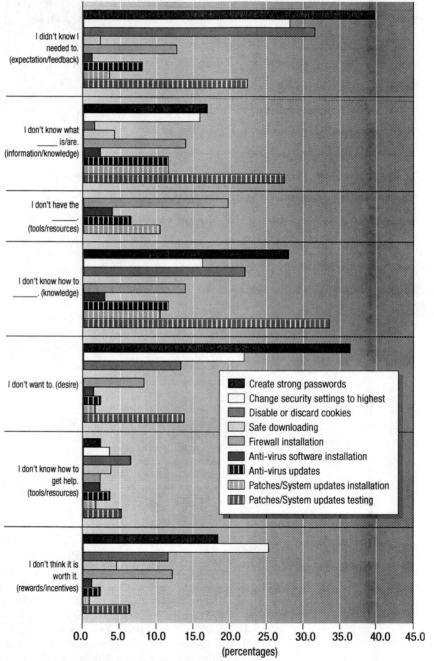

FIGURE 8-4 Cause analysis summary by cause category and content area

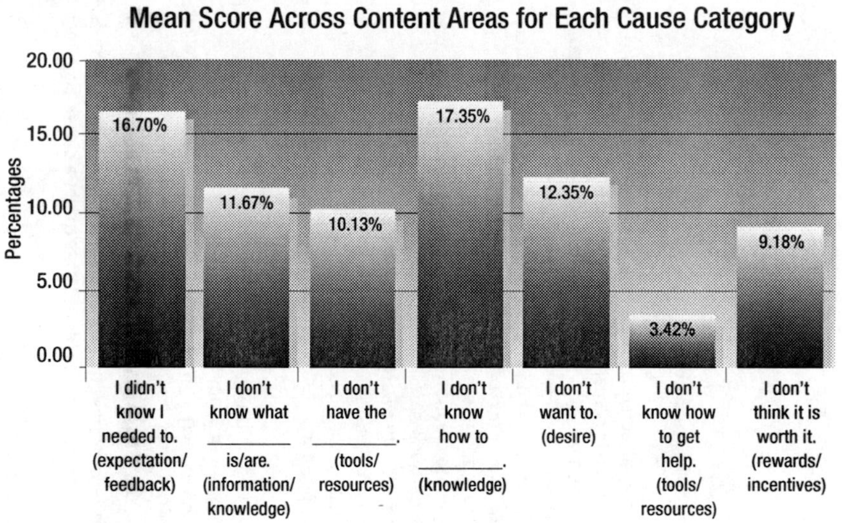

Mean Score Across Content Areas for Each Cause Category

FIGURE 8-5 Mean content score for each cause category

Averages were created for each category in order to make comparisons among the different root causes. Figure 8-5 shows the mean score across all content areas for each cause category. What these data show are that a lack of knowledge/skill is the largest cause of failure to take desired action, followed by lack of expectations/feedback, then desire, and so on. These data provide the human performance technologist with detailed information about the nature and focus of the intervention.

INTERVENTION SELECTION, DESIGN, AND DEVELOPMENT

Using the output of the cause analysis as a design blueprint for the performance intervention, the next step was to select or design/develop the intervention. In selecting or designing/developing interventions, the first task was developing a list of suggested solutions. Because resources were limited, a cause prioritization was conducted. This cause prioritization was based on five factors. The first was coverage—the possibility for the solution to address multiple root causes. The second was capability—the capability of the IT department to execute the solution given the skills/knowledge of its staff. The third was access and control—a rating of the ability of the IT department to directly cause the solution to be developed and implemented versus having to rely upon other parties. The fourth was efficacy—the belief that the solution will address the problem effectively. The fifth was cost—the projected cost of developing, implementing, and evaluating the solution. IT staff were asked to rate each solution based on these five factors using a scale of 1–5 with 5 being strongly agree and 1 being strongly disagree. Table 8-6 shows a sample of the suggested solutions for the 'StudentNet Users Not Creating Strong Passwords' performance gap (it was not possible to show all of the suggested solutions here). Table 8-7 shows the mean rating for the suggested

TABLE 8-6   **Partial Sample of Suggested Solutions**

Performance Gap	Cause Statement	Cause Type	Solution Category	Specific Solution Suggestions
StudentNet users not creating strong passwords	40% of users are not aware they need to create strong passwords	Expectation/ feedback	Job aid/feedback system/newsletter	1. On the login screen, post a message about the need and expectation for creating strong passwords. Highlight a scenario where a weak password has created hardship for a student and the university. 2. Make the tutorial on creating strong passwords mandatory for students. This sends the message that users need to do this and it is important. 3. Enforce the creation of strong passwords by rejecting weak passwords. 4. Hold a security awareness week once a year and include these expectations as part of the event. 5. E-mail a personalized reminder to each student about the importance of strong passwords.
	36.6% of users have no desire to create strong passwords	Desire	Reprimand system/ reward system	1. At the beginning of each month include a news release in the student e-newsletter that highlights how many computers were compromised the past month due to weak passwords and the effects it had on the students.
	28% of users do not know how to create strong passwords	Knowledge/skill	Tutorial/training	1. Create a brief on-line tutorial on creating strong passwords. Make it mandatory for all students to get a career account.
	18.4% of users do not think creating strong passwords is worthwhile	Rewards/ incentives	Newsletter/feedback system	1. At the beginning of each month include a news release in the student e-newsletter that highlights how many computers were compromised the past month due to weak passwords and the effects it had on the students affected. 2. E-mail a personalized reminder to each student about the importance of strong passwords.
	16.8% of users are not aware of what strong passwords are	Information/ knowledge	Tutorial/newsletter	1. Create a brief on-line tutorial on creating strong passwords. 2. Reinforce the attributes of strong passwords in the e-newsletter to students. 3. Hold a security awareness week once a year and include these expectations as part of the event.

TABLE 8-7   **Solution Rating and Ranking**

Solution	Coverage	Capability	Access and Control	Efficacy	Low Cost	Total Score
On the login screen, post a message about the need and expectation for XXX. Highlight a scenario where XXX created hardship for a student and the university.	5	4.7	5	2	5	21.7
Enforce the creation of strong passwords by rejecting weak passwords.	1	5	5	5	5	21
At the beginning of each month include a news release in the student e-newsletter that highlights how many computers were compromised the past month due to XXX and the effects it had on the students.	5	5	3.4	3.4	3.3	20.1
Create a tutorial on XXX. Make the tutorial on XXX mandatory for students. This sends the message that users need to do this and it is important.	5	3.4	3.5	5	3	19.9
E-mail a personalized reminder to each student about the importance of XXX.	5	5	5	3	1.3	19.3
Hold a security awareness week once a year and include these expectations as part of the event.	4	4	4	4	2	18

solutions presented in Table 8-6; the solutions are ranked from highest to lowest scoring. The interventions that the university decided to design/develop and implement are highlighted in gray. Formative evaluation was conducted at this step to ensure that the interventions aligned to root causes and also to the criteria for managing change.

INTERVENTION IMPLEMENTATION AND CHANGE

The next step was to develop a project/change management plan. The project/change management plan included a timeline with key milestones as well as a list of criteria for how the change process was to be managed. An excerpt from the larger project/change management plan is provided in Table 8-8.

EVALUATION

The last step in completing the HPT process is the evaluation. The formative evaluation was actually started during the intervention selection, design, and development phase. The formative evaluation consisted of expert review. The experts selected to provide review included content experts,

TABLE 8-8   Project/Change Management Plan

Solution	Subtask	Owner	Time	Need for intervention–individuals	Need for intervention–organizational	Recognition of change	Reward for change/consequence for lack of change
On the login screen, post a message about the need and expectation for XXX. Highlight a scenario where XXX created hardship for a student and the university.	Create login message and scenario	Bob	May 31	X	X		
	Review and revise	Policy expert	June 30				
	Execute	Mary	August 15				
Enforce the creation of strong passwords by rejecting weak passwords.	Change policy settings	Mary	August 15			X	X
At the beginning of each month include a news release in the student e-newsletter that highlights how many computers were compromised the past month due to XXX and the effects it had on the students, including diminishing impacts over time.	Develop e-newsletter template	Lance	May 31	X	X	X	X
	Write newsletter content	Bob	2nd Friday of every month beginning in June				
	Review and revise	Content and marketing experts	3rd Friday of every month				
	Distribute	Mary	1st Monday every month				
Create a tutorial on XXX. Make the tutorial on XXX mandatory for students. This sends the message that users need to do this and it is important. Students must score 85% or higher. Provide congratulatory feedback in the way of a free mouse pad to students who pass with a score of 85% or higher.	Create objectives	Sue	May 31	X	X	X	X
	Create assessment items	Sue	June 15				
	Develop materials	Sue	August 1				
	Pilot test and revise	Content and training experts	August 15				
	Implement tutorial	Sue	September 1				
	Evaluate	Committee	October 15				

TABLE 8-9 **Summative and Confirmative Evaluations**

Metric	Summative	Confirmative	Baseline	Target	Evaluation Design	Data Collection Methods
Knowledge of how to create strong passwords	X		57%	100%	Pre-post survey	After the intervention was implemented, a post survey was used to determine how many students reported that they knew how to create a strong password. Data were compared to the baseline data collected during the performance assessment.
Creation of strong passwords	X	X	8.1%	100%	Longitudinal (Pre-post-post-post...)	Once operational, periodically sample passwords, testing for strength and compliance with policy.
Knowledge of how to disable or discard cookies	X		59.5%	100%	Pre-post survey	After the intervention was implemented, a post survey was used to determine how many students reported that they knew how to disable or discard cookies. Data were compared to the baseline data collected during the performance assessment.
Disabling and discarding cookies	X	X	44.2%	100%	Pre-post-post	After the intervention was implemented, a post survey was administered to determine how many students reported disabling or discarding cookies. The survey was then repeated 3 months later. Data were compared to the baseline data collected during the performance assessment.
% of machines compromised		X	28%	<5%	Pre-post-post	Data were collected 3, 6, and 12 months after the intervention and compared with baseline data.
# of machines infected by mailhub viruses		X	2,000 last 5 out-breaks	0	Pre-post-post	Data were collected 3, 6, and 12 months after the intervention and compared with baseline data.
# of IT FTE reallocated from security to other IT projects		X	7	3	Pre-post-post	Data were collected 12 and 24 months after the intervention and compared with baseline data.

policy experts, training experts, and marketing/communications experts. The content experts provided feedback on the accuracy and completeness of the content included in the e-newsletter and the tutorial. The policy experts provided feedback on the structure and content of the policy posted on the login screen, the training experts provided feedback on the structure and elements of the tutorial, and the marketing/communication experts provided feedback on the design, layout, and readability of the e-newsletter. The formative evaluation was conducted using one-to-one evaluation with direct feedback being provided to the owner of that task.

The summative and confirmative evaluations consisted of several metrics. Table 8-9 shows a sample of various metrics classified as summative, confirmative, or both, the evaluation design, and corresponding data collection methods. Notice that the first four metrics listed are the direct results of the intervention, whereas the next three metrics are organizational impact metrics.

Suggested Readings

Human Performance Technology Principles, International Society for Performance Improvement. Available at *http://www.ispi.org/*

Lei, K., Schmidt, T., Um, E., & Schaffer, S. (2004). Performance analysis: A case study on computer security. *Proceedings of the Association for Educational Communications Technology Conference.* Chicago: The Association.

Performance Improvement Journal. Available at *http://www.ispi.org/*

What is HPT? International Society for Performance Improvement. Available at *http://www.ispi.org/*

The Provision of Defenses Against Internet-Based Attacks

LI-CHIOU CHEN

Pace University

THOMAS A. LONGSTAFF AND KATHLEEN M. CARLEY

Carnegie Mellon University

Dr. Li-Chiou Chen received her PhD from Carnegie Mellon University in Engineering and Public Policy. She is an Assistant Professor at the Department of Information Systems in the School of Computer Science and Information Systems, Pace University. Her dissertation, entitled "Computational Models for Defenses against Internet-Based Attacks," utilizes a network-based simulation tool to analyze the policy and economic issues in the provision of defenses against distributed denial-of-service attacks. Her current research interests are focused on combining artificial intelligence and agent-based modeling to conduct technological and policy analysis in the area of information security.

Dr. Thomas A. Longstaff received his PhD in 1991 at the University of California, Davis in Software Environments. He is a senior member of the technical staff in the Network Situational Awareness Program at the Software Engineering Institute (SEI), Carnegie Mellon University. He is currently managing research and development in network infrastructure security for the program. His publication areas include information survivability, insider threat, intruder modeling, and intrusion detection.

Dr. Kathleen M. Carley received her PhD from Harvard. She is a Professor at the Institute for Software Research International, Carnegie Mellon University. Her research combines cognitive science, social networks, and computer science. Specific research areas are dynamic network analysis, computational social and organization theory, adaptation and evolution, computational text analysis, and the impact of telecommunication technologies and policy on behavior and disease contagion within and among groups. Her models meld multi-agent technology with network dynamics and empirical data. Illustrative large-scale multi-agent network models she and the CASOS team have developed are: BioWar—a scale model of weaponized biological attacks; OrgAhead—a strategic and natural organizational adaptation model; and DyNet—a change in covert networks model.

Overview

In mid 2003, Internet Security Systems estimated that there were in excess of three million hackers in the U.S. There are at least that many in the rest of the world. That means over six million hackers world wide, who could at any minute turn their sights on your organization. Are you ready? In this reading, the authors turn their attention to the examination of defenses against attacks that target the organization from the Internet. With the increase in electronic commerce, and the use of the Internet for organizational communications, organizations must increasingly work to secure their connection to this insecure network. The authors examine common attacks such as denial-of-service and distributed denial-of-service attacks, with special attention to how these attacks are conducted, and then provide defenses against these attacks.

Introduction

Internet-based attacks have become an important concern to the government and business since more systems are reliant upon the Internet to exchange information. Without a secure Internet infrastructure, neither e-commerce such as online purchasing nor e-democracy services such as online voting can be conducted successfully. For business, both Internet worms and distributed denial-of-service attacks were listed among top ten security concerns of more than 1,230 organizations globally.[1] For government, preventing Internet-based attacks has been an important issue in national plans to secure critical infrastructure.[2]

Among various Internet-based attacks, distributed denial-of-service (DDOS) attacks have emerged as a prevalent way to compromise the availability of online services. These attacks have imposed financial losses for e-commerce businesses. For example, in February 2000, over a period of three days, a 15-year-old hacker launched DDOS attacks against several high-profile e-commerce Web sites including Yahoo, eBay, and Amazon.com.[3] The Yankee Group estimates that the financial losses imposed by the attacks on these companies totaled more than $1 billion.[4] The CSI/FBI survey[5] shows that 17% of respondents in the last 12-month period have detected DDOS attacks and the financial losses are estimated as more than $26 million.

DDOS attacks are usually sent from wide-spread sources. Since most attack tools are now designed to scan and exploit vulnerabilities automatically, the spread of attack tools is faster and easier. For example, Code-Red worm attacks in August 2001 highlight the potential risk of large-scale DDOS attacks launched from wide-spread sources. Moreover, in order to generate attacks from distributed sources, these attack tools usually form a network of attack bots by exploiting vulnerable computers over the Internet. An Internet security survey from Symantec reveals that the number of computers infected with attack bots increased from under 2,000 to more than 30,000 among their customers in the first six months of 2004.[6]

We investigated the technological factors and economic factors in providing defenses against DDOS attacks. We asked how Internet Service Providers (ISPs) can provide DDOS defenses to their subscribers. Many defenses that mitigate the effect of ongoing DDOS attacks have been proposed, but none of them have been widely deployed on the Internet infrastructure at this point because of a lack of understanding in the tradeoffs inherent in the complex system of attacks and defenses. The problem is not just technical but is a management and policy problem as well, involving setting policies and meeting the needs of diverse subscribers with different priorities.[7,8] Security services, such as Virtual Private Networks or firewalls, have been provided by ISPs as optional network services to deal with the secrecy of data transportation. In this case, the services that provide DDOS defenses ensure the availability of online services.

We will provide recommendations for subscribers, ISPs, and policy makers in making decisions about deploying DDOS defenses. The effectiveness of DDOS defenses depends on many factors, such as the nature of the network's topology, the specific attack scenario, and the settings of the network routers, because the attacks are distributed in nature and the scale of the attacks can vary. Understanding the nature and severity of these tradeoffs will assist attack victims, network providers, and public policy makers in making security policy decisions while they are assessing potential defenses against these attacks. This reading aims to increase our understanding of these tradeoffs and to derive insights that will enable a more secure infrastructure.

Background of the Distributed Denial-of-Service Attack

Distributed denial-of-service (DDOS) attacks are an Internet-based attack that aims at compromising the availability of computers or network resources. A denial-of-service (DOS) attack is considered to take place only when access to a computer or network resource is intentionally blocked or degraded as a result of malicious actions taken by another user. These attacks do not necessarily damage data directly, or permanently, but they intentionally compromise the availability of the resource.[9]

In a DDOS attack, an attacker could trigger tens of thousands of concurrent attacks on either one or a set of targets by using unprotected Internet nodes around the world to coordinate these attacks.[10] A DDOS attack can unfold in the following way. Referring to Figure 9-1, suppose that DDOS attacks are launched against Yahoo's Web servers both from the computers connected to the DSL line provided by the Internet Access Provider's (IAP's)

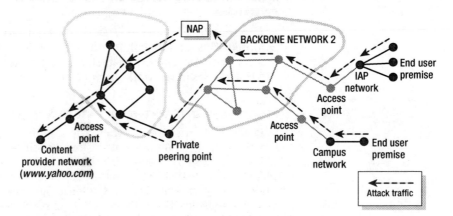

FIGURE 9-1 An illustration of a DDOS attack

network and from the computers inside the campus network in the backbone network 1. These computers are attack sources and the IAP network is the source network, while Yahoo's Web servers are attack victims and Yahoo's network is the victim network. In this example, to maintain the availability of Yahoo's Web servers during such an attack, the mitigation strategy is to detect and filter out the attack traffic at some points of the routing path from the IAP network to Yahoo's network.

Several obstacles have made tracing and filtering DDOS attacks difficult. First, IP spoofing conceals the true origins of attacks. IP spoofing means attackers use false source IP addresses in attack packets to conceal their origins. The source addresses of IP packets are not required for IP routing since the routers need only the destination addresses in order to forward the IP packets. Senders of IP packets can forge the source addresses in order to hide their true identities. The forged source addresses make it difficult to trace and to determine the true origins of DDOS attack traffic within the current IP routing environment. Secondly, tracing and filtering attacks is not only a technical problem but also a policy and economic problem since attack sources can be distributed across multiple administrative domains. Since vulnerability-scanning tools have been automated as mentioned earlier, attackers can exploit the vulnerable computers across the Internet and utilize them as attack sources. As a result, attack sources can be distributed across multiple administrative domains. In this case, attack tracing and blocking is more difficult since it involves the cooperation of multiple network providers and subscribers. Under this circumstance, attack tracing and filtering is a policy and economic problem among various network providers. Thirdly, filtering attack traffic has a side effect on legitimate traffic because attack tools utilize various vulnerabilities in IP protocols that make it harder to distinguish attack traffic from legitimate traffic. Many tools have been used to launch DDOS attacks,[11,12] and several characteristics in these attack tools make it hard to distinguish attack traffic from legitimate traffic.[13]

Defenses Against Distributed Denial-of-Service Attacks

In responding to ongoing DDOS attacks, a variety of defenses have been proposed. This section will provide an overview of the current solutions to DDOS attacks. A detailed characterization of automatic responses against DDOS attacks is in the works from Chen, Longstaff, and Carley.[14]

REACTION POINTS: NETWORK-BASED VS. HOST-BASED

Reaction points refer to where the responses against attacks take place. Reaction points could be network-based such as those on network routers, or host-based such as those on servers that the attack targets. Host-based defenses refer to the defenses that are deployed on the machines that are potential targets of attacks, and defenses are used to increase the tolerance of the targets to the attacks. The methods proposed in the works of Spatscheck and Peterson[15] and Yan and Early et al.[16] are in this category. These methods can only mitigate the impact of attacks on the services that the attack targets provide, but not actually block attacks. When attack traffic is large enough to deplete the resources used for mitigating the attacks, additional methods for blocking attacks are needed. Network-based methods are deployed on the points where packets route through the network connections to the targets, such as routers or proxy servers.[17–24] These methods are used to either trace or block attack traffic. Our analysis later will focus on network-based defenses.

TYPE OF RESPONSE: ACTIVE VS. PASSIVE

A few defenses are designed to actively respond to the attack traffic, while the majority are designed to passively trace/log attack traffic. Tracing back to the real sources of attacks has been an established part of DDOS defense studies.[25–30] These methods could facilitate future liability assignments if source IP addresses of attack packets are forged. These methods are for identifying the sources of attacks, not for stopping ongoing attack traffic. In contrast, other defenses are designed to actively reduce the amount of ongoing attack traffic.[31–36] However, even with these responses, an ISP can only trace and respond against attack traffic within the boundary of its own network. Technically, an ISP needs the assistance of upstream or downstream ISPs to stop attack traffic at another network. Legally, an ISP can only trace the suspicious attack traffic within its own network under the U.S. Wiretap Act.[37] Our analysis later will focus on the responses that actively reduce ongoing attack traffic within the boundary of an ISP's network.

ATTACK TRAFFIC SAMPLING: PROBABILISTIC SAMPLING VS. CHECK-EVERYTHING

Since examining every packet that goes through a router may impose an enormous storage or computational power requirement, some defenses sample network packets probabilistically to reduce the number of packets to be examined and logged.[38] Our analysis later will focus on the defenses that check everything once they are triggered.

REACTION TIMING: CONSTANT VS. EVENT-TRIGGERED

Some defenses needed to be active all the time in order to detect suspicious packets. Egress[39] and ingress filtering[40] are deployed at local edge routers to examine all incoming and outgoing packets. However, if a defense can be automatically turned on whenever an attack is launched, the overhead could be limited to a certain time period. However, it is difficult to determine the exact timing to trigger a defensive response. A few defenses are triggered based on the congestion level of network links.[41–44] Our analysis later will model both constant- and event-triggered responses.

DETECTION CRITERIA: ATTACK SIGNATURES, CONGESTION PATTERN, PROTOCOLS, OR SOURCE IP ADDRESSES

It is hard to distinguish attack packets from legitimate packets, especially when both types are sent to the same destination. Many different criteria have been examined. Each criterion has a tradeoff in terms of the number of false positives[45] and false negatives associated with the outcome. Moreover, some criteria are only effective at identifying certain types of attack packets. For example, most intrusion detection systems detect attacks based on anomaly pattern matching or statistical measures of attack signatures.[46] The pushback method treats traffic aggregates as attack flows.[47,48] A revised TCP state machine has been used to identify TCP SYN packet flood.[49] A route-based method detects attack packets with spoofed source IP addresses based on the knowledge of the network's topology on core routers.[50]

DEPLOYMENT LOCATION: A SINGLE POINT, ATTACK PATH, OR DISTRIBUTED POINTS

Deployment location refers to where a defense is placed and triggered. If a defense is placed at the firewall or the proxy server in a subscriber's network,[51] it will help the subscriber to discover attacks but will not be effective when the bandwidth of the subscriber's network is saturated. The pushback method triggers filters along the path that the aggregated traffic has traversed[52,53] if the routers on this path have deployed such a defense in advance. A defense can be gradually deployed at distributed locations across a network.[54–56] To prevent the attack detection from slowing down the backbone network, CenterTrack routs suspicious traffic to an additional overlay network.[57] Our analysis later will distinguish such systems as source filtering (filtering at the upstream of the attack sources) and destination filtering (filtering at the upstream of the victim's networks).

The Provision of DDOS Defenses

The provision of DDOS defenses involves both technological and economic factors. Technically, the effectiveness of DDOS defenses depends on the false positives of the detection algorithms, the type of network topology, the type of attacks, and whether all ISPs are compliant in establishing defenses. Economically, once an ISP decides to deploy the defenses on its network, the provision of the service is influenced by the cost of the provision, the willingness to pay of the subscribers, and the cooperation of interconnected ISPs. Since little is known about the interactions among these factors, the service provision model for deploying the defenses is still unclear.

A SIMULATION MODEL OF DDOS ATTACKS AND DEFENSES

To study these problems, we built a model for simulating DDOS attacks given a network topology. Figure 9-2 is an overview of the components in this model. This simulation tool consists of four sets of input parameters, including parameters that quantify the network scenario, the attack scenario, the attack detection, and the attack response. The network scenario parameters model how network traffic is transported on a network. Attack scenario parameters decide the number of victim networks and attack source networks for a scenario. The attack detection parameters and attack response parameters describe a given defense mechanism.

Three sets of output parameters are generated from this tool, which include performance measures, cost measures, and topology measures. Performance measures are for the analysis of the performance impact of the

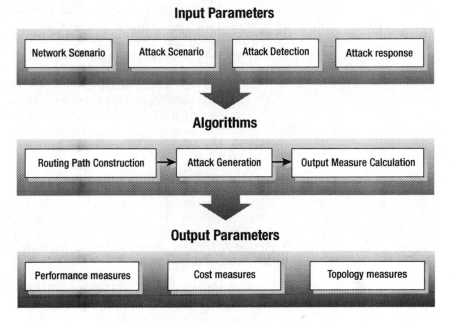

FIGURE 9-2 The simulation model of DDOS attacks and defenses

defenses. Cost measures are for the analysis of the economic cost of operating the service. Topology measures are for the analysis of the correlation between network topology and other output measures.

The tool has three sets of algorithms. During a simulation, the attack generation algorithm sets the packet rate of attack traffic, and selects attack source networks, legitimate source networks, and victim networks. After simulated attacks are determined, the routing path construction algorithm calculates the routing path between attack source networks, legitimate source networks, and victim networks. At the end, for each attack scenario and each defense, the output measure calculation algorithm calculates performance measures and cost measures for the further analyses.

ASSUMPTIONS

Using this tool, we studied three issues for providing DDOS defenses: 1) the service models for dealing with the technological uncertainty in defenses, 2) the economic incentives for providing the services, and 3) the incentives for cooperation with other ISPs. The assumptions for our analyses are as follows:

- The DDOS attacks saturate the network connections of subscribers to their backbone networks or take down servers inside the network of the subscribers.
- Network subscribers would pay based on the utility received from the defense. The utility that a subscriber derives from DDOS defenses is the expected value of losses that would be incurred from DDOS attacks.

▧ Providers would like to provide DDOS defenses to their subscribers if the operational benefit is larger than the operational cost.

▧ Statistical data about DDOS attacks to subscribers of ISPs are hard to obtain due to confidentiality and technical difficulty of data collection. The DDOS data and the Code-Red data[58,59] used in this study are the closest approximation to the probability of attacks using publicly available data. However, using their proprietary data, ISPs can adopt our model to estimate their benefit and cost of providing defense services. The network topology data is that of ISPs listed in *The Board Watch Magazine*,[60] which is a simplified version of each ISP's actual network topology.

We analyzed the benefits and the costs of the stakeholders in the provisioning of DDOS defenses. The stakeholders include the subscribers that originate attacks (attack sources), the ISPs of the attack sources (upstream ISPs), the subscribers that are victims of attacks (victims), and the ISPs of the victims (downstream ISPs). We provide a list of recommendations for these stakeholders as well as public policy makers based on the evidence found in our study.[61]

RECOMMENDATIONS TO NETWORK SUBSCRIBERS

Several recommendations are provided for network subscribers when considering the DDOS defenses.

1) Subscribers need to recognize the attack tolerance of their online servers in order to estimate the availability of their servers during attacks. Since none of the current defenses can filter out attack traffic without posing an impact on legitimate traffic, network providers would be able to tune the defenses based on the availability of the servers to meet the needs of the subscribers. In particular, when the subscriber has a capacity that is larger than the packet rate of the attack traffic, maintaining a certain tolerance to attacks can minimize any additional dropping of the legitimate traffic.

2) Subscribers should provide online services that are closer to where their clients are located when DDOS defenses are implemented in order to maintain the availability of the online service to legitimate clients. For example, distributed content storage systems can provide online content closer to legitimate clients.

3) Subscribers should implement defenses on the outbound traffic of an access network. The defenses will ensure the accessibility of legitimate clients to other online services, which is better than having the victim network filter out legitimate traffic.

RECOMMENDATIONS TO NETWORK PROVIDERS

To provide the defenses, ISPs need to consider the service models for dealing with the technological uncertainty in defenses, the economic incentives for providing the services, and incentives for cooperation with other ISPs. These issues are explained as follows.

To provide DDOS defenses, ISPs should consider the following recommendations regarding technological uncertainty:

1) Network providers should design services that focus on adjusting the filtering rate of the attack traffic to meet the needs of different

subscribers when providing defenses that are congestion-based and are dynamically enforced. The filter location and the filtering rate of attack traffic are the most sensitive variables for such defenses.

2) Network providers should design services that focus on the false positive rate of attack detection when providing defenses that are anomaly-based and are statically enforced. The false positive rate of attack detection is the most sensitive variable for such defenses.

3) In order to improve the quality of the defenses when attacks are distributed, network providers should cooperate with highly influential network providers. For attack detection, they should cooperate with administrative domains that have the largest reachable source IP addresses. For attack filtering, they should cooperate with the ones where the most attacks originate. Possible incentives for cooperation include the increase in the quality of the defense service, the increase in reputation because of conducting the best practice, and economic incentives for providing the services.

To introduce the new service for their subscribers, network providers need to ensure that the operational profit in the long term would justify their capital investment. We have found several reasons to expect that the operational benefits will be higher than the operational costs of the service. Here is a sequence of actions for a provider to implement the services of DDOS defenses.

First, at the initial stage when few providers are able to deploy the service (monopoly market assumption), the provider should implement a differential pricing scheme. By doing this, the provider can benefit from the different levels of expected loss experienced by subscribers, from the different levels of the attack frequency, and from the different quality of defenses demanded.

Secondly, when more and more providers are able to provide the service (competitive market assumption), no single provider can benefit from differential pricing since subscribers have more choices and can switch to another provider. In this case, the providers should consider the following:

1) Providers should set the filter location closer to the attack source since it is more beneficial for both the subscribers and the providers. This result is more significant when the network of the provider is capacity constrained.

2) Providers should provide the destination filtering service for free if the fixed cost per subscribers can be recovered from the additional income from additional subscribers to network transport services in a competitive market.

3) Providers should provide source filtering when attacks are launched at high packet rates and when subscribers that originate attacks suffer losses, such as losses due to liability assignment. Offering source filtering is more beneficial than offering destination filtering since the probability of originating attacks is higher than the probability of being attacked. This result is true even when the loss to originating networks is only 1% of the expected loss of attack victims. Source filtering is also more beneficial when the network of the provider is less connected and has a long average path length.

RECOMMENDATIONS TO POLICY MAKERS

The market mechanism is enough to sustain the provision of DDOS defenses. To facilitate cooperation among ISPs to reach a critical mass for providing the DDOS defense service, several recommendations are made for policy makers:

1) Policy makers should set up a program helping the industry to acquire the technologies that can detect and react against attack traffic at sources. The technologies for conducting source filtering at subscribers' networks are still underdeveloped. Even though ISPs would like to provide the services to their subscribers, the technologies are not ready at this moment. For example, ingress filtering may not be feasible in several situations.[62,63]

2) Policy makers should provide capital incentives for highly influential ISPs to deploy the defenses once new DDOS defenses are available. Capital incentives are necessary to initiate the service provision for DDOS defenses, although ISPs have an economic incentive to continue to operate the services. The initiation of the services becomes important for an overall service deployment. It is in the ISPs' interest to cooperate on the provision of the services once a critical mass is created for deploying the defenses.

3) Policy makers should consider laws that assign liability to the attack sources because liability assignment creates an incentive for subscribers to reduce the attacks originating from their networks. In this case, subscribers who subscribe to source filtering should be exempted from liability, since they have conducted the best practice. Several technical issues about conducting the best practice to prevent DDOS have been documented in IETF RFC2013[64] and in the works of Greene and Morrow.[65] To whom the liability of Internet-based attacks should be assigned is an ongoing debate in both academia and public policy making. In the future, if the liability is assigned to the software companies for buggy programs and if the liability assignment manages to improve the quality of software, the benefit of deploying DDOS defenses would be reduced because the risk of Internet-based attacks would be lower. However, assigning liability to software companies may not necessarily improve the quality of software. Before the debate is resolved, we propose to assign the liability to the sources of attacks since the liability assignment is an incentive for cooperation in providing DDOS defenses.

Future Trends

In the future, changes in both technology and legislation would inevitably alter the assumptions upon which the conclusions are drawn in this paper. For example, adaptive attackers would result in more dynamic scenarios of attacks. Our model does not consider the situation where attackers change attack sources dynamically during an attack in order to avoid filtering. The proposed model would have to be revised to capture the dynamic strategy of defending attacks that avoid filtering or prevent routers from detecting and filtering attacks.

Several future research areas can be conducted based on our study. First, attacks to network routers or attacks that cause the instability of global routing[66] are another threat to network providers. In this case, the providers are attack victims themselves. The deployment of defenses will bring more obvious performance benefits to network providers in addition to the economic benefits mentioned in this paper. Secondly, liability assignment on the attack sources should be considered as a future research issue for cyber laws. Thirdly, calibrating the probability of attacks using security incident records is important for pricing security services. Finally, the assessment of the utility function of subscribers is important for determining the price of DDOS defenses.

Conclusions

We described our study on the technological and economic factors in the provision of defenses against distributed denial-of-service attacks. Recommendations are provided for subscribers, Internet service providers, and public policy makers.

There are a large number of possible benefits of the tool that we developed. First, the proposed service provision framework for DDOS defenses will help ISPs and subscribers to consider the benefits of providing DDOS defenses and to recognize the tradeoffs in DDOS defenses. Secondly, the simulation model provides a systematic framework for thinking through the tradeoffs in defense strategies in the complex attack-defense system. Thus, this work has direct bearing on security policy decisions at the router level for a critical infrastructure. Thirdly, our research framework provides a new method to evaluate the costs imposed by various attack scenarios and defenses since it is neither cost effective nor ethical to conduct real world experiments of DDOS attacks on a large network. Finally, this approach provides a theoretical basis for evaluating the provision of security service, DDOS defenses in this case.

Our study has several limitations. First, the quantitative analysis in our study provides an order of magnitude benefit and cost comparison among defenses. However, the real dollar value of the cost will depend on the implementation of these defenses. Secondly, our cost model is based on the router overhead and the bandwidth consumption costs by either attack traffic or defenses. Other implementation costs are not examined since we focus on examining the operational benefit and the operational cost caused by defenses. Finally, our simulation model is intended to provide decision support for tradeoffs in DDOS defenses only. This model would need further revision to analyze defenses for other types of Internet-based attacks.

Acknowledgments

This work was supported in part by the NSF/ITR 0218466 and the Pennsylvania Infrastructure Technology Alliance, a partnership of Carnegie Mellon, Lehigh University, and the Commonwealth of Pennsylvania's Department of Economic and Community Development. Additional support was provided by ICES (the Institute for Complex Engineered Systems) and CASOS—the Center for Computational Analysis of Social and

Organizational Systems at Carnegie Mellon University (*http://www.casos.cs.cmu.edu*). The views and conclusions contained in this document are those of the authors and should not be interpreted as representing the official policies, either expressed or implied, of the National Science Foundation, the Commonwealth of Pennsylvania, or the U.S. government.

References

[1]Ernst, & Young. (2004). *Global information security survey.*

[2]The White House. (2003). *The national strategy to secure cyberspace.*

[3]Tran, K. T. L. (2000, February 8). Yahoo! Portal is shutdown by web attack. *Wall Street Journal*, 6.

[4]The Yankee Group. (2000). *$1.2 billion impact seen as a result of recent attacks launched by Internet hackers.*

[5]Gordon, L. A., Loeb, M. P., Lucyshyn, W., & Richardson, R. (2004). *CSI/FBI computer crime and security survey.* Computer Security Institute.

[6]Symantec. (2004). *Symantec Internet security threat report.*

[7]The White House. (2003). *The national strategy to secure cyberspace.*

[8]McCurdy, D. (2004). *The DHS infrastructure protection division: Public-private partnerships to secure critical infrastructures.* IS Alliance.

[9]Howard, J. D. (1997). *An analysis of security incidents on the Internet.* Doctorate dissertation, Carnegie Mellon University.

[10]CERT Coordination Center. (1999). *Distributed denial of service tools.* Pittsburgh, PA:Software Engineering Institute, Carnegie Mellon University.

[11]Dietrich, S., Long, N., & Dittrich, D. (2000, December 3–8). *Analyzing distributed denial of service tools: The shaft case.* New Orleans, LA: Paper presented at the USENIX Systems Administration Conference.

[12]Dittrich, D. Distributed denial of service tools. Available from *http://staff.washington.edu/dittrich/misc/ddos/*

[13]Houle, K. J., & Weaver, G. M. (2001). *Trends in denial of service attack technology.* Pittsburgh, PA:CERT Coordination Center, Software Engineering Institute, Carnegie Mellon University.

[14]Chen, L. C., Longstaff T. A., & Carley, K. M. (2003). Characterization of DDOS defense mechanisms. *Computers & Security.*

[15]Spatscheck, O., & Peterson, L. L. (1998, Winter). Defending against denial of service in scout. *Operating Systems Review.*

[16]Yan, J., Early, S., & Anderson, R. (2000). *The xenoservice—a distributed defeat for distributed denial of service.* Paper presented at the Information Survivability Workshop.

[17]Ferguson, P., & Senie, D. (1998). *Network ingress filtering: Defeating denial of service attacks which employ IP source address spoofing.* IETF RFC2267.

[18]Bellovin, S. M. (2000). *ICMP traceback message.* Internet draft: draft-bellovin-itrace-00.txt.

[19]Burch, H., & Cheswick, B. (2000, December). *Tracing anonymous packets to their approximate source.* New Orleans, LA: Paper presented at the LINUX System Administration Conference.

[20]Savage, S., Wetherall, D., Karlin, A., & Anderson, T. (2001). Practical network support for IP traceback. *ACM/IEEE Transactions on Networking 9* (3), 226–237.

[21]Stone, R. (2000, July). *Centertrack: An IP overlay network for tracking DOS.* Denver, CO: Paper presented at the USENIX Security Symposium.

[22]Mahajan, R., Bellovin, S. M., Floyd, S., Ioannidis, J., Paxson, V., & Shenker, S. (2001). Controlling high bandwidth aggregate in the network. *Computer Communications Review.*

[23]Park, K., & Heejo L. (2001, December 3). *On the effectiveness of route-based packet filtering for distributed DOS attack prevention in power-law Internet.* San Diego, CA: Paper presented at the ACM SIGCOMM'01.

[24]Ioannidis, J., & Bellovin, S. M. (2002, February 6–8). *Implementing pushback: Router defense against DDOS attacks.* Paper presented at the Network and Distributed System Security Symposium.

[25]Bellovin, S. M. (2000). *ICMP traceback message.* Internet Draft: draft-bellovin-itrace-00.txt.

[26]Burch, H., & Cheswick, B. (2000, December). *Tracing anonymous packets to their approximate source.* New Orleans, LA: Paper presented at the LINUX System Administration Conference.

[27]Savage, S., Wetherall, D., Karlin, A., & Anderson, T. (2001). Practical network support for IP traceback. *ACM/IEEE Transactions on Networking 9* (3), 226–237.

[28]Park, K., & Lee, H. (2001). *On the effectiveness of probabilistic packet marking for IP traceback under denial of service attack.* Paper presented at the Proceedings of IEEE INFOCOM.

[29]Snoeren, A. C., Partridge, C., Sanchez, L. A., Jones, C. E., Tchakountio, F., Kent, S. T., & Strayer, W. T. (2001). *Hash-based IP traceback.* Paper presented at the ACM SIGCOMM.

[30]Song, D. X., & Perrig, A. (2001). *Advanced and authenticated marking schemes for IP traceback.* Paper presented at the IEEE Inforcom.

[31]Ferguson, P., & Senie, D. (1998). *Network ingress filtering: Defeating denial of service attacks which employ IP source address spoofing.* IETF RFC2267.

[32]Mahajan, R., Bellovin, S. M., Floyd, S., Ioannidis, J., Paxson, V., & Shenker, S. (2001). Controlling high bandwidth aggregate in the network. *Computer Communications Review.*

[33]Park, K., & Lee, H. (2001, December 3). *On the effectiveness of route-based packet filtering for distributed DOS attack prevention in power—Law Internet.* San Diego, CA: Paper presented at the ACM SIGCOMM'01.

[34]Ioannidis, J., & Bellovin, S. M. (2002, February 6–8). *Implementing pushback: Router defense against DDOS attacks.* Paper presented at the Network and Distributed System Security Symposium.

[35]Sung, M., & Xu, J. (2002, November). *IP traceback-based intelligent packet filtering: A novel technique for detecting against Internet DDOS attacks.* Paper presented at the IEEE International Conference on Network Protocols.

[36]Yaar, A., Perrig, A., & Song, D. (2003). *Pi: A path identification mechanism to defend against DDOS attack.* Paper presented at the IEEE conference on security and privacy.

[37]18 U. S. C. §2510; 18 U. S. C. §2511.

[38]Huang, Y., & Pullen, J. M. (2001). *Countering denial-of-service attacks using congestion triggered packet sampling and filtering.* Paper presented at the 10th International Conference on Computer Communications and Networks.

[39]SANS Institute. (2000). *Egress filtering, V 0.2.*

[40]Ferguson, P., & Senie, D. (1998). *Network ingress filtering: Defeating denial of service attacks which employ IP source address spoofing.* IETF RFC2267.

[41]Huang, Y., & Pullen, J. M. (2001). *Countering denial-of-service attacks using congestion triggered packet sampling and filtering.* Paper presented at the 10th International Conference on Computer Communications and Networks.

[42]Mahajan, R., Bellovin, S. M., Floyd, S., Ioannidis, J., Paxson, V., & Shenker S. (2001). Controlling high bandwidth aggregate in the network. *Computer Communications Review.*

[43]Xiong, Y., Liu, S., & Sun, P. (2001). On the defense of the distributed denial of service attacks: An on-off feedback control approach. *IEEE Transaction on Systems, Man, and Cybernetics—Part A: Systems and Humans 31* (4), 282–293.

[44]Ioannidis, J., & Bellovin, S. M. (2002, February 6–8). *Implementing pushback: Router defense against DDOS attacks.* Paper presented at the Network and Distributed System Security Symposium.

[45]False positive here means the rate of mistakenly regarding normal packets as attack packets.

[46]Debar, H., Dacier, M., & Wespi, A. (1999). Toward a taxonomy of intrusion detection systems. *Computer Networks 31* (8).

[47]Mahajan, R., Bellovin, S. M., Floyd, S., Ioannidis, J., Paxson, V., & Shenker, S. (2001). Controlling high bandwidth aggregate in the network. *Computer Communications Review.*

[48]Ioannidis, J., & Bellovin, S.M. (2002, February 6–8). *Implementing pushback: Router defense against DDOS Attacks.* Paper presented at the Network and Distributed System Security Symposium.

[49]Schuba, C. L., Krsul, I. V., Kuhn, M. G., Spafford, E. H., Sundaram, A., & Zamboni, D. (1997). *Analysis of a denial of service attack on TCP.* Paper presented at the IEEE Symposium on Security and Privacy.

[50]Park, K., & Lee, H. (2001, December 3). *On the effectiveness of route-based packet filtering for distributed DOS attack prevention in power—Law Internet.* San Diego, CA: Paper presented at the ACM SIGCOMM'01.

[51]Schuba, C. L., Krsul, I. V., Kuhn, M. G., Spafford, E. H., Sundaram, A. & Zamboni. D. (1997). *Analysis of a denial of service attack on TCP.* Paper presented at the IEEE Symposium on Security and Privacy.

[52]Mahajan, R., Bellovin, S. M., Floyd, S., Ioannidis, J., Paxson, V., & Shenker, S. (2001). Controlling high bandwidth aggregate in the network. *Computer Communications Review.*

[53]Ioannidis, J., & Bellovin, S.M. (2002, February 6–8). *Implementing pushback: Router defense against DDOS attacks.* Paper presented at the Network and Distributed System Security Symposium.

[54]Schnackenberg, D., & Djahandari, K. (2000, January 25–27). *Infrastructure for intrusion detection and response.* Paper presented at the DARPA Information Survivability Conference and Exposition (DISCEX).

[55]Park, K., & Lee, H. (2001, December 3). *On the effectiveness of route-based packet filtering for distributed DOS attack prevention in power—Law Internet.* San Diego, CA: Paper presented at the ACM SIGCOMM'01.

[56]Ioannidis, J., & Bellovin, S. M. (2002, February 6–8). *Implementing pushback: Router defense against DDOS attacks.* Paper presented at the Network and Distributed System Security Symposium.

[57]Stone, R. (2000, July). *Centertrack: An IP overlay network for tracking DOC.* Denver, CO: Paper presented at the USENIX Security Symposium.

[58]Moore, D., Voelker, G. M., & Savage, S. (2001, August). Inferring Internet denial-of-service activity. Washington, DC: Paper presented at the USENIX Security Symposium.

[59]Moore, D. (2001). *The spread of the code-red worm (Crv2).* Available from www.caida.org/analysis/security/code-red/

[60]Directory of Internet service providers. (2001, Spring). *The Board Watch Magazine.*

[61]Chen, L. C. (2003). *Computational models for defenses against Internet-based attacks.* Carnegie Mellon University.

[62]Ferguson, P., & Senie, D. (1998). *Network ingress filtering: Defeating denial of service attacks which employ IP source address spoofing.* IETF RFC2267.

[63]CISCO. (2003). *The IP source tracker.* CISCO Systems.

[64]Killalea, T. (2000). *Recommended Internet service provider security services and procedures.* IETF RFC2013.

[65]Greene, R. B., Morrow, C. L., & Gemberling, B. W. (2002). *ISP security—real world techniques.* The North American Network Operators' Group.

[66]Cowie, J., Ogielski, A., Premore, B. J., & Yuan, Y. (2001). *Global routing instabilities triggered by code red II and nimda worm attacks.* Renesys Corporation.

Trust, Controls, and Information Security

IRENE WOON AND ATREYI KANKANHALLI
National University of Singapore

Dr. Irene Woon holds the appointment of Senior Lecturer in the School of Computing at the National University of Singapore (NUS). She obtained her Bachelor of Business Administration from the University of Singapore and her MSc and PhD from Aston University in the UK. Prior to joining NUS, she was employed in the information technology industry. She has worked in a wide variety of roles ranging from software development to project management and project consultancy. She has provided information technology consultancy services to agencies such as the Ministry of Education, the Public Utilities Board (now known as Singapore Power), and the Commission of European Communities.

Dr. Atreyi Kankanhalli is Assistant Professor in the Department of Information Systems at the National University of Singapore (NUS). She obtained her B. Tech. from the Indian Institute of Technology Delhi, her MS from the Rensselaer Polytechnic Institute, New York, and her PhD from NUS. Prior to joining NUS, she had considerable experience in industrial R&D. She has consulted for a number of organizations including the World Bank. Her work has been published in journals such as the Journal of the American Society for Information Science and Technology, Communications of the ACM, *and* Decision Support Systems. *She serves on several information systems conference committees and the editorial board of the* International Journal of Knowledge Management. *Her research focuses on investigating the individual, organizational, and societal impacts of information and knowledge sharing systems.*

Overview

While it is possible for an organization to secure its systems, what happens when that organization is required—by merger, hostile takeover, or collaborative agreement—to connect those systems to those of another organization? Inherent in the connection of the computer and personal systems between these two entities is a requirement for trust. While trust may be necessary, it should not be blind to the risks of one system compromising the information of the other. In this article the authors examine the role of managerial trust and controls in the context of information security. They focus on the complex interplay between trust, controls, and information security effectiveness in organizations, and establish a model for trust—and provide a justification for that model—by surveying IT professionals. They further examine the role of trust and controls based on social theory.

Introduction

The threat of computer security breaches is of great concern to organizations. Sources of security breaches may be external (e.g., hackers) or internal (e.g., employees) to the organization. While recent surveys show that security breaches from external sources are rising, insider threats remain an important source of vulnerabilities. The Computer Security Institute/FBI computer crime and security survey in 2004 found that 59% of respondent organizations detected insider abuse of network access.[1] According to a survey by PriceWaterhouseCoopers, over one-third of UK businesses said that the source of their worst security incidents was internal.[2]

In response to internal threats, organizations increase the level of security controls in their attempt to ensure information security effectiveness. In general, it is believed that information security controls have a positive effect on information security effectiveness by acting as deterrents or preventives to committing computer crimes.[3] Individuals with the intent to commit crimes can be dissuaded by the administration of deterrents relevant to these acts.[4] Individuals calculate the risk involved in a criminal activity and, if they perceive that they are likely to be punished for their misbehavior, this has a significant deterrent effect on them. The level of deterrence is greater when offenders are aware of the certainty and severity of punishment, which may create fear and result in compliance with rules. Preventive measures such as access controls can also reduce security crimes by obstructing potential computer abusers. By making potential abusers expend more resources towards breaching security, they can reduce the likelihood of computer crimes.

However, while management exercises controls on employees to reduce internal threats to security, managers also need to trust and depend on employees to accomplish work goals. Trust provides the conditions that facilitate cooperation and working together.[5] However, trust also implies accepting risk and vulnerability based upon the positive expectations of employees' intentions or behavior. When managers trust employees, this trust carries the risk of betrayal.[6] In the context of information security, such betrayal may be in the form of security breaches. Hence trust and controls are likely to be intertwined in the relationship between managers and employees and in their effect on information security effectiveness.

From the employee point of view, higher levels of trust can lead to higher levels of job satisfaction and organizational commitment and consequently to lower levels of organizational crime, i.e., trust may have a positive effect on security. In order to tease out the apparently contradictory effects of trust on information security effectiveness, a study was designed to examine the relationships between managers' trust in employees, controls exercised on employees, and information security effectiveness. Although trust has been studied in a variety of contexts, it has not been investigated in the context of security controls and information security effectiveness. This article provides a review of related literature, then a description and test of a model to explain the role of trust and controls in information security, followed by future trends and implications.

Background

This section provides a review of the literature related to the concepts of control, trust, and information security effectiveness. The literature on information security controls is viewed in the context of general organizational controls. Trust is described in terms of beliefs in the trustee, antecedents to trust, and manager-employee trust. The inter-relationships of trust, controls, and information security effectiveness are discussed.

CONTROLS

Organizational controls are regulatory processes by which organizational elements are made more predictable in the pursuit of a desired organizational objective or state.[7,8] Control may be achieved through formal processes or informally through social processes.

Formal organizational controls such as policies, rewards, and work structures aim to invoke conformance to organizational requirements that are thought necessary to accomplish organizational goals. In the context of information security, formal controls refer to the definition and enforcement of organizational procedures and mechanisms designed to determine and influence employees' appropriate use of information assets. NIST categorizes controls into management controls, operational controls, and technical controls.[9] Management controls are techniques addressing the management of the organization's security program, e.g., security policy and risk management models. Operational controls are security controls that are implemented and executed by people to control operations, e.g., security awareness and technical training, security reviews, and physical access controls. Technical controls refer to controls that are implemented and executed by systems, e.g., anti-virus software and intrusion detection systems.

Informal control processes reside in the social relationships among people in the workplace, e.g., organizational norms,[10] feeling of belonging. Such controls can increase compliance to organizational policies and reduce opportunistic behavior of employees.

Research in information security has traditionally focused on formal controls. Empirical studies (e.g., those by Straub in 1990)[11] based on general deterrence theory[12] have studied the effect of formal preventive and deterrent security measures on computer abuse. However formal controls do not appear to do enough, as the frequency and sophistication of computer abuse continues to increase. As a result, researchers and practitioners are beginning to look at the role of informal controls in security. For example, Lee and Lee[13] stress the need for paying more attention to the relationships among organizational members in the context of security.

Two theories in support of a social perspective towards security are social bond theory[14] and social learning theory.[15] Social bond theory proposes that the probability that employees will engage in a crime is lower when their social bonds (i.e., attachment, commitment, involvement, and belief in the organization) are strong. Empirical studies have shown that social bonds have been critical in reducing delinquency.[16] Social learning theory looks at the "bonding" of the individual to a specific group rather than the organization as a whole. The theory states that people are more likely to engage in criminal or deviant behavior when they associate with others who commit criminal behavior. Conversely, appropriate (compliant) behavior can be encouraged by positive associations. Previous empirical studies have found a positive relationship between delinquency and interaction with undesirable peers.[17] Therefore, informal (social) security controls may involve ensuring better bonding of employees to the organization and association with desirable peers in order to reduce probability of crime. According to this perspective, trust can be related to social security controls since it can foster bonding between management and employees.

TRUST

A commonly accepted definition of interpersonal trust is the willingness of one party to be vulnerable to another party. Trust implies that one party is willing to depend on the other party for certain resources or action, even though negative consequences are possible.[18] Empirical studies have shown that interpersonal trust consists of several beliefs.[19,20]

Beliefs in Trustee

Researchers have suggested that there are three main trusting beliefs, i.e., benevolence, integrity, and competence.[21,22] Additionally, reliability has been considered as a trusting belief.[23] Hence, a trustor will trust a trustee if the trustor believes in the benevolence, integrity, competence, and reliability of the trustee.

Benevolence is the demonstration of consideration and sensitivity for another's needs and interests. It implies acting in a way that protects another's interests and refraining from exploiting others for the benefit of one's own interests.[24-26] Integrity refers to honesty, uprightness, and promise-keeping attributes of an individual. Individuals who are observed to demonstrate higher levels of integrity are likely to be trusted more.

Competence is defined to be the individual's skill and ability in dealing with their job. According to Becerra and Gupta, a person's competence has a positive effect on the trustor.[27] Reliability is the consistency in behavior over time and across situations. If individuals behave reliably, others will be better able to predict their future behavior. Predictable behavior can in turn increase the level of trust in the relationship.

Antecedents of Trust

Antecedents of trust include certain attributes of the trustor such as the trustor's disposition to trust and the previous experience with the trustee. Disposition to trust is the extent to which a person displays a tendency to be willing to depend on others across a broad spectrum of situations and persons.[28] This is a general personality trait that conveys how trusting one is, and is assumed to be stable over the relationship. A manager's disposition to trust affects the level of trust in the employee.[29]

However, interpersonal trust strengthens or weakens as a function of the cumulative interaction between the two parties. Trustors update their thoughts and feelings about the trustee's trustworthiness as a result of their experiences with the trustee, whether positive or negative.[30] Positive displays of employees' benevolence, integrity, competence, and reliability are likely to strengthen trust while negative experiences will have the opposite effect.

Manager-Employee Trust

Previous literature has investigated trust in the workplace from the employees' perspective, i.e., how employees view their managers and the organization. Researchers such as Whitener and Korsgaard have identified organizational factors (e.g., human resource policies) and individual factors (e.g., disposition to trust) that influence employees' perceptions of trust.[31] Previous studies, for example by McAllister, have also investigated trust from the manager's viewpoint, i.e., how managers view their peers and subordinates.[32] Interpersonal trust has been demonstrated to have a significant impact on a number of organizational variables such as cooperation, as shown by Blau,[33] and performance, as shown by Earley.[34] The negative repercussions of trust have been less studied.

TRUST AND CONTROL

There is a natural tension between trust and control, which translates to the context of information security. On one hand, managers or employers may be motivated to minimize an employee's opportunistic behavior by exercising tight control and close monitoring of the employee's activities. This perspective is espoused by agency theory by Eisenhardt, which contends that employees are motivated by their own interests rather than the interests of the firm and therefore need to be monitored and controlled to obtain desired behavior.[35] On the other hand, managers may be motivated to informally control employees by promoting trust and identification in the workplace. This viewpoint gets support from social exchange theory articulated by Cook and Emerson, wherein managers engaged in reciprocal exchanges with employees on a voluntary, informal basis can develop social relationships that result in positive job outcomes.[36] Both these perspectives point to the moderating role of trust on the relationship between controls and desired behavior.

SECURITY EFFECTIVENESS

From the industry perspective, a commonly accepted security standard is the ISO17799 (*http://www.iso17799world.com/*), which evolved from the BS7799 standard. This standard is regarded as a comprehensive catalog of practices that organizations can follow to secure their assets. Security effectiveness can be achieved by compliance to these standards. From the academic perspective, studies have conceptually and empirically investigated the organizational and individual level factors that contribute to the security effectiveness of organizations. Dhillon and Torkzadeh empirically derive a broad set of factors (e.g., human resource practices, ethical environment, and management development practices) that are instrumental in shaping a favorable security outcome for the organization.[37] Kankanhalli defines security effectiveness as the ability of information security measures to protect the organization against unauthorized or deliberate misuse of information assets by people.[38] More specifically, they investigate the protection of hardware, software, data, and computer services assets of the organization.

Model and Data Analysis

Previous literature is integrated into a model shown in Figure 10-1. This explains the role of trust in the relationship between controls and security effectiveness. In line with the previous discussions, we expect trust to moderate the relationship between controls and security effectiveness, i.e., a higher level of trust should strengthen the relationship between controls and security effectiveness. The model also examines the antecedents of a manager's trust in employees. Such trust is likely to depend on the manager's disposition to trust and previous experience with employees.

The behavioral model was operationalized and empirically tested using a field survey.[39] Measures for controls included degree of management, operational, and technical controls in the organization. Trust was measured in terms of a manager's beliefs in the benevolence, integrity, competence, and reliability of employees. Disposition to trust was assessed as a manager's belief that people in general are benevolent, honest, competent, and reliable. Past experience is measured based on a manager's previous experience of employees misusing IT assets. Security effectiveness was assessed in terms of protection of hardware, software, data, and services in the organization. The survey data was collected from 199 information systems managers from a number of IT organizations, with the majority of respondents belonging to two large multi-national organizations.

Partial least squares analysis (Falk and Miller 1992) was used to assess the model.[40] The survey data analysis indicated that the model had good explanatory and predictive power for trust and security effectiveness. Further, all relationships between antecedents of trust, controls, and security effectiveness proposed in the model were supported (statistically significant at a 0.05 level). In other words, controls were positively related to security effectiveness moderated by trust. Trust in turn was determined by the manager's disposition to trust and previous experience with employees. The findings can be discussed in terms of the relationships between the constructs in the model.

Discussion

CONTROLS, TRUST, AND SECURITY EFFECTIVENESS

The study indicates that controls are positively related to information security effectiveness contingent on the manager's trust in employees, i.e., the higher the level of trust, the stronger the relationship between controls and security effectiveness. In other words, management, operational, and technical controls can influence employees' behavior. However, where employees have shown that they can be trusted, controls will be more effective than in low trust situations. For instance, even if a particular control fails or is ineffective, trusted employees may report its failure and not take advantage of it.

ANTECEDENTS OF TRUST

Based on the findings of the study, managers' disposition to trust has a positive effect on their trust in employees under their control. This result is consistent with previous studies, which show that a person's general level of trust affects the level of trust he or she has in a specific individual, whether or not there have been interactions with that individual. This state of trust will be tested and revised through interactions with the employees over time, as also shown by research in other contexts.[41,42] The experience with employees will influence managers' trust in them.

IMPLICATIONS FOR THEORY AND PRACTICE

Theoretically, the model underscores the role of trust as a moderator on the effect that controls have on security effectiveness. In doing so, the model redefines and tests the constructs of controls, trust, and its antecedents, in the security context. Trust is proposed to have four dimensions, with reliability added to the three most often used dimensions of benevolence, integrity,

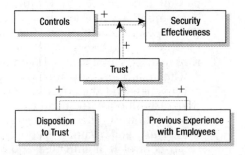

FIGURE 10-1 Model for trust, controls, and information security effectiveness

and competence. Overall, the model can provide a basis for investigating the role of trust in the context of information security.

The results have practical implications for managers in suggesting ways to increase information security effectiveness in organizations. To increase the level of security in organizations, management controls (such as security policy and risk management), operational controls (such as security awareness and training), and technical controls (such as intrusion detection systems) can be enhanced. However, as trust plays a role in moderating the relationship between controls and security effectiveness, it is also worthwhile to foster a high trust work environment to support the impact of controls. The findings suggest that trust can be enhanced by increasing managers' positive experiences with employees. Since managers' disposition to trust is difficult to change, emphasis should be placed on increasing positive interactions with employees. Other ways of increasing trust include hiring employees with appropriate competence, assessing their reliability and integrity prior to hiring, and aligning their interests with organizational goals after recruitment.

Future Trends

Several avenues for future investigation could be derived from the proposed model. First, additional factors such as trustee attributes and monitoring of controls can be introduced in the model. Trustee attributes can serve as additional antecedents to manager-employee trust, which are partly encapsulated in the manager's experience with the employee. The current model can also be extended to include the effect of employees' trust in managers on the relationship between controls and security effectiveness. When employees have greater trust in their managers, they tend to be more satisfied with their job.[43] This satisfaction may result in reduced dysfunctional behavior and, hence, less security breaches.

It would also be fruitful to study the impact controls have on trust as this would signal the level of controls an organization should impose. Other types of controls could also be studied using this model in different organizational settings. In the future, as the ongoing tussle between security breaching techniques and prevention techniques continues, informal controls may make a difference. This study provides insights to organizations about the psychological and sociological factors in the workplace that could complement formal controls.

Conclusion

The objective of this article was to examine the role of managerial trust and controls in the context of information security. It focused on the complex interplay between trust, controls, and information security effectiveness in organizations. A review of previous literature provided the background for the proposed model that integrated concepts from diverse perspectives. The model was tested through a field survey. Responses from 199 information systems managers from various IT companies were used to validate the model.

The results indicate that controls have a positive effect on security effectiveness and the effect is strengthened by managerial trust. In addition, disposition to trust and past experience are found to positively affect managerial trust. These findings serve to extend previous theory on controls, trust, and security effectiveness. The role of trust as an informal social control is highlighted and suggested as a complement to formal security controls, which have not proved completely effective in ensuring information security. As an extension of the socio-technical perspective of information security that has gained ground in recent years, this article outlines measures in the social realm to enhance security effectiveness.

References

[1]Computer Security Institute. (2004). CSI/FBI computer abuse and security survey. San Francisco, CA CSI. Retrieved October 7, 2004 at *http://www.securitymanagement.com/library/CSI_FBI_ComputerCrime0904.pdf.*

[2]PriceWaterhouseCoopers. (2004). DTI information security breaches survey. Retrieved October 7, 2004 at *http://www.infosec.co.uk/files/DTI_Survey_Report.pdf.*

[3]Straub, D. W. (1990). Effective IS security: An empirical study. *Information Systems Research 1* (3), 255–276.

[4]Blumstein, A. (1978). Introduction. In A. Blumstein, J. Cohen, & D. Nagin (Eds.). *Deterrence and incapacitation: Estimating the effects of criminal sanctions on crime rates.* Washington, DC: National Academy of Sciences.

[5]Dirks, K. T., & Ferrin, D. L. (2001). The role of trust in organizational settings. *Organization Science 12* (4), 450–467.

[6]Atuahene-Gima, K., & Li, H. (2002). When does trust matter? Antecedents and contingent effects of superviser trust on performance in selling new products in China and the United States. *Journal of Marketing 66* (3), 61–82.

[7]Leifer, R., & Mills, P. K. (1996). An information processing approach for deciding upon control strategies and reducing control loss in emerging organizations. *Journal of Management 22* (1), 113–137.

[8]Das, T. K., & Teng, B. S. (1998). Between trust and control: Developing confidence in partner cooperation in alliances. *Academy of Management Review 23* (3), 491–512.

[9]National Institute of Standards and Technology. (1995). *An introduction to computer security: A NIST handbook, special publication 800-12.* Retrieved October 7, 2004, at *http://http://csrc.nist.gov/publications/nistpubs/index.html.*

[10]Gilliland, D. I., & Manning, K. C. (2002). When do firms conform to regulatory control? The effect of control processes on compliance and opportunism. *Journal of Public Policy 21* (2), 319–331.

[11]Straub, D. W. (1990). Effective IS security: An empirical study. *Information Systems Research 1* (3), 255–276.

[12]Blumstein, A. (1978). Introduction. In A. Blumstein, J. Cohen, & D. Nagin, (Eds.). *Deterrence and incapacitation: Estimating the effects of criminal sanctions on crime rates.* Washington, DC: National Academy of Sciences.

[13]Lee J., & Lee, L. (2002). A holistic model of computer abuse within organizations *Information Management and Computer Security 10* (2), 57–63.

[14]Hirschi, T. (1969). *Causes of delinquency.* Berkeley, CA University of California Press.

[15]Akers R. L., Krohn, M. D., Lanza-Kaduce, L., & Radosevich, M. (1979). Social learning and deviant behavior: a specific test of a general theory. *American Sociological Review 44,* 636–655.

[16]Agnew, R. (1995). Testing the leading crime theories: an alternative strategy focusing on motivational process. *Journal of Research in Crime and Delinquency 32* (4), 363–398.

[17]Krohn M. D., Skinner, W. F., Massey, J. L., & Akers, R. L. (1985). Social learning theory and adolescent cigarette smoking: a longitudinal study. *Social Problems 32* (5), 455–471.

[18]Mayer R.C., Davis, J. H., & Schoorman, F. D. (1995). An integration model of organizational trust. *Academy of Management Review 20* (3), 709–734.

[19]Ibid.

[20]McKnight D. H., Choudhury, V., & Kacmar, C. (2002). Developing and validating trust measures for e-commerce: An integrative typology. *Information Systems Research 13* (3), 334–359.

[21]Mayer R. C., Davis, J. H., & Schoorman, F. D. (1995). An integration model of organizational trust. *Academy of Management Review 20* (3), 709–734.

[22]McKnight, D. H.,Choudhury, V., & Kacmar, C. (2002). Developing and validating trust measures for e-commerce: An integrative typology. *Information Systems Research 13* (3), 334–359.

[23]Whitener, E. M., Brodt, S. E., Korsgaard, M. A., & Werner, J. M. (1998). Managers as initiators of trust: An exchange relationship framework for understanding managerial trustworthy behavior. *Academy of Management Review 23* (3), 513–530.

[24]Whitener, E. M., Brodt, S. E., Korsgaard, M. A., & Werner, J. M. (1998). Managers as initiators of trust: An exchange relationship framework for understanding managerial trustworthy behavior. *Academy of Management Review 23* (3), 513–530.

[25]McKnight, D. H., Choudhury, V., & Kacmar, C. (2002). Developing and validating trust measures for e-commerce: An integrative typology. *Information Systems Research 13* (3), 334–359.

[26]Suh, B., & Han, I. (2003). The impact of customer trust and perception of security control. *Acceptance of Electronic Commerce 7* (3), 135–161.

[27]Becerra, M., & Gupta, A. K. (2003). Perceived trustworthiness within the organization: The moderating impact of communication frequency on trustor and trustee effects. *Organization Science 14* (1), 32–44.

[28]McKnight, D. H., Choudhury, V., & Kacmar, C. (2002). Developing and validating trust measures for e-commerce: An integrative typology. *Information Systems Research 13* (3), 334–359.

[29]Jarvenpaa, S. L., Knoll, K., & Leidner, D. E. (1998). Is anybody out there? Antecedents of trust in global virtual teams. *Journal of Management Information Systems 14* (4), 29–64.

[30]Williams, M. (2001). In whom we trust: Group membership as an affective context for trust development. *Academy of Management Review 26* (3), 377–396.

[31]Korsgaard, M. A., Brodt, S. E., & Whitener, E. M. (2002). Trust in the face of conflict: The role of managerial trustworthy behavior and organizational context. *Journal of Applied Psychology 87* (2), 312–319.

[32]McAllister, D. J. (1995). Affect and cognition-based trust as foundations for interpersonal cooperation in organizations. *Academy of Management Journal 38* (1), 24–59.

[33]Blau, P. M. (1964). *Exchange and power in social life New York:* Wiley.

[34]Earley, P. C. (1986). Trust, perceived importance of praise and criticism and work performance: An examination of feedback in the United States and England. *Journal of Management 12*, 457–473.

[35]Eisenhardt, K. M. (1989). Agency theory: An assessment and review. *Academy of Management Review 14*, 57–74.

[36]Cook, K. S., & Emerson, R. M. (1978). Power, equity and commitment in exchange networks. *American Sociological Review 43*, 721–739.

[37]Dhillon, G., & Torkzadeh, R. (2001). *Value-focused assessment of information system security in organizations.* New Orleans, LA: Proceedings of the International Conference on Information Systems.

[38]Kankanhalli, A., Teo, H. H., Tan, C. Y., & Wei, K. K. (2003). An integrative study of information systems security effectiveness. *International Journal of Information Management 23* (2), 139–167.

[39]Low, W. L. (2004). *Trust, control and security in organizations: An empirical analysis.* Unpublished honors thesis, National University of Singapore.

[40]Falk, R. F., & Miller, N. B. (1992). *A primer for soft modeling.* Akron, Ohio University of Akron Press.

[41]Mayer, R. C., Davis, J. H., & Schoorman, F. D. (1995). An integration model of organizational trust. *Academy of Management Review 20* (3), 709–734.

[42]Ring, P. S., & Van de Ven, A. H. (1994). Developmental processes of cooperative interorganizational relationships. *Academy of Management Review 19* (1), 90–118.

[43]Brockner, J., Siegel, P. A., Daly, J., Tyler, T., & Martin, C. (1997, September 3). When trust matters: The moderating effect of outcome favorability. *Administrative Science Quarterly 42*, 558–583.

Hierarchical Model of Organizational Work in the Sphere of Information Security

ALEXANDER ANISIMOV

Department of Physics and Technology, Ural State Technical University (Ekaterinburg, Russia)

Alexander Anisimov is an assistant professor at the Ural State Technical University (Ekaterinburg, Russia). His major research interests are in the sphere of managerial problems related to practical usage of contemporary information systems. Information security management is one of the major areas of his research and methodological work.

Overview

As a method to protect the organization's information, security must complement the organization's work methods. Failure to do so can result in a compromise in the information security posture. It is a well-known truism that when security and business conflict, security loses. The organization may become frustrated with inefficient or excessive security and bypass or remove security measures. In order to understand the best way to integrate information security into the organization's work processes, the information security professional must first understand the very nature of work itself. In this chapter, the author examines models of work, with an interpretation of the role of information security within those models.

Introduction

The major perspective of this chapter is to present the overview of the most important aspects of organizational work in the sphere of information security. It should support clear understanding of the fact that managerial work in information security may be performed at different organizational levels and may have different aims. At the same time, all the directions of this work are more or less closely connected and require consistent methodological and managerial support.

The purpose of this chapter is to develop and present the overall hierarchical model of organizational work in the sphere of information security that could reflect all the major levels and situations at which organizational issues are usually important. We also consider practical importance of this model and the perspectives of its further development and usage.

Background

It is well known that organizational work plays a crucial role in the ensuring of information security in different organizations and information systems. Appropriate organizational and managerial support provides consistency across different technologies and allows them to operate efficiently and safely. Among the most important tasks of managerial work in the sphere of computer information security are the following:

- Coordination of different activities (development of technical solutions, adjustment of business processes and procedures, etc.)
- Development and ongoing improvement of analytical and methodological background (that includes risk analysis, organizational structures, economic analysis, and other similar aspects[1])
- Development of regulatory rules and documents (such as laws, directives, instructions, and others)
- Decrease of the influences of the so called "human factor" (various approaches to the enforcement of security policies and regulatory rules introduced)

The major purpose of management in the sphere of information security is to guarantee that all the important elements of the corporate information infrastructure are protected during all work on information systems and in all possible situations.[2] In practice, this task is very complicated; there are no universal solutions to this problem, as each particular solution in each particular case significantly depends on different specific conditions such as, for example, the current situation in the business environment (and consequently the current value of information that is to be protected), the current level of development of information technologies, the availability of information protection tools, etc. This is why information security management almost always requires usage of complicated methodologies and approaches and the attraction of qualified and experienced specialists. Moreover, such complexity also explains why managerial and organizational problems cannot be handled only on the level of particular companies and institutions, but these problems also require support at higher organizational levels in more advanced organizational forms such as, for example, national governments, non-governmental organizations (NGOs), and companies whose business has global importance, as well as cooperation between business entities that do not have common business interests but have common problems, etc.

In this reading we present an overview of the organizational approaches that are used for handling the most complicated problems of information security assurance: coordination of the methodological work in this sphere, mutual support of different entities involved in the cyber infrastructure, and other activities that make information technologies and protection tools more efficient and safer. It should help to understand why the information security of particular institutions and entities depends not only on their own efforts and adequacy of information protection tools they use, but also on the efficiency of organizational work and managerial methods that are used at higher organizational levels.

The Major Levels of Organizational Work

In practice there are several relatively separate levels of organization in the range from the global scale to the scale of particular organizations and departments. Each of these levels concentrates on specific tasks, responsibilities, and problems; consequently, each of them is usually considered separately.

The major such organizational levels are:

- Organizations (usually non-profit and non-governmental ones) that influence the overall IT and business community (on a global scale)
- Global IT companies (usually commercial ones)—particularly large firms—that influence the overall situation in the sphere of information security (such as, for example, suppliers of widely used computer operating systems or communication tools)
- Particular states (governments) and international cooperation between governments
- The business community that consists of separate organizations and departments (the lowest level)

There is also an additional intermediary level that involves different, more or less independent, consultants, researchers, and advisers that provide technical and methodological support in the sphere of information security for organizations that need it.

The levels described are presented in Figure 11-1. Let us briefly describe each of these levels. The top level includes several well-known organizations (usually non-governmental) that employ specialists and researchers. These organizations serve to coordinate the methodological work of specialists from different countries and different institutions that are involved with forming and advancing the agendas of their respective fields. Such organizations also may be based upon research departments of large universities. The second level also has almost global importance. It includes the major multi-national companies' software products and information services that are used by a large number of customers in many places around the world. The third level, states, includes different

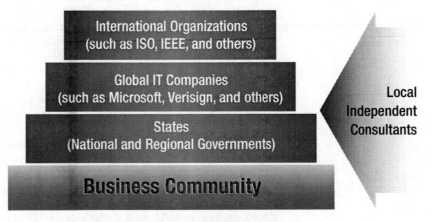

FIGURE 11-1 The major levels of organizational work

governmental agencies and departments as well as committees of legislative bodies concerned with different aspects of information security at both national and international levels (legislation, law enforcement, official certifications, control, and others).[3] Usually activities of such bodies have importance only for corresponding countries in which they are enacted. The lowest level is represented by information security departments and other forms of organizational work in particular companies and institutions.[4]

Separate consideration of these levels is objectively conditioned by the significant differences between them and absence of direct functional connections. Consequently, it is usually more convenient to analyze organizational behavior at particular levels apart from others. That is why there is no single universal organizational theory that could describe all the issues of management in the sphere of information security.

Nevertheless, in our opinion, analysis of all the major levels of organizational work as a single system has significant importance for information security management. It should provide a basis for more consistent management of technology—both at the level of particular companies and at the level of national and regional policies—by helping coordinate development of efficient software and hardware information-protection tools, regulate usage of cryptographical methods, etc.

But before we dive into the analysis of connections and dependencies between different levels, let us briefly analyze the methods and functions that are typical to each of these levels. The hierarchy introduced is the basis for such analysis of the overall range of specific approaches and techniques.

Methods of Managerial Work

Each of the levels described has its specific functions and roles in the overall information security infrastructure. For further analysis we assume that the information security infrastructure includes all the conditions for the safety of information assets: availability of consultants and specialists, availability of efficient software and hardware protection tools on the open market, existence of different efficient agreements between the major entities involved in the information interchange, efficient legal system (law enforcement, flexible legislation, justice, etc.), and others. In other words, information security infrastructure helps (more or less directly) to make protective measures in different companies and institutions more efficient. To understand better the methods, functions, and roles of different members of this community, it is reasonable to assume that the entities that operate on the highest levels usually work for support and improvement of this infrastructure (or its certain elements), e.g., development and promotion of common rules of information interchange and processing, support of technical and organizational standards, and support of education and certification systems, among others.

The level of the the business community, consisting of both commercial and non-commercial entities, possesses information assets requiring protective measures. As such it relies on this global infrastructure, not just on the managerial efforts of separate companies, while doing business. To rely upon this infrastructure and use its different elements is one of the most promising directions of practical work in this sphere.

Besides that, governmental organizations also may rely upon this infrastructure in their work up to a certain level. The structure of these functions and relations is presented in Figure 11-2.

This scheme conceptually explains why organizational work at different levels is characterized by the involvement of different methods and techniques. In particular, different levels of information security management and different organizations involved in the overall information protection infrastructure usually require different approaches to information security management. Besides that, organizational work at different levels is usually concentrated on different aspects of information security and on different elements of information security infrastructure. The major characteristics of managerial work at different organizational levels are analyzed in Table 11-1.

As we may see from this table, each level has its specific aims and supports information security accordingly. The differences in the primary aims and methods commonly used highlight the reasons these organizational levels are very different and do not have methodologies of coordination of their activities.

Dependencies Between Different Levels

Although all the levels of organizational work are separated from each other, in our opinion all the elements of the information security landscape have more or less strong connections, influence each other, and depend on each other (not only in the way that is presented in Figure 11-1 and described earlier). That is why it is important for IT specialists and managers to clearly understand all the hierarchy of all the major entities involved in the overall information security infrastructure, the organizational and

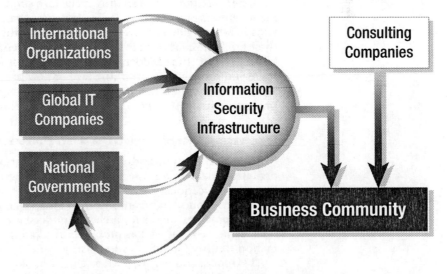

FIGURE 11-2 Interrelations between different organizational levels

TABLE 11-1   **Methods of Organizational Work**

Level	Aims and roles	Specific methods
International organizations	Development of rules (such as, for example, information exchange protocols) and agreements that have importance for the overall IT community	Coordination of work of different specialists, experts, researchers, and companies whose involvement may be valuable
Global IT companies	Methodological and organizational support of the products and services that are provided	Constant improvement of products and services Flexible communications with users (user support, analysis of feedback)
Governmental organizations	Regulation of activities of different entities involved in information interchange so that they could not damage interests of other entities, as well as protection of interests of governmental institutions and integrity of the information infrastructure	Development of national and international regulations and rules Implement tools for control other than information infrastructure Law enforcement
Business community	Protection of own information assets	Development (adoption) of internal regulatory rules Distribution of tasks and responsibilities between managers and specialists

managerial. One of the major and most important connection in the overall hierarchy of organizational work is the support of the overall information security infrastructure (international, national, regional, etc.) by global organizations and governmental institutions that in turn helps the business community to manage information security at the level of particular companies. Certain other connections and dependencies between different levels that, in our opinion, have particular significance and should be analyzed and controlled are presented in Table 11-2.

As we may see from this table, different levels of organizational work in the sphere of information security make up a single system in which each element depends on the others. It clearly demonstrates that there are numerous ways in which different levels influence each other, although at first glance these levels are connected in the way that is presented earlier in Figure 11-1.

Analysis of these hidden connections and interdependencies becomes more and more important in the face of new threats, challenges, and risks, and management of such connections may open new opportunities for the improvement of efficiency of information security protection.

Practical Implications and Future Trends

Such classification and systematic presentation of different aspects of organizational work in the sphere of information security has importance from the educational point of view (it may be used as a framework for an educational course in organization and management of information security) and provides a basis for a clearer understanding of organizational and managerial tasks, as well as problems and methods in the sphere of information security for both IT specialists and field managers.

This model also may be used as a methodological basis for further development of different relatively clear and efficient techniques and methods

TABLE 11-2   **Connections and Dependencies Between Different Organizational Levels**

Level	Organizational tasks and functions	Influence on other levels
International organizations	Development of common rules, methodologies, and agreements Support of professional conferences for IS specialists, magazines, databases, and other forms of exchange of professional information	Open opportunities for the development of unified IT products (software, hardware, and services) Enforce and support the introduction of advanced methods and techniques of information protection Allow efficient communication between specialists in different companies, suppliers of different solutions, and consultants
Global IT companies	Support and promotion of products and services provided	Increase efficiency of the usage of technologies and services provided Decrease expenses for information security (at the level of the business community)
	Development of new solutions, technologies, and methodologies in the sphere of information technology	Open new opportunities for the development of commonly accepted standards and rules that could improve the security of global information exchange (influences all the levels including independent information security consultants)
Governmental organizations	Prevention of unlawful and destructive practices Regulation of business directly connected with information security	Guarantee a certain level of safety of the information infrastructure (for the level of the business community) Determine conditions for work of suppliers of IT solutions (for the level of global IT companies)
	Development and introduction of internal information-protection systems, regulations, and methodologies in governmental organizations (as a part of the overall homeland security policy)	Set up standards for IT and the business community (levels of protection with which different business practices may be and usually are compared) Growth of the information protection tools and services market Recognize the importance of information security by society and the business community
Business community	Development of improved internal practices and culture in the sphere of information security	Motivate improvement of global information infrastructure, new information security products, and governmental regulations Inform the IT community about new threats and solutions developed
	Demonstration of advances in the sphere of information security (as a part of the overall public relations policy and promotion of services and products)	Participate in the work of international organizations and in the life of the IT community (experience sharing, publications in professional magazines, participation in professional conferences and seminars, etc.)

of coordination and stimulation of managerial work at different organizational levels (such as, for example, coordination of national policies with interests of the business community). Moreover, it may be used as a starting point for the development of criteria for the assessment of efficiency of different organizational levels (and different structures within these levels) in the overall information security infrastructure. For example, such assessment may be important for such activities as:

- Governmental support of non-governmental organizations that make the most important contribution to the improvement and support of security of information infrastructure
- Support of business entities that make the most significant contribution to the work of global organizations

It is also necessary to note that the model presented in this chapter is a framework model. It may be extended: additional sublevels may be introduced in the model, additional dependencies between different levels may be found and highlighted, and so on.

Conclusion

We have analyzed the overall system of organizational work in the sphere of information security. This analysis explains that responsibility for information security cannot be taken only by separate companies—owners of the information assets and information infrastructure. It also should be taken by the overall IT community, in which a certain hierarchy exists and all the levels of this hierarchy depend on each other. And only an efficient interaction between these levels may ensure a significant level of protection against threats within the contemporary world.

It is obvious that the model introduced is important for education and in particular for complex understanding of information security management at different organizational levels. But it also may have practical importance: clear understanding of such dependencies should be a base for the development of more advanced techniques of information security management. Nevertheless, the practical usage of the model described will completely depend on the commitment of corresponding managers and stakeholders and their personal attitude.

References

[1]Domrev, V. V. (2002). *Security of information technologies*, Moscow: Diasoft.

[2]Schnier, B. (2000). *Secrets and lies: Digital security in a networked world.* Wiley Computer Publishing.

[3]Grinberg, A. S., Gorbachev, N. N., & Teplyakov, A. A. (2003). *Protection of governmental information assets.* Moscow: Unity

[4]Koneev, I. R., & Belyaev, A. V. (2003). *Information security of enterprises*, St. Petersburg, FL: BHV-Petersburg.

Transparency in Information Security System Design

MICHAEL E. WHITMAN AND HERBERT J. MATTORD

Kennesaw State University

Herbert Mattord, MBA, CISSP is an Instructor of Information Systems in the Computer Science and Information Systems Department at Kennesaw State University, Kennesaw, Georgia. Professor Mattord completed 24 years of IT industry experience prior to moving to academia. During his career as an IT practitioner, he served as adjunct professor at numerous institutions. Professor Mattord is also the Operations Manager of the KSU Center for Information Security Education and Awareness (infosec.kennesaw.edu), as well as the coordinator for the KSU Certificate in Information Security and Assurance. He currently teaches undergraduate courses in Information Security, Data Communications, Database, Project Management, Systems Analysis and Design, and Information Resources Management and Policy. He was formerly the Manager of Corporate Information Technology Security at Georgia-Pacific Corporation, where much of the practical knowledge found in this textbook was acquired. Professor Mattord is also the co-author of Management of Information Security, Readings and Cases in the Management of Information Security, *and* The Hands-On Information Security Lab Manual, *all published by Course Technology.*

Michael Whitman, PhD, CISSP, is a Professor of Information Systems in the Computer Science and Information Systems Department at Kennesaw State University, Kennesaw, Georgia, where he is also the Director of the Master of Science in Information Systems and the Director of the KSU Center for Information Security Education (infosec.kennesaw.edu). Dr. Whitman is an active researcher in Information Security Curriculum Development and Policy and Ethics. He currently teaches graduate and undergraduate courses in Information Security, Local Area Networking, and Data Communications. Dr. Whitman is also the co-author of Management of Information Security, Readings and Cases in the Management of Information Security, *and* The Hands-On Information Security Lab Manual, *all published by Course Technology. Prior to his career in academia, Dr. Whitman was an armored cavalry officer in the United States Army.*

Overview

In this short essay, the tradeoffs in the objectives for information system design techniques are discussed and a proposal for an innovation in the design of information systems to assure improved security and privacy is proposed.

Introduction

Sed Quis Custodiet Ipsos Custodes?
(But who will guard the guards themselves?)

—FROM *SATIRES* (C. 120 AD) BY THE ROMAN AUTHOR JUVENAL
(DECIMUS JUNIUS JUVENALIS, C. 60–140 AD)

Information system capabilities continue to expand. In two particular areas, that of the surveillance records and personal data, a public policy debate is underway. This debate regards the relationship between the rights of the individual to freedom from unwanted observation and the rights of the organization to collect and use data for its own legitimate purposes. This discussion encompasses privacy as well as a broader concern with what life could be like in a surveillance-based society.

The fundamental question facing information systems designers is whether or not to use the contemporary approach of striving for secrecy, or to look for some novel way to assure security and privacy without secrecy. While government regulation and public opinion will no doubt be significant factors, other drivers explored in this essay may play a role.

Future systems will implement surveillance and data gathering capabilities far beyond those in use today, and thus these systems will pose new challenges to our current thinking about privacy. These systems will collect and process data that are threats to individual privacy and will be exposed to all of the risks expected in the operation of information systems. Will these systems, often used in the context of information security or national security, be designed to reinforce the power of select individuals or oligarchies or will these systems be designed to improve the security and privacy of society as a whole?

The phrase from Juvenal, "But who will guard the guards themselves?" encapsulates the problem presented when any person or small group has been assigned to roles that give decision-making powers or control over wealth. Those who are trusted to protect the common good are faced with the temptation of abusing their positions for personal gain—as per Lord Acton, "Power corrupts, absolute power corrupts absolutely." It is a natural human drive to seek and retain power and the rewards that accompany that power. In the information-driven age of the 21st century, control of information systems and their contents is already one of the most powerful and valuable roles in society. The challenge that faces the designers of such information systems is to make sure that the resulting systems perform as designed while also meeting security and transparency needs. Thus means that systems should provide essential confidentiality, integrity, and availability as indicated by organizational policy, are resistant to unauthorized uses, and that they also do not have the unintended consequences of misuse by those seeking to gain or retain power at the expense of the privacy rights of the various constituencies that may use the systems.

System Capabilities

One of the more contentious debates at the opening of the 21st century is that of the inability of the individual to retain any semblance of privacy in a world filled with pervasive surveillance, omnipresent information systems, and the highly automated routine of daily life. Try to envision a single day in the life of any Western democracy where an individual is not in contact with one of the modern totems of the digital world: the wireless phone, the personal digital assistant, the laptop computer, the automated teller machine, or the point-of-sale terminal.

System processing capabilities and their capacity to store information continue to grow at exponential rates. Driven by Moore's Law[1] and society's appetite for online capabilities, organizations capture and store ever more data, organizing it into information needed to continue to operate. One of the reasons for the emergence of massive-capacity disk drives in the near term is the desire to capture and store vast quantities of data. The amount of data online has grown exponentially since the opening of the digital age. In fact, one study observes that society used print, film, magnetic, and optical storage media to store roughly five exabytes[2] of new information in 2002. Over 90% of the new information stored is placed on magnetic media and is thus accessible by computers either immediately or with little extra effort. What's more, roughly 18 exabytes of data flowed through electronic channels in that same year.[3] No one expects the volume of information transmitted and stored to decrease in the future.

One of the foundations for the current debate about privacy and the expectations of individuals is the use of surveillance data from IT and IT-related systems deployed across society. As these systems have been designed and deployed to meet many and diverse business and governmental objectives, a common thread has been an increase in the quantity and quality of the surveillance data collected and used. The sense of alarm about pervasive surveillance and its potential abuses has generated research and commentary, as socially aware computer scientists and social critics weigh in on the topic. A July 2004 special edition of *IEEE Spectrum* contained a series of articles in a special report titled "Sensor Nation" (*IEEE*, 2004). As the preface to this special edition notes, "For most of our history, privacy was a luxury...clustering together in caves, our distant ancestors knew who the best hunters were, and who was sleeping with whom. Later, in the fiefs, villages, and towns, everybody knew who was dependable, who was a drunk, who had money. Amid such intimacy, anonymous sociopathology was pretty hard to pull off. Later on, when we didn't really need to huddle for security, we came to see privacy as "a fundamental human right". .... As...this special report makes clear, our ideas about privacy, and our privacy itself, seem to be under siege. [The authors] trace the assault to several connected technology developments, [such as] hugely improved sensors...the emergence of enormous databases of personal information... [and the] availability of a cheap, easy way to instantly spread personal information and data gathered by sensors to every corner of the planet: it's called the Internet." (*IEEE*, 2004)

While the use of video surveillance of public places has received some coverage from the media and has encountered some discussion in the public sphere, the collection and use of less obvious forms of surveillance data has not had as much scrutiny. Under debate here is the routine audit data collection in the more mundane information systems that populate the electronic networks of modern organizations. Few have discussed the tradeoffs inherent in the design objectives for information systems in an era when ubiquitous surveillance is rapidly becoming the norm.

Almost every non-trivial information system implemented today will encompass one or more features or sub-systems that involve direct surveillance of users or the recording of data that provide surveillance-like capabilities. Even mundane bookkeeping systems include auditor-mandated logging capabilities that could be construed as surveillance. Other information systems may strike the issue of surveillance more centrally. Information security systems, as a class, often include elaborate logging capabilities as well as information feeds to link sensor systems to central analysis systems. These types of capabilities in these types of systems are not limited to the obvious intrusion detection components, but rather encompass even mundane systems like policy management or user privilege management systems.

Framing the Debate

This is not a new discussion, nor is it a new phenomenon. In 1890, Brandeis and Warren cautioned us in the *Harvard Law Review* about how technology impinges on the rights of the individual.[4] There is no question that systems exist now and are being deployed that, by design or as a byproduct of operation, generate surveillance data. Another related issue is that of the quality of the data collected. When traffic-management system cameras observe blobs of color and light to gauge a relative density of traffic, there is little opportunity for personally identifying information being captured. On the other hand, as technology improves and higher resolution cameras are deployed in the same role, or the role evolves to include systems that can issue citations for traffic infractions (which have already been deployed in Europe), the image quality becomes sufficient for personally identifying data to be harvested and used. Likewise, when an auditing system records a few dozen bytes about each transaction, the capabilities for surveillance by data aggregation are limited. As larger capacity storage subsystems enable more data about each transaction to be recorded, the entire sequence of every transaction with all the reconstruction of all of its details will be possible.

Some systems are designed with the intent of collecting surveillance data, and others produce surveillance data as a byproduct. Intentional surveillance data systems include those information systems used to support security missions as well as still and video image-processing applications, like traffic enforcement and physical security surveillance. Other systems, like banking, credit, or accounting systems, may collect significant surveillance data that is incidental to the primary objectives of the system, such as ATM still or video-image capture systems. Other systems can be used to create surveillance-like data, including the auditing subsystems found in most financial applications, and where good design principles are followed, any other information system that provides accountability for transactional integrity.

The design choice in front of the IT developer is not whether IT systems in general or information security systems in particular will engage in surveillance data collection, but rather how the information collected is used and by whom. All systems are designed to manage the surveillance data in specific ways, whether this is done with intent or as the result of assumptions absorbed from the culture of the organization. Even systems built for sale as packaged solutions will integrate surveillance data collection as either explicit features of the products to be marketed or as implicit elements used for internal purposes. This cultural bias, or set of assumptions, is likely founded on the perceived relationship of the users of the system to the operating authority of the system. The nature of this grouping of assumptions, whether founded unconsciously on the authority relationship implied in the design or explicitly as a design feature for the product, will naturally fall on a continuum of open versus closed access to surveillance data. The closed model has almost always been the norm, and few designers are even conscious of the existence of other design options. Few designers consider any but the organizational default choice to handle surveillance data. In this, it means that all surveillance data (explicit as surveillance information or implicit from auditing objectives) is treated as highly confidential system-level data and thus is protected as if it were of the same value or even a higher value as the content data the system is designed to process. The alternate extreme, making all surveillance data collected openly available to anyone with a legitimate claim to access (called transparency) it is not usually even considered an option.

Defining Transparency

In his landmark book *The Transparent Society: Will Technology Force Us to Choose Between Privacy and Freedom"?*[5] David Brin opens the door to the concept of surveillance data transparency. His book defines transparency and takes his readers on an exploration of some of the social impact of this design choice. The groundbreaking aspect of Brin's thesis is that pervasive surveillance will undoubtedly become common. The only question is to determine who will control the information from the surveillance system. To make this discussion concrete, he uses a parable of two cities; one city where the police and government agencies control all access to the surveillance data, and another city where all surveillance data is available to all members of society, with police authorities just another user alongside other government agencies, individual citizens, and public interest groups. At the end of his analysis, the people living in both cities are subject to pervasive surveillance in public places. However, the people in the first city are subject to the whims of the powerful, while the people in the second city have the same access to the information that is used to subjugate the people in the first city and are able to keep the police agencies under control using the information they now possess.

In fact, much of what Brin forecasts about pervasive surveillance has come to pass. From the ubiquitous surveillance of openly public places such as train stations and shopping malls, many more surveillance systems are in place today. The complete list of purposeful surveillance systems would make a long list indeed and is left to the reader to contemplate. Regarding who controls these information systems, they are most often under the complete control of government agencies, often agencies of law enforcement. Brin elaborates by saying, "Transparency is not about eliminating privacy. It is about giving us the power to hold accountable those who violate it."[6]

Another revealing approach about how the emergence of pervasive surveillance will affect society is given in an article by Brock N. Meeks. As Meeks writes, "... the watched become the watchers. At every traffic stop the cop knows he is being monitored, by someone, somewhere"[7] (e.g., Rodney King). To summarize the prognostication of Meeks, "Privacy is a quid pro quo now. If my tax returns are made public, so are yours and those of your neighbors. If that galls you, know that your elected officials will have to cough up their tax returns, too, as well as the fat cats of corporate America."[8]

Design Options

So, what is to be done about the systems that are created in the early years of the 21st century? Each system will be designed on a control contin-uum. At one end are the systems of the past where all control of access to all data is in the hands of the system's owner. At the other end of the spec-trum, some system will be designed such that certain data will become fully transparent, available to all who have the interest and time to spend in accessing it. In between are many options, with two choices at the polar extremes: sole control by one person and complete transparency.

First, the traditional approach is to design the control of the system using a hierarchical approach. In this model, complete control is wielded by individuals granted that level of access by the owner of the information system. This is very much in keeping with the way in which the earliest sys-tems were designed to operate in the mainframe environment of the past.

A second option is to introduce broader shared control. The result is more openness but still severe limits on how much any specific user of a system will be permitted to know. One example of this might be to implement shared-authorization for critical system functions such as that used for key-recovery operations of a PKI system. No one person exerts complete control over all system functions; rather, many of the functions are delegated and distributed and those functions that cannot be delegated are shared.

The third approach is achieved by creating a peer-based access model, and allowing anyone who is a member of the group about which data is collected to access some or all of that data. There should perhaps be some limits to access of another person's intimate details. This would achieve a limited form of transparency and might be called data translucency.

Finally, the option that David Brin and others have proposed as an answer to the police state—full transparency.

Two arguments against transparency that come readily to mind are per-formance and cultural acceptance. Any system that has to provide security controls will incur overhead as the rules for access are evaluated. The cost to a system for providing transparency may be a slightly higher cost for data retrieval. In a fully transparent situation, this may be more than offset by lower costs when access requests are no longer evaluated but all requests are honored.

The subject of cultural acceptance for full or even partial transparency may preclude its adoption. There are many latent fears of employee monitoring. This has not stopped employers from collecting and using surveillance data, but does keep them from publicizing its existence. The complete scope of these systems is a dirty little secret within some organizations. Lucas Introna notes that by December 2000, 45% of major U.S. firms were performing workplace surveillance of some form.[9]

The degree of transparency designed into a system is another requirement of the system design that the systems analyst must identify, quantify, and document. The degree of transparency designed into a system will depend on government regulations, cultural assumptions in the developing organization, and the conflicting needs of the individual constituents and the collective group.

Conclusion

Balance is needed, even when systems are designed with full transparency in mind. As Introna concludes, limits on transparency are needed to assure fairness to all concerned. The interest of the individual's need for privacy is balanced against the interest of the collective's need for transparency. While the collective needs to acquire and use information to coordinate and control the overall activities, the individual seeks to control how and to what purpose the information collected about him or her is used. It appears that there are significant opportunities for additional research into the area of privacy and the rights of the individual to be balanced against transparency needs of the collective. Brin and others have articulated the idea that perhaps transparency offers a way to build systems that are effective and are immune to abuses of power or privilege, if individuals can acquire a taste for a new approach to dealing with the privacy of personal data.

References

[1]Moore, G. (2004). *Moore's Law*. Retrieved September, 24, 2004, from *http://www.intel.com/research/silicon/mooreslaw.htm*

[2]An **exabyte** (derived from the SI prefix *exa-*) is a unit of measurement in computers of one million million million bytes. Its abbreviation is **EB**. Because of irregularities in definition and usage of the kilobyte, the exact number in common practice could be either of the following:

1. 1,000,000,000,000,000,000 bytes — 1000^6, or 10^{18}.
2. 1,152,921,504,606,846,976 bytes — 1024^6, or 2^{60}. This is the definition most often used in computer science and computer programming.

As of 2004, exabytes of data are almost never encountered in a practical context. For example the total amount of printed material in the world is estimated to be around a fifth of an exabyte. Exabytes may also appear to be encountered if a computer's file system is corrupt and displaying incorrect file sizes. However, one may hear of 16 exabytes (or 16 times 10^{18}) of address space when discussing various 64-bit architectures.

To clarify the distinction between decimal and binary prefixes, the International Electrotechnical Commission (IEC), a standards body, in 1998 defined new prefixes by combining the International System of Units (SI) prefixes with the word "binary" (see Binary prefix). Thus meaning (2) is called by the IEC an *exbibyte* (EiB), and meaning (1) is called by the IEC an exabyte. This naming convention has not, as of 2004, been widely adopted.

An exabyte is 1000 petabytes using the first definition, while an exbibyte is 1024 pebibytes using the second definition.

1 petabyte = 1000 terabyte

1 exabyte = 1000 petabyte

1 zettabyte = 1000 exabyte

The prefix *exa* is an alteration of *hexa*, the Greek word for 6, because in $10^{18} = (10^3)^6$.

— taken from *http://en.wikipedia.org/wiki/Exabyte*

[3]Lyman P., Varian, H., & Swearingen, K. (2003). *How much information 2003?* Retrieved on September 16, 2004, from *http://www.sims.berkeley.edu/research/projects/how-much-info-2003/acknowledgments.htm*

[4]Warren S. D., & Brandeis, L. D. (1890). The right to privacy. *Harvard Law Review, 4* (5), 193–220.

[5]Brin, D. (1999). *Will technology force us to choose between privacy and freedom? The transparent society:* Perseus Publishing.

[6]Brin, D. (1999). *Will technology force us to choose between privacy and freedom? The transparent society:* Perseus Publishing.

[7]Meeks, B. N. (2001, March). Accountability through transparency: Life in 2050. *Communications of the ACM 44* (3), 96–97.

[8]Meeks, B. N. (2001, March). Accountability through transparency: Life in 2050. *Communications of the ACM 44* (3), 96–97.

[9]Introna, L. D. (2000, December). Workplace surveillance, privacy and distributive justice. *Computers and Society,* 33–39.

Cases in the Management of Information Security

Objective

The following set of six cases provides the instructor a suite of fictional organizations to use as teaching aids in the field of information security management. Some of the cases in this section represent very simple organizational structures, allowing students to perform a variety of information security management projects using the information presented. Others are meant to be springboards for group discussion or writing assignments.

Computer Gaming Technologies—CGT Inc.

Overview

This case is meant to provide the student with an opportunity to prepare a bid response to a request for a comprehensive security review. Sufficient detail is provided to enable the student, working independently or in a team, to prepare a suitably detailed response. Students are encouraged to make and then document in the proposal any assumptions that are not contraindicated by the text of the case.

About Computer Gaming Technologies Inc.

CGT Inc. is a premier developer and publisher of games and entertainment software. Thanks to an experienced staff and creative environment CGT has developed an impressive string of successful titles. By combining cutting-edge technology, enchanting graphics, and superior game design, CGT has become a leading force in the world of interactive software.

CGT Inc. develops and publishes titles for PC, Macintosh, and popular video game systems that include Nintendo 64, Sega Saturn, and the Sony PlayStation. The company employs a diverse staff of people whose talents range from computer programming and game design, to writing screenplays and composing sound tracks.

History

In 1992, Mike Edwards set to work in a garage in Las Vegas. From those humble beginnings came CGT Inc., one of the most successful entertainment software companies in the history of the industry. Among its early creations were Space Saga, Robo-Wars, Coldrake, and Quest of the Staffs, which garnered the young company its first taste of widespread recognition at home and abroad.

In 1995, the company merged with Software-4-All, which enabled CGT Inc. to become a software publisher in its own right and to enjoy Software-4-All's superior worldwide distribution network. It was also the year CGT released two now-legendary titles in the gaming world: Fantastica and the game that defined the real-time strategy genre, Destiny. Soon after came Seek and Destroy and Seek and Destroy: Dark Nights, which set sales records all over the world and redefined the real-time strategy genre.

In 1998, the company relocated to Atlanta, Georgia, in order to take advantage of potential new talent in the software programming fields. Acting on faith, the CEO relocated the programming facilities to a remote area north of Atlanta, in order to provide a higher quality of life for CGT's employees. With the implementation of new education initiatives, Georgia's higher education institutes are expected to begin providing companies in the state with a superior high technology employee in both software development and hardware technologies.

CGT set new standards last year with the release of Hacker, which combined groundbreaking graphic technologies with a depth of storytelling rarely seen in computer games. Also last year, the Seek and Destroy series topped the 10 million-unit sales mark, a rare achievement in the interactive entertainment industry. Today CGT stands at the forefront of the industry with the upcoming release of Seek and Destroy: Suicide Squad and Destiny II: Afterlife.

Still headed by the visionary who started in a garage, CGT Inc. is already exploring new technologies and developing the games that will set trends well into the next millennium.

Organization

CGT Inc. is currently organized into three divisions to support past, present, and future software offerings.

- Division 1 (Development) handles new software development. A series of three five-member teams each address the various aspects of the different game packages under development. These programmers use their specialized graphical design workstation to integrate video, computer-generated graphics, and multimedia formats to create the high-impact games most popular in today's market.

- Division 2 (Testing) handles new software in-house testing. Once Division 1 creates and delivers a coded product, the Div 2 Test Specialists assist in identifying and diagnosing system-critical code defects. Once a "kill list" is compiled, the Development teams work through the bugs to create an improved program. This division is also responsible for the identification and application of external product testers. These individuals are identified from the local area and brought into a specially prepared test lab, where they are encouraged to "stress test" the packages. The Testing specialists work with the Development team to collect and catalog additional deficiencies in the coding. If Management is so inclined, the testing specialists then post the revised packages in leased Web sites to allow additional testing by any interested party. Testing also handles the collection and cataloging of comments and suggestions from these testers.

- Division 3 (Technical Support) handles call-in problems from customers. They use a series of stand-alone diagnostic workstations to identify and provide resolution on a number of problems resulting from the installation, conduct, or removal of a CGT product. Essentially they handle the thousands of questions individuals might have as to the installing and running of the games. Currently Technical Support does not have the facilities to provide "game hints" or other play tips.

The Networking Operations Group (NetOps) (when staffed) will be responsible for the installation, maintenance, and change of any and all hardware, software, and networking equipment used internally by CGT. The NetOps will be expected to maintain a standing inventory of systems and peripheral components to facilitate instantaneous support through its 24-hour helpdesk. Employees will be able to call, e-mail, or just stop by with a problem, and a support representative will be expected to be available to answer their questions, resolve their problems, or replace their defective systems. Currently the company does not have this Network Operations staff. It is the intent of the management to identify the needs of the company with respect to networking, and to design and hire a staff capable of supporting present and future network needs.

Most of the administrative support for CGT Inc. is provided by Administrative Systems of Atlanta (ASA). ASA is a specialized company focused on providing high-quality administrative services to its clientele. ASA provides complete accounting functions (accounts payable, receivable, and general ledger) as well as traditional human resources functions (payroll, benefits, insurance management, and retirement benefits) at extremely reasonable cost to the business, freeing them up to focus on their competitive strengths. The Service Level Agreement for this contract requires ASA to accept all responsibility for the systems used to support these functions. Disruptions to any of these systems will cause CGT to experience reduced capability to do business and is estimated to cost $10,000 per hour of downtime. In the past life of the contract, ASA has experienced an average of one outage each six months that took four hours to restore to normal operations.

CGT provides connectivity to the Internet from company LAN segments through a local ISP using a dedicated T-3 circuit. But, CGT has outsourced all provisioning of World Wide Web services using a company called Pinnacle Web Services, Inc. (PWS). PWS provides Web authoring and content management services to: 1) advertise current and forthcoming titles, 2) provide technical support, 3) provide online "hints" and "tips," and 4) provide information about the organization. CGT does not currently conduct business (sales) through the WWW site. All employees have access to the technical support servers that PWS provides for the contract through an intranet connection, but development is done on desktop systems and LAN file servers and the CGT database. PWS does not provide FTP, telnet, or e-mail services; these are all implemented by CGT staff using the LAN file servers as dual function devices. The Service Level Agreement for this contract requires PWS to accept all responsibility for the systems used to support these functions. Disruptions to any of these systems will cause CGT to experience reduced capability to do business and is estimated to cost $45,000 per hour of downtime. In the past life of the contract, PWS has experienced an average of one outage each nine months that took six hours to restore to normal operations.

CGT occupies a single floor of Class A office space for its corporate headquarters. The floor plan of the corporate headquarters is shown in Figure A-1, and details about the usage of the rooms is provided in Table A-1. The current organizational structure of CGT is shown in Figure A-2.

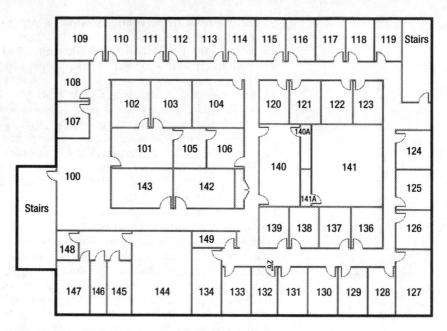

FIGURE A-1 Floor plan for CGT corporate headquarters

Technical Infrastructure

Currently CGT has 12 TCP protocol LANs implemented throughout the organization, with primary and backup file servers for each LAN with PIII-1.4 GHz, 1 GB RAM, quad 300 GB HDs (mirrored in 2s). The LAN is a 100BaseT Ethernet over Cat5 UTP. The system uses a pair of HP Procurve 2424M switches as a collapsed backbone. Currently there are 250 client desktop computer systems, one primary and one backup database server (same specifications as above), a dial-up (RRAS) server with 24 inbound lines (specification unknown), and a VPN server using Windows Server 2003 VPN services to enable inbound remote connectivity. There is currently no firewall or DMZ present.

E-mail is perceived as a critical business function. When e-mail is not available an outside auditor estimates CGT loses $1,500 per hour of downtime. In the past, CGT has experienced an outage an average of every three weeks lasting an average of one hour and 45 minutes. FTP and telnet access is less critical. The CIO estimates that interruptions to these services cause reduced productivity that costs CGT $125 per hour. In the past these services have been interrupted an average of once every eight weeks and required an average of nine hours to restore.

The company has a degree of physical security in place to protect the valuable software under development. All employees are issued a photo ID keycard used to enter the facility and property. All visitors to the facility must be coordinated through the corporate office, and escorted on the premises at all times. A physical security review was recently completed, and it was estimated that a physical security breach would cause losses of from $25,000 to $75,000 and is likely to happen once every three years.

(Text continued on A-7)

TABLE A-1   **Legend of Rooms for CGT Corporate Headquarters**

Room	Title	Owner	# of PCs
100	Foyer	PM	0
101	Receptionist	CEO	2
102	Chief Executive Officer	CEO	2
103	Chief Operations Officer	CEO	2
104	Chief Information Officer (plus Admin Asst)	CEO	3
105	Mail Room	CEO	0
106	Work Room	CEO	1
107	Programmer	D1M	1
108	Programmer	D1M	1
109	Division 1 Manager	D1M	1
110	Division 1 Admin Asst	D1M	1
111	Programmer	D1M	1
112	Programmer	D1M	1
113	Programmer	D1M	1
114	Programmer	D1M	1
115	Programmer	D1M	1
116	Programmer	D1M	1
117	Programmer	D1M	1
118	Programmer	D1M	1
119	Programmer	D1M	1
120	Programmer	D1M	1
121	Programmer	D1M	1
122	Programmer	D1M	1
123	Programmer	D1M	1
124	Technical Support Specialist	D3M	1
125	Technical Support Specialist	D3M	1
126	Division 3 Manager	D3M	1
127	Division 3 Admin Asst	D3M	1
128	Technical Support Specialist	D3M	1
129	Technical Support Specialist	D3M	1
130	Technical Support Specialist	D3M	1
131	Technical Support Specialist	D3M	1
132	Technical Support Specialist	D3M	1
133	Technical Support Specialist	D3M	1
134	Division 2 Manager	D2M	1

continued

TABLE A-1   **Legend of Rooms for CGT Corporate Headquarters—cont'd**

Room	Title	Owner	# of PCs
135	Storage	D2M	1
136	Testing Specialist	D2M	1
137	Testing Specialist	D2M	1
138	Testing Specialist	D2M	1
139	Testing Specialist	D2M	1
140	Conference Room	CEO	1
140A	Storage	CEO	0
141	Testing Lab	D2M	20
141A	Storage	D2M	0
142	Mens Room	PM	0
143	Ladies Room	PM	0
144	Network Operations (Network Support Specialists)	NetAdmin	5
145	Network Administrator	NetAdmin	2
146	Server Room	NetAdmin	10
147	Storage	NetAdmin	0
148	Wiring Closet	NetAdmin	0
149	Storage	NetAdmin	10

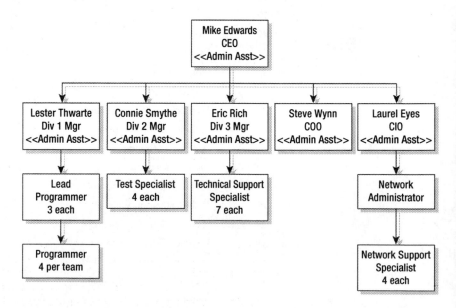

FIGURE A-2 CGT organization chart

There are no current policy, standards, or guidelines identified or implemented.

Responding to a Request for Proposal

Your assignment is to prepare a proposal in response to the following Request for Proposal that CGT issued to your consulting firm:

Request for Proposal

Thank you for your interest in supporting the ongoing goals of CGT Inc. In order to support our desire for continued growth, we here at CGT recognize the need for both the efficient access and exchange of information and limited technological resources, as well as the exploration of the gaming medium of the future, the Internet. In order to pursue these growth ideals, we have determined that it is imperative that we solicit recommendations for an integrated security solution for both our internal operations, and as a means to manage our risk in our Internet presence.

While it is certainly not my intent to expose our internal activities to the potential threats of access from unauthorized users, I recognize the need to support both off-site productivity, and flexible schedules. As a result, CGT currently has a network which allows each employee to work from home, one day per week. Our concern is that the network must provide adequate protection both from external miscreants, and internal and most probably accidental employee activities.

Our WWW presence is currently outsourced to our ISP. Not every employee has desktop access to the WWW. We have a WWW networking facility, open to employees, where employees can manage Web sites, post information on coming attractions, research information on competitive products, and experience a degree of mental relaxation. Employees do have integrated e-mail with an internal e-mail client that also allows them to check their e-mail from home.

For planning purposes, we have several standards for PCs, and these system specifications are available from Ms. Laurel Eyes, the CIO, on request. In each office or lab there is a dedicated printer. We have detailed diagrams of office layouts and a building floor plan, which I have included in this Request for Proposals.

I do not have a set budget for this project yet. I will evaluate all proposals and make a decision on each proposal's ability to meet our security needs, at a reasonable price. In your decision process, I would also ask you to consider a recommendation for a security administration staff, and any necessary physical plant facilities. If you need to use existing space for this facility please formulate a business plan as to the need for use of this facility (say an existing office or lab), a plan to relocate the contents into other facilities, and a plan for future use.

Please formulate your proposal using the enclosed templates. I expect to see the deliverables as specified in the accompanying project specifications. Any proposed budget should conform to the structure provided, and should be both detailed and properly formatted (include hard copy of items recommended, either from sales brochures, or Internet specifications). Finally, prepare a log of your activities, showing time spent and CGT employees involved.

I would like these proposals as specified in the project specification; please make sure these are professionally organized and presented. I may require a short presentation by each company bidding for our business. This presentation, if required, should be no longer than 5–10 minutes (emphasis on the shorter) and should highlight the important points (layout, cost, benefits).

If you need any additional information please feel free to contact me by e-mail for all correspondence. Be aware that I am not a security specialist, and that any questions I deem too technical or specialized in focus will probably be responded to with a degree of sarcasm. I have been told I have a caustic wit, and little tolerance for inefficient uses of my time. Please do not take offense, but craft your questions carefully. Questions that require a simple yes or no work best.

Proposal Format for Computer Gaming Technologies Networking RFP

Unless superseded by additional written project specifications, the following sections should guide the development and submission of the proposal. The final document will be submitted in a three-ring binder and single-spaced, with standard margins and fonts. Each major and minor section should be properly tabbed, organized, and structured with appropriate headers. Each new section and subsection should begin on a fresh page. All pages should be numbered, and an index placed at the beginning of the document. The group members' names should be prominently displayed on the front cover. For each section, address the subjects or components outlined beneath it. If a component requires a separate binder or document, create it as needed.

SECTION I: Investigation and Needs Analysis
  A. Overview of CGT: company history, including an organization chart, physical plant layout (blank), and general description of organization's computing resources
  B. Problem definition: a summary of the situation leading to the instigation of the analysis and design project. Specify specific organizational needs, and situations demanding resolution
  C. User requirements (non-technical): task functions, document form and flow, message/data volume, recommended improvements or changes, and organizational rules
  D. Feasibility study: An examination of the economic, technical, and behavioral feasibilities affecting the selection and implementation of networks
  E. Outline of project scope/goals
  F. Estimate of costs
  G. List Existing resources
  H. Feasibility analysis
  I. Copy of Enterprise Information Security policy

SECTION II: Analysis of Requirements
  A. Assessment of current system against plan developed in Phase 1
  B. Preliminary system requirements

    C. Considerations/challenges for integration of new system with existing system
    D. Documentation of findings and updated feasibility analysis
    E. Analysis of existing security policies and programs
    F. Analysis of current threats and controls
    G. Identification of legal issues impacting program
    H. Risk analysis

SECTION III: Logical and Physical Security Design
Logical Design
    A. Assessment of current business needs against plan developed in Phase 2
    B. Identification of key applications and technologies
    C. Presentation of multiple solutions with recommendations for selection of best solutions
    D. Document of findings and updated feasibility analysis
    E. Security blueprint
    F. Incident response plan outline
    G. Disaster Recover and Business Continuity Plan outline
    H. Feasibility Recommendation for continuing and/or outsourcing the project
Physical Design
    A. General description of technologies needed to support solutions developed in Phase 3
    B. Identification of optimal solution
    C. Recommendations for 'make or buy' components
    D. Documentation of findings and updated feasibility analysis
    E. Identification of specific technologies needed to support security blueprint
    F. Physical security measures to support technological solutions
    G. Design managerial review and approval document

SECTION IV: Implementation Strategies
    A. Recommendations for "make or buy" software
    B. Specifications for component vendors
    C. Documentation of the system
    D. Plan to train users
    E. Updated feasibility analysis
    F. Discussion of plan to present system to users
    G. Plan for system testing and performance review
    H. Implementation plan management approval document

SECTION V: Security Maintenance and Change
    A. Plan and recommendations for system support
    B. Plan and recommendations for periodic system review
    C. Plan for upgrade and patch management
    D. Description of Security Management Model to be deployed (Fault, Configuration, Accounting, Performance. . .)

Appendix A: Project Log

Include a calendar of events that actually occurred, include group meetings, labs, and any event that brought the group together to perform any of the activities necessary to complete this project. Each entry should specify the date, members present, activities discussed, and activities accomplished.

Appendix B: Copies of Pricing Sources

If you cite a price in the budget, include a photocopy of the item, price, and vendor. Web printouts are acceptable.

Assessing and Mitigating the Risks to a Hypothetical Computer System

National Institute of Standards and Technology (NIST),
Technology Administration, U.S. Department of Commerce

Overview

This case has been extracted in its entirety from NIST Special Publication 800-12: The Computer Security Handbook. *This document was authored by a number of individuals as referenced in the Acknowledgement section. Chapter 20 of SP 800-12 (presented here) is a case study on computer security.*

This case illustrates how a hypothetical government agency (HGA) deals with computer security issues in its operating environment. It follows the evolution of HGA's initiation of an assessment of the threats to its computer security system all the way through to HGA's recommendations for mitigating those risks. In the real world, many solutions exist for computer security problems. No single solution can solve similar security problems in all environments. Likewise, the solutions presented in this example may not be appropriate for all environments.

This case study is provided for illustrative purposes only, and should not be construed as guidance or specific recommendations to solving specific security issues. Because a comprehensive example attempting to illustrate all Handbook topics would be inordinately long, this example necessarily simplifies the issues presented and omits many details. For instance, to highlight the similarities and differences among controls in the different processing environments, it addresses some of the major types of processing platforms linked together in a distributed system: personal computers, local area networks, wide area networks, and mainframes; it does not show how to secure these platforms.

Introduction

This example can be used to help understand how security issues are examined, how some potential solutions are analyzed, how their cost and benefits are weighed, and ultimately how management accepts responsibility for risks.

This section also highlights the importance of management's acceptance of a particular level of risk—this will, of course, vary from organization to organization. It is management's prerogative to decide what level of risk is appropriate, given operating and budget environments and other applicable factors.

Initiating the Risk Assessment

HGA has information systems that comprise and are intertwined with several different kinds of assets valuable enough to merit protection. HGA's systems play a key role in transferring U.S. government funds to individuals in the form of paychecks; hence, financial resources are among the assets associated with HGA's systems. The system components owned and operated by HGA are also assets, as are personnel information, contracting and procurement documents, draft regulations, internal correspondence, and a variety of other day-to-day business documents, memos, and reports. HGA's assets include intangible elements as well, such as the reputation of the agency and the confidence of its employees that personal information will be handled properly and that the wages will be paid on time.

A recent change in the directorship of HGA has brought in a new management team. Among the new Chief Information Officer's first actions was appointing a Computer Security Program Manager who immediately initiated a comprehensive risk analysis to assess the soundness of HGA's computer security program in protecting the agency's assets and its compliance with federal directives. This analysis drew upon prior risk assessments, threat studies, and applicable internal control reports. The Computer Security Program Manager also established a timetable for periodic reassessments.

Since the wide area network and mainframe used by HGA are owned and operated by other organizations, they were not treated in the risk assessment as HGA's assets. And although HGA's personnel, buildings, and facilities are essential assets, the Computer Security Program Manager considered them to be outside the scope of the risk analysis.

After examining HGA's computer system, the risk assessment team identified specific threats to HGA's assets, reviewed HGA's and national safeguards against those threats, identified the vulnerabilities of those policies, and recommended specific actions for mitigating the remaining risks to HGA's computer security. The following sections provide highlights from the risk assessment. The assessment addressed many other issues at the programmatic and system levels. However, this case focuses on security issues related to the time and attendance application.

HGA's Computer System

HGA relies on the distributed computer systems and networks shown in Figure B-1. They consist of a collection of components, some of which are systems in their own right. Some belong to HGA, but others are owned and operated by other organizations. This section describes these components, their role in the overall distributed system architecture, and how they are used by HGA.

SYSTEM ARCHITECTURE

Most of HGA's staff (a mix of clerical, technical, and managerial staff) are provided with personal computers (PCs) located in their offices. Each PC includes hard disk and floppy-disk drives.

The PCs are connected to a local area network (LAN) so that users can exchange and share information. The central component of the LAN is a

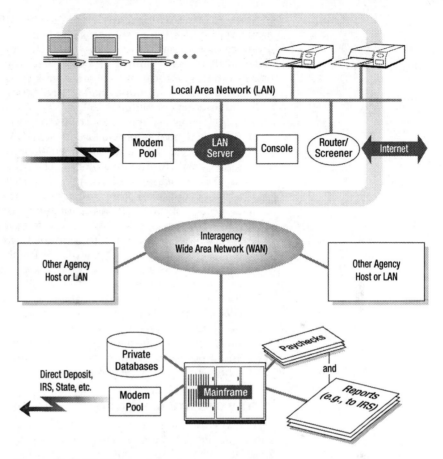

FIGURE B-1 HGA's computer systems

LAN server, a more powerful computer that acts as an intermediary between PCs on the network and provides a large volume of disk storage for shared information, including shared application programs. The server provides logical access controls on potentially sharable information via elementary access control lists. These access controls can be used to limit user access to various files and programs stored on the server. Some programs stored on the server can be retrieved via the LAN and executed on a PC; others can only be executed on the server.

To initiate a session on the network or execute programs on the server, users at a PC must log into the server and provide a user identifier and password known to the server. Then they may use files to which they have access.

One of the applications supported by the server is electronic mail (e-mail), which can be used by all PC users. Other programs that run on the server can only be executed by a limited set of PC users.

Several printers, distributed throughout HGA's building complex, are connected to the LAN. Users at PCs may direct printouts to whichever printer is most convenient for their use.

Since HGA must frequently communicate with industry, the LAN also provides a connection to the Internet via a router. The router is a network interface device that translates between the protocols and addresses associated with the LAN and the Internet. The router also performs network packet filtering, a form of network access control, and has recently been configured to disallow non–e-mail (e.g., file transfer remote log in) between LAN and Internet computers.

The LAN server also has connections to several other devices:

- A modem pool is provided so that HGA's employees on travel can "dial in" via the public switched (telephone) network and read or send e-mail. To initiate a dial-in session, a user must successfully log in. During dial-in sessions, the LAN server provides access only to e-mail facilities; no other functions can be invoked.
- A special console is provided for the server administrators who configure the server, establish and delete user accounts, and have other special privileges needed for administrative and maintenance functions. These functions can only be invoked from the administrator console; that is, they cannot be invoked from a PC on the network or from a dialup session.
- A connection to a government agency X.25-based wide area network (WAN) is provided so that information can be transferred to or from other agency systems. One of the other hosts on the WAN is a large multiagency mainframe system. This mainframe is used to collect and process information from a large number of agencies while providing a range of access controls.

SYSTEM OPERATIONAL AUTHORITY/OWNERSHIP

The system components contained within the large dashed rectangle shown in Figure B-1 are managed and operated by an organization within HGA known as the Computer Operations Group (COG). This group includes the PCs, LAN, server, console, printers, modem pool, and router. The WAN is owned and operated by a large commercial telecommunications company that provides WAN services under a government contract. The mainframe is owned and operated by a federal agency that acts as a service provider for HGA and other agencies connected to the WAN.

SYSTEM APPLICATIONS

PCs on HGA's LAN are used for word processing, data manipulation, and other common applications, including spreadsheet and project management tools. Many of these tasks are concerned with data that are sensitive with respect to confidentiality or integrity. Some of these documents and data also need to be available in a timely manner.

The mainframe also provides storage and retrieval services for other databases belonging to individual agencies. For example, several agencies, including HGA, store their personnel databases on the mainframe; these databases contain dates of service, leave balances, salary and W-2 information, and so forth.

In addition to their time and attendance application, HGA's PCs and the LAN server are used to manipulate other kinds of information that may be sensitive with respect to confidentiality or integrity, including personnel-related correspondence and draft-contracting documents.

Threats to HGA's Assets

Different assets of HGA are subject to different kinds of threats. Some threats are considered less likely than others, and the potential impact of different threats may vary greatly. The likelihood of threats is generally difficult to estimate accurately. Both HGA and the risk assessment's authors have attempted to the extent possible to base these estimates on historical data, but have also tried to anticipate new trends stimulated by emerging technologies (e.g., external networks).

PAYROLL FRAUD

As with most large organizations that control financial assets, attempts at fraud and embezzlement are likely to occur. Historically, attempts at payroll fraud have almost always come from within HGA or the other agencies that operate systems on which HGA depends. Although HGA has thwarted many of these attempts, and some have involved relatively small sums of money, it considers preventing financial fraud to be a critical computer security priority, particularly in light of the potential financial losses and the risks of damage to its reputation with Congress, the public, and other federal agencies.

Attempts to defraud HGA have included the following:

- Submitting fraudulent time sheets for hours or days not worked, or for pay periods following termination or transfer of employment. The former may take the form of overreporting compensatory or overtime hours worked, or underreporting vacation or sick leave taken. Alternatively, attempts have been made to modify time sheet data after being entered and approved for submission to payroll.
- Falsifying or modifying dates or data on which one's "years of service" computations are based, thereby becoming eligible for retirement earlier than allowed, or increasing one's pension amount.
- Creating employee records and time sheets for fictitious personnel, and attempting to obtain their paychecks, particularly after arranging for direct deposit.

PAYROLL ERRORS

Of greater likelihood, but of perhaps lesser potential impact on HGA, are errors in the entry of time and attendance data; failure to enter information describing new employees, terminations, and transfers in a timely manner; accidental corruption or loss of time and attendance data; or errors in interagency coordination and processing of personnel transfers.

Errors of these kinds can cause financial difficulties for employees and accounting problems for HGA. If an employee's vacation or sick leave balance became negative erroneously during the last pay period of the year, the employee's last paycheck would be automatically reduced. An individual who transfers between HGA and another agency may risk receiving duplicate paychecks or no paychecks for the pay periods immediately following the transfer. Errors of this sort that occur near the end of the year can lead to errors in W-2 forms and subsequent difficulties with the tax collection agencies.

INTERRUPTION OF OPERATIONS

HGA's building facilities and physical plant are several decades old and are frequently under repair or renovation. As a result, power, air conditioning, and LAN or WAN connectivity for the server are typically interrupted several times a year for periods of up to one work day. For example, on several occasions, construction workers have inadvertently severed power or network cables. Fires, floods, storms, and other natural disasters can also interrupt computer operations, as can equipment malfunctions.

Another threat of small likelihood, but significant potential impact, is that of a malicious or disgruntled employee or outsider seeking to disrupt time-critical processing (e.g., payroll) by deleting necessary inputs or system accounts, misconfiguring access controls, planting computer viruses, or stealing or sabotaging computers or related equipment. Such interruptions, depending upon when they occur, can prevent time and attendance data from getting processed and transferred to the mainframe before the payroll processing deadline.

DISCLOSURE OR BROKERAGE OF INFORMATION

Other kinds of threats may be stimulated by the growing market for information about an organization's employees or internal activities. Individuals who have legitimate work-related reasons for access to the master employee database may attempt to disclose such information to other employees or contractors or to sell it to private investigators, employment recruiters, the press, or other organizations. HGA considers such threats to be moderately likely and of low to high potential impact, depending on the type of information involved.

NETWORK-RELATED THREATS

Most of the human threats of concern to HGA originate from insiders. Nevertheless, HGA also recognizes the need to protect its assets from outsiders. Such attacks may serve many different purposes and pose a broad spectrum of risks, including unauthorized disclosure or modification of information, unauthorized use of services and assets, or unauthorized denial of services.

As shown in Figure B-1, HGA's systems are connected to the three external networks: (1) the Internet, (2) the Interagency WAN, and (3) the public switched (telephone) network. Although these networks are a source of security risks, connectivity with them is essential to HGA's mission and to the productivity of its employees; connectivity cannot be terminated simply because of security risks.

In each of the past few years before establishing its current set of network safeguards, HGA had detected several attempts by outsiders to penetrate its systems. Most, but not all of these, have come from the Internet, and those that succeeded did so by learning or guessing user account passwords. In two cases, the attacker deleted or corrupted significant amounts of data, most of which were later restored from backup files. In most cases, HGA could detect no ill effects of the attack, but concluded that the attacker may have browsed through some files. HGA also conceded that its systems did not have audit logging capabilities sufficient to track an attacker's activities. Hence, for most of these attacks, HGA could not accurately gauge the extent of penetration.

In one case, an attacker made use of a bug in an e-mail utility and succeeded in acquiring System Administrator privileges on the server—a significant breach. HGA found no evidence that the attacker attempted to exploit these privileges before being discovered two days later. When the attack was detected, COG immediately contacted HGA's Incident Handling Team, and was told that a bug fix had been distributed by the server vendor several months earlier. To its embarrassment, COG discovered that it had already received the fix, which it then promptly installed. It now believes that no subsequent attacks of the same nature have succeeded. Although HGA has no evidence that it has been significantly harmed to date by attacks via external networks, it believes that these attacks have great potential to inflict damage. HGA's management considers itself lucky that such attacks have not harmed HGA's reputation and the confidence of the citizens its serves. It also believes the likelihood of such attacks via external networks will increase in the future.

OTHER THREATS

HGA's systems also are exposed to several other threats that, for reasons of space, cannot be fully enumerated here. Examples of threats and HGA's assessment of their probabilities and impacts include those listed in Table B-1.

Current Security Measures

HGA has numerous policies and procedures for protecting its assets against the above threats. These are articulated in HGA's Computer Security Manual, which implements and synthesizes the requirements of many federal directives, such as Appendix III to OMB Circular A-130, the Computer Security Act of 1987, and the Privacy Act. The manual also includes policies

TABLE B-1   **Examples of Threats to HGA's Systems**

Potential Threat	Probability	Impact
Accidental Loss/Release of Disclosure-Sensitive Information	Medium	Low/Medium
Accidental Destruction of Information	High	Medium
Loss of Information due to Virus Contamination	Medium	Medium
Misuse of System Resources*	Low	Low
Theft	High	Medium
Unauthorized Access to Telecommunications Resources*	Medium	Medium
Natural Disaster	Low	High

*HGA operates a PBX system, which may be vulnerable to (1) hacker disruptions of PBX availability and, consequently, agency operations, (2) unauthorized access to outgoing phone lines for long-distance services, (3) unauthorized access to stored voice-mail messages, and (4) surreptitious access to otherwise private conversations/data transmissions.

for automated financial systems, such as those based on OMB Circulars A-123 and A-127, as well as the Federal Managers' Financial Integrity Act. Several examples of those policies follow, as they apply generally to the use and administration of HGA's computer system and specifically to security issues related to time and attendance, payroll, and continuity of operations.

GENERAL USE AND ADMINISTRATION OF HGA'S COMPUTER SYSTEM

HGA's Computer Operations Group (COG) is responsible for controlling, administering, and maintaining the computer resources owned and operated by HGA. These functions are depicted in Figure B-1 enclosed in the large, dashed rectangle. Only individuals holding the job title System Administrator are authorized to establish log-in IDs and passwords on multi-user HGA systems (e.g., the LAN server). Only HGA's employees and contract personnel may use the system, and only after receiving written authorization from the department supervisor (or, in the case of contractors, the contracting officer) to whom these individuals report.

COG issues copies of all relevant security policies and procedures to new users. Before activating a system account for a new user, COG requires that they (1) attend a security awareness and training course or complete an interactive computer-aided-instruction training session, and (2) sign an acknowledgment form indicating that they understand their security responsibilities. Authorized users are assigned a secret log-in ID and password, which they must not share with anyone else. They are expected to comply with all of HGA's password selection and security procedures (e.g., periodically changing passwords). Users who fail to do so are subject to a range of penalties.

Users creating data that are sensitive with respect to disclosure or modification are expected to make effective use of the automated access control mechanisms available on HGA computers to reduce the risk of exposure to unauthorized individuals. (Appropriate training and education are in place to help users do this.) In general, access to disclosure-sensitive information is to be granted only to individuals whose jobs require it.

PROTECTION AGAINST PAYROLL FRAUD AND ERRORS: TIME AND ATTENDANCE APPLICATION

The time and attendance application plays a major role in protecting against payroll fraud and errors. Since the time and attendance application is a component of a larger automated payroll process, many of its functional and security requirements have been derived from both government-wide and HGA-specific policies related to payroll and leave. For example, HGA must protect personal information in accordance with the Privacy Act. Depending on the specific type of information, it should normally be viewable only by the individual concerned, the individual's supervisors, and personnel and payroll department employees. Such information should also be timely and accurate.

Each week, employees must sign and submit a time sheet that identifies the number of hours they have worked and the amount of leave they have taken. The Time and Attendance Clerk enters the data for a given group of employees and runs an application on the LAN server to verify the data's validity and to ensure that only authorized users with access to the Time and Attendance Clerk's functions can enter time and attendance data. The application performs these security checks by using the LAN server's access control and identification and authentication (I&A) mechanisms. The application compares the data with a limited database of employee information to detect incorrect employee identifiers, implausible numbers of hours worked, and so forth. After correcting any detected errors, the clerk runs another application that formats the time and attendance data into a report, flagging exception/out-of-bound conditions (e.g., negative leave balances).

Department supervisors are responsible for reviewing the correctness of the time sheets of the employees under their supervision and indicating their approval by initialing the time sheets. If they detect significant irregularities and indications of fraud in such data, they must report their findings to the Payroll Office before submitting the time sheets for processing. In keeping with the principle of separation of duty, all data on time sheets and corrections on the sheets that may affect pay, leave, retirement, or other benefits of an individual must be reviewed for validity by at least two authorized individuals (other than the affected individual).

Protection Against Unauthorized Execution

Only users with access to Time and Attendance Supervisor functions may approve and submit time and attendance data—or subsequent corrections thereof—to the mainframe. Supervisors may not approve their own time and attendance data.

Only the System Administrator has been granted access to assign a special access control privilege to server programs. As a result, the server's operating system is designed to prevent a bogus time and attendance application created by any other user from communicating with the WAN and, hence, with the mainframe.

The time and attendance application is supposed to be configured so that the clerk and supervisor functions can only be carried out from specific PCs attached to the LAN and only during normal working hours. Administrators are not authorized to exercise functions of the time and attendance application apart from those concerned with configuring the accounts, passwords, and access permissions for clerks and supervisors. Administrators are expressly prohibited by policy from entering, modifying, or submitting time and attendance data via the time and attendance application or other mechanisms. (Technically, System Administrators may still have the ability to do so. This highlights the importance of adequate managerial reviews, auditing, and personnel background checks.)

Protection against unauthorized execution of the time and attendance application depends on I&A and access controls. While the time and attendance application is accessible from any PC, unlike most programs run by PC users, it does not execute directly on the PC's processor. Instead, it executes on the server, while the PC behaves as a terminal, relaying the user's keystrokes to the server and displaying text and graphics sent from the server. The reason for this approach is that common PC systems do not provide I&A and access controls and, therefore, cannot protect against unauthorized time and attendance program execution. Any individual who has access to the PC could run any program stored there.

Another possible approach is for the time and attendance program to perform I&A and access control on its own by requesting and validating a password before beginning each time and attendance session. This approach, however, can be defeated easily by a moderately skilled programming attack, and was judged inadequate by HGA during the application's early design phase.

Recall that the server is a more powerful computer equipped with a multi-user operating system that includes password-based I&A and access controls. Designing the time and attendance application program so that it executes on the server under the control of the server's operating system provides a more effective safeguard against unauthorized execution than executing it on the user's PC.

Protection Against Payroll Errors

The frequency of data entry errors is reduced by having Time and Attendance clerks enter each time sheet into the time and attendance application twice. If the two copies are identical, both are considered error free, and the record is accepted for subsequent review and approval by a supervisor. If the copies are not identical, the discrepancies are displayed, and for each discrepancy, the clerk determines which copy is correct. The clerk then incorporates the corrections into one of the copies, which is then accepted for further processing. If the clerk makes the same data-entry error twice, then the two copies will match, and one will be accepted as correct, even though it is erroneous. To reduce this risk, the time and attendance application could be configured to require that the two copies be entered by different clerks.

In addition, each department has one or more Time and Attendance supervisors who are authorized to review these reports for accuracy and to approve them by running another server program that is part of the time and attendance application. The data are then subjected to a collection of "sanity checks" to detect entries whose values are outside expected ranges. Potential anomalies are displayed to the supervisor prior to allowing approval; if errors are identified, the data are returned to a clerk for additional examination and corrections.

When a supervisor approves the time and attendance data, this application logs into the interagency mainframe via the WAN and transfers the data to a payroll database on the mainframe. The mainframe later prints paychecks or, using a pool of modems that can send data over phone lines, it may transfer the funds electronically into employee-designated bank accounts. Withheld taxes and contributions are also transferred electronically in this manner.

The Director of Personnel is responsible for ensuring that forms describing significant payroll-related personnel actions are provided to the Payroll Office at least one week before the payroll processing date for the first affected pay period. These actions include hiring, terminations, transfers, leaves of absences and returns from such, and pay raises.

The Manager of the Payroll Office is responsible for establishing and maintaining controls adequate to ensure that the amounts of pay, leave, and other benefits reported on pay stubs and recorded in permanent records and those distributed electronically are accurate and consistent with time and attendance data and with other information provided by the Personnel Department. In particular, paychecks must never be provided to anyone who is not a bona fide, active-status employee of HGA. Moreover, the pay of any employee who terminates employment, who transfers, or who goes on leave without pay must be suspended as of the effective date of such action; that is, extra paychecks or excess pay must not be dispersed.

Protection Against Accidental Corruption or Loss of Payroll Data

The same mechanisms used to protect against fraudulent modification are used to protect against accidental corruption of time and attendance data—namely, the access-control features of the server and mainframe operating systems.

COG's nightly backups of the server's disks protect against loss of time and attendance data. To a limited extent, HGA also relies on mainframe administrative personnel to back up time and attendance data stored on the mainframe, even though HGA has no direct control over these individuals. As additional protection against loss of data at the mainframe, HGA retains copies of all time and attendance data online on the server for at least one year, at which time the data are archived and kept for three years. The server's access controls for the online files are automatically set to read-only access by the time and attendance application at the time of submission to the mainframe. The integrity of time and attendance data will be protected by digital signatures as they are implemented.

The WAN's communications protocols also protect against loss of data during transmission from the server to the mainframe (e.g., error checking). In addition, the mainframe payroll application includes a program that is automatically run 24 hours before paychecks and pay stubs are printed. This program produces a report identifying agencies from whom time and attendance data for the current pay period were expected but not received. Payroll department staff are responsible for reviewing the reports and immediately notifying agencies that need to submit or resubmit time and attendance data. If time and attendance input or other related information is not available on a timely basis, pay, leave, and other benefits are temporarily calculated based on information estimated from prior pay periods.

PROTECTION AGAINST INTERRUPTION OF OPERATIONS

HGA's policies regarding continuity of operations are derived from requirements stated in OMB Circular A-130. HGA requires various organizations within it to develop contingency plans, test them annually, and establish appropriate administrative and operational procedures for supporting them. The plans must identify the facilities, equipment, supplies, procedures, and personnel needed to ensure reasonable continuity of operations under a broad range of adverse circumstances.

COG Contingency Planning

COG is responsible for developing and maintaining a contingency plan that sets forth the procedures and facilities to be used when physical plant failures, natural disasters, or major equipment malfunctions occur sufficient to disrupt the normal use of HGA's PCs, LAN, server, router, printers, and other associated equipment.

The plan prioritizes applications that rely on these resources, indicating those that should be suspended if available automated functions or capacities are temporarily degraded. COG personnel have identified system software and hardware components that are compatible with those used by two nearby agencies. HGA has signed an agreement with those agencies, whereby they have committed to reserving spare computational and storage capacities sufficient to support HGA's system-based operations for a few days during an emergency.

No communication devices or network interfaces may be connected to HGA's systems without written approval of the COG Manager. The COG staff is responsible for installing all known security-related software patches in a timely manner and for maintaining spare or redundant PCs, servers, storage devices, and LAN interfaces to ensure that at least 100 people can simultaneously perform word-processing tasks at all times.

To protect against accidental corruption or loss of data, COG personnel back up the LAN server's disks onto magnetic tape every night and transport the tapes weekly to a sister agency for storage. HGA's policies also stipulate that all PC users are responsible for backing up weekly any significant data stored on their PC's local hard disks. For the past several years, COG has issued a yearly memorandum reminding PC users of this responsibility. COG also strongly encourages them to store significant data on the LAN server instead of on their PC's hard disk so that such data will be backed up automatically during COG's LAN server backups.

To prevent more limited computer equipment malfunctions from interrupting routine business operations, COG maintains an inventory of approximately 10 fully equipped spare PCs, a spare LAN server, and several spare disk drives for the server. COG also keeps thousands of feet of LAN cable on hand. If a segment of the LAN cable that runs through the ceilings and walls of HGA's buildings fails or is accidentally severed, COG technicians will run temporary LAN cabling along the floors of hallways and offices, typically restoring service within a few hours for as long as needed until the cable failure is located and repaired.

To protect against PC virus contamination, HGA authorizes only System Administrators approved by the COG Manager to install licensed, copyrighted PC software packages that appear on the COG-approved list. PC software applications are generally installed only on the server. (These stipulations are part of an HGA assurance strategy that relies on the quality of the engineering practices of vendors to provide software that is adequately robust and trustworthy.) Only the COG Manager is authorized to add packages to the approved list. COG procedures also stipulate that every month System Administrators should run virus-detection and other security-configuration validation utilities on the server and, on a spot-check basis, on a number of PCs. If they find a virus, they must immediately notify the agency team that handles computer security incidents.

COG is also responsible for reviewing audit logs generated by the server, identifying audit records indicative of security violations, and reporting such indications to the Incident-Handling Team. The COG Manager assigns these duties to specific members of the staff and ensures that they are implemented as intended.

The COG Manager is responsible for assessing adverse circumstances and for providing recommendations to HGA's Director. Based on these and other sources of input, the Director will determine whether the circumstances are dire enough to merit activating various sets of procedures called for in the contingency plan.

Division Contingency Planning

HGA's divisions also must develop and maintain their own contingency plans. The plans must identify critical business functions, the system resources and applications on which they depend, and the maximum acceptable periods of interruption that these functions can tolerate without significant reduction in HGA's ability to fulfill its mission. The head of each division is responsible for ensuring that the division's contingency plan and associated support activities are adequate.

For each major application used by multiple divisions, a chief of a single division must be designated as the application owner. The designated official (supported by his or her staff) is responsible for addressing that application in the contingency plan and for coordinating with other divisions that use the application.

If a division relies exclusively on computer resources maintained by COG (e.g., the LAN), it need not duplicate COG's contingency plan, but is responsible for reviewing the adequacy of that plan. If COG's plan does not adequately address the division's needs, the division must communicate its concerns to the COG Director. In either situation, the division must make known the criticality of its applications to the COG. If the division relies on computer resources or services that are not provided by COG, the division is responsible for (1) developing its own contingency plan or (2) ensuring that the contingency plans of other organizations (e.g., the WAN service provider) provide adequate protection against service disruptions.

PROTECTION AGAINST DISCLOSURE OR BROKERAGE OF INFORMATION

HGA's protection against information disclosure is based on a need-to-know policy and on personnel hiring and screening practices. The need-to-know policy states that time and attendance information should be made accessible only to HGA employees and contractors whose assigned professional responsibilities require it. Such information must be protected against access from all other individuals, including other HGA employees. Appropriate hiring and screening practices can lessen the risk that an untrustworthy individual will be assigned such responsibilities. The need-to-know policy is supported by a collection of physical, procedural, and automated safeguards, including the following:

- Time and attendance paper documents must be stored securely when not in use, particularly during evenings and on weekends. Approved storage containers include locked file cabinets and desk drawers—to which only the owner has the keys. While storage in a container is preferable, it is also permissible to leave time and attendance documents on top of a desk or other exposed surface in a locked office (with the realization that the guard force has keys to the office). (This is a judgment left to local discretion.) Similar rules apply to disclosure-sensitive information stored on floppy disks and other removable magnetic media.

■ Every HGA PC is equipped with a key lock that, when locked, disables the PC. Although not discussed in this example, recognize that technical "spoofing" can occur. When information is stored on a PC's local hard disk, the user to whom that PC was assigned is expected to (1) lock the PC at the conclusion of each work day and (2) lock the office in which the PC is located.

■ The LAN server operating system's access controls provide extensive features for controlling access to files. These include group-oriented controls that allow teams of users to be assigned to named groups by the System Administrator. Group members are then allowed access to sensitive files not accessible to nonmembers. Each user can be assigned to several groups according to need to know. (The reliable functioning of these controls is assumed, perhaps incorrectly, by HGA.)

■ All PC users undergo security awareness training when first provided accounts on the LAN server. Among other things, the training stresses the necessity of protecting passwords. It also instructs users to log off the server before going home at night or before leaving the PC unattended for periods exceeding an hour.

PROTECTION AGAINST NETWORK-RELATED THREATS

HGA's current set of external network safeguards has only been in place for a few months. The basic approach is to tightly restrict the kinds of external network interactions that can occur by funneling all traffic to and from external networks through two interfaces that filter out unauthorized kinds of interactions. As indicated in Figure B-1, the two interfaces are the network router and the LAN server. The only kinds of interactions that these interfaces allow are (1) e-mail and (2) data transfers from the server to the mainframe controlled by a few special applications (e.g., the time and attendance application).

Figure B-1 shows that the network router is the only direct interface between the LAN and the Internet. The router is a dedicated, special-purpose computer that translates between the protocols and addresses associated with the LAN and the Internet. Internet protocols, unlike those used on the WAN, specify that packets of information coming from or going to the Internet must carry an indicator of the kind of service that is being requested or used to process the information. This makes it possible for the router to distinguish e-mail packets from other kinds of packets—for example, those associated with a remote log-in request (although not discussed in this example, recognize that technical "spoofing" can occur). The router has been configured by COG to discard all packets coming from or going to the Internet, except those associated with e-mail. COG personnel believe that the router effectively eliminates Internet-based attacks on HGA user accounts because it disallows all remote log-in sessions, even those accompanied by a legitimate password.

The LAN server enforces a similar type of restriction for dial-in access via the public-switched network. The access controls provided by the server's operating system have been configured so that during dial-in sessions, only the e-mail utility can be executed. (HGA policy, enforced by periodic checks, prohibits installation of modems on PCs, so that access must be through the LAN server.) In addition, the server's access controls have been configured so that its WAN interface device is accessible only to programs that possess a special access-control privilege. Only the System Administrator can assign this privilege to server programs, and only a handful of special-purpose applications, like the time and attendance application, have been assigned this privilege.

PROTECTION AGAINST RISKS FROM NON–HGA COMPUTER SYSTEMS

HGA relies on systems and components that it cannot control directly because they are owned by other organizations. HGA has developed a policy to avoid undue risk in such situations. The policy states that system components controlled and operated by organizations other than HGA may not be used to process, store, or transmit HGA information without obtaining explicit permission from the application owner and the COG Manager. Permission to use such system components may not be granted without written commitment from the controlling organization that HGA's information will be safeguarded commensurate with its value, as designated by HGA. This policy is somewhat mitigated by the fact that HGA has developed an issue-specific policy on the use of the Internet, which allows for its use for e-mail with outside organizations and access to other resources (but not for transmission of HGA's proprietary data).

Vulnerabilities Reported by the Risk Assessment Team

The risk assessment team found that many of the risks to which HGA is exposed stem from (1) the failure of individuals to comply with established policies and procedures or (2) the use of automated mechanisms whose assurance is questionable because of the ways they have been developed, tested, implemented, used, or maintained. The team also identified specific vulnerabilities in HGA's policies and procedures for protecting against payroll fraud and errors, interruption of operations, disclosure and brokering of confidential information, and unauthorized access to data by outsiders.

VULNERABILITIES RELATED TO PAYROLL FRAUD

Falsified Time Sheets

The primary safeguards against falsified time sheets are review and approval by supervisory personnel, who are not permitted to approve their own time and attendance data. The risk assessment has concluded that, while imperfect, these safeguards are adequate. The related requirement that a clerk and a supervisor must cooperate closely in creating time and attendance data and submitting the data to the mainframe also safeguards against other kinds of illicit manipulation of time and attendance data by clerks or supervisors acting independently.

Unauthorized Access

When a PC user enters a password to the server during I&A, the password is sent to the server by broadcasting it over the LAN "in the clear." This allows the password to be intercepted easily by any other PC connected to the

LAN. In fact, so-called "password sniffer" programs that capture passwords in this way are widely available. Similarly, a malicious program planted on a PC could also intercept passwords before transmitting them to the server. An unauthorized individual who obtained the captured passwords could then run the time and attendance application in place of a clerk or supervisor. Users might also store passwords in a log-on script file.

Bogus Time and Attendance Applications

The server's access controls are probably adequate for protection against bogus time and attendance applications that run on the server. However, the server's operating system and access controls have only been in widespread use for a few years and contain a number of security-related bugs. Worse, the server's access controls are ineffective if not properly configured, and the administration of the server's security features in the past has been notably lax.

Unauthorized Modification of Time and Attendance Data

Protection against unauthorized modification of time and attendance data requires a variety of safeguards because each system component on which the data are stored or transmitted is a potential source of vulnerabilities.

First, the time and attendance data are entered on the server by a clerk. On occasion, the clerk may begin data entry late in the afternoon, and complete it the following morning, storing it in a temporary file between the two sessions. One way to avoid unauthorized modification is to store the data on a diskette and lock it up overnight. After being entered, the data will be stored in another temporary file until reviewed and approved by a supervisor. These files, now stored on the system, must be protected against tampering. As before, the server's access controls, if reliable and properly configured, can provide such protection (as can digital signatures, as discussed later) in conjunction with proper auditing.

Second, when the Supervisor approves a batch of time and attendance data, the time and attendance application sends the data over the WAN to the mainframe. The WAN is a collection of communications equipment and special-purpose computers called "switches" that act as relays, routing information through the network from source to destination. Each switch is a potential site at which the time and attendance data may be fraudulently modified. For example, an HGA PC user might be able to intercept time and attendance data and modify the data en route to the payroll application on the mainframe. Opportunities include tampering with incomplete time and attendance input files while stored on the server, interception and tampering during WAN transit, or tampering on arrival to the mainframe prior to processing by the payroll application.

Third, on arrival at the mainframe, the time and attendance data are held in a temporary file on the mainframe until the payroll application is run. Consequently, the mainframe's I&A and access controls must provide a critical element of protection against unauthorized modification of the data.

According to the risk assessment, the server's access controls, with prior caveats, probably provide acceptable protection against unauthorized modification of data stored on the server. The assessment concluded that a WAN-based attack involving collusion between an employee of HGA and an employee of the WAN service provider, although unlikely, should not be dismissed entirely, especially since HGA has only cursory information about the service provider's personnel security practices and no contractual authority over how it operates the WAN.

The greatest source of vulnerabilities, however, is the mainframe. Although its operating system's access controls are mature and powerful, it uses password-based I&A. This is of particular concern, because it serves a large number of federal agencies via WAN connections. A number of these agencies are known to have poor security programs. As a result, one such agency's systems could be penetrated (e.g., from the Internet) and then used in attacks on the mainframe via the WAN. In fact, time and attendance data awaiting processing on the mainframe would probably not be as attractive a target to an attacker as other kinds of data or, indeed, disabling the system, rendering it unavailable. For example, an attacker might be able to modify the employee database so that it disbursed paychecks or pensions checks to fictitious employees. Disclosure-sensitive law enforcement databases might also be attractive targets.

The access control on the mainframe is strong and provides good protection against intruders breaking into a second application after they have broken into a first. However, previous audits have shown that the difficulties of system administration may present some opportunities for intruders to defeat access controls.

VULNERABILITIES RELATED TO PAYROLL ERRORS

HGA's management has established procedures for ensuring the timely submission and interagency coordination of paperwork associated with personnel status changes. However, an unacceptably large number of troublesome payroll errors during the past several years have been traced to the late submission of personnel paperwork. The risk assessment documented the adequacy of HGA's safeguards, but criticized the managers for not providing sufficient incentives for compliance.

VULNERABILITIES RELATED TO CONTINUITY OF OPERATIONS

COG Contingency Planning

The risk assessment commended HGA for many aspects of COG's contingency plan, but pointed out that many COG personnel were completely unaware of the responsibilities the plan assigned to them. The assessment also noted that although HGA's policies require annual testing of contingency plans, the capability to resume HGA's computer-processing activities at another cooperating agency has never been verified and may turn out to be illusory.

Division Contingency Planning

The risk assessment reviewed a number of the application-oriented contingency plans developed by HGA's divisions (including plans related to time and attendance). Most of the plans were cursory and attempted to delegate nearly all contingency planning responsibility to COG. The assessment criticized several of these plans for failing to address potential disruptions caused by lack of access to (1) computer resources not managed by COG and (2) nonsystem resources, such as buildings, phones, and other facilities. In particular, the contingency plan encompassing the time and attendance application was criticized for not addressing disruptions caused by WAN and mainframe outages.

Virus Prevention

The risk assessment found HGA's virus-prevention policy and procedures to be sound, but noted that there was little evidence that they were being followed. In particular, no COG personnel interviewed had ever run a virus scanner on a PC on a routine basis, though several had run them during publicized virus scares. The assessment cited this as a significant risk item.

Accidental Corruption and Loss of Data

The risk assessment concluded that HGA's safeguards against accidental corruption and loss of time and attendance data were adequate, but that safeguards for some other kinds of data were not. The assessment included an informal audit of a dozen randomly chosen PCs and PC users in the agency. It concluded that many PC users store significant data on their PCs hard disks, but do not back them up. Based on anecdotes, the assessment's authors stated that there appear to have been many past incidents of loss of information stored on PC hard disks and predicted that such losses would continue.

VULNERABILITIES RELATED TO INFORMATION DISCLOSURE/BROKERAGE

HGA takes a conservative approach toward protecting information about its employees. Since information brokerage is more likely to be a threat to large collections of data, HGA risk assessment focused primarily, but not exclusively, on protecting the mainframe.

The risk assessment concluded that significant, avoidable information brokering vulnerabilities were present—particularly due to HGA's lack of compliance with its own policies and procedures. Time and attendance documents were typically not stored securely after hours, and few PCs containing time and attendance information were routinely locked. Worse yet, few were routinely powered down, and many were left logged into the LAN server overnight. These practices make it easy for an HGA employee wandering the halls after hours to browse or copy time and attendance information on another employee's desk, PC hard disk, or LAN server directories.

The risk assessment pointed out that information sent to or retrieved from the server is subject to eavesdropping by other PCs on the LAN. The LAN hardware transmits information by broadcasting it to all connection points on the LAN cable. Moreover, information sent to or retrieved from the server is transmitted in the clear—that is, without encryption. Given the widespread availability of LAN "sniffer" programs, LAN eavesdropping is trivial for a prospective information broker and, hence, is likely to occur.

Last, the assessment noted that HGA's employee master database is stored on the mainframe, where it might be a target for information brokering by employees of the agency that owns the mainframe. It might also be a target for information brokering, fraudulent modification, or other illicit acts by any outsider who penetrates the mainframe via another host on the WAN.

NETWORK-RELATED VULNERABILITIES

The risk assessment concurred with the general approach taken by HGA, but identified several vulnerabilities. It reiterated previous concerns about the lack of assurance associated with the server's access controls and pointed out that these play a critical role in HGA's approach.

The assessment noted that the e-mail utility allows a user to include a copy of any otherwise accessible file in an outgoing mail message. If an attacker dialed in to the server and succeeded in logging in as an HGA employee, the attacker could use the mail utility to export copies of all the files accessible to that employee. In fact, copies could be mailed to any host on the Internet. The assessment also noted that the WAN service provider may rely on microwave stations or satellites as relay points, thereby exposing HGA's information to eavesdropping. Similarly, any information, including passwords and mail messages, transmitted during a dial-in session is subject to eavesdropping.

Recommendations for Mitigating the Identified Vulnerabilities

The discussions in the following subsections were chosen to illustrate a broad sampling of handbook topics. (Some of the controls, such as auditing and access controls, play an important role in many areas. The limited nature of this example, however, prevents a broader discussion.) Risk management and security program management themes are integral throughout, with particular emphasis given to the selection of risk-driven safeguards.

MITIGATING PAYROLL FRAUD VULNERABILITIES

To remove the vulnerabilities related to payroll fraud, the risk assessment team recommended the use of stronger authentication mechanisms based on smart tokens to generate one-time passwords that cannot be used by an interloper for subsequent sessions. (Note that, for the sake of brevity, the process of evaluating the cost-effectiveness of various security controls is not specifically discussed.) Such mechanisms would make it very difficult for outsiders (e.g., from the Internet) who penetrate systems on the WAN to use them to attack the mainframe. The authors noted, however, that the mainframe serves many different agencies, and HGA has no authority over the way the mainframe is configured and operated. Thus, the costs and procedural difficulties of implementing such controls would be substantial. The assessment team also recommended improving the server's administrative procedures and the speed with which security-related bug fixes distributed by the vendor are installed on the server.

After input from COG security specialists and application owners, HGA's managers accepted most of the risk assessment team's recommendations. They decided that since the residual risks from the falsification of time sheets were acceptably low, no changes in procedures were necessary. However, they judged the risks of payroll fraud due to the interceptability of LAN server passwords to be unacceptably high, and thus directed COG to investigate the costs and procedures associated with using one-time passwords for Time and Attendance Clerks and supervisor sessions on the server.

Other users performing less sensitive tasks on the LAN would continue to use password-based authentication.

While the immaturity of the LAN server's access controls was judged a significant source of risk, COG was only able to identify one other PC LAN product that would be significantly better in this respect. Unfortunately, this product was considerably less friendly to users and application developers, and incompatible with other applications used by HGA. The negative impact of changing PC LAN products was judged too high for the potential incremental gain in security benefits. Consequently, HGA decided to accept the risks accompanying use of the current product, but directed COG to improve its monitoring of the server's access control configuration and its responsiveness to vendor security reports and bug fixes.

HGA concurred that risks of fraud due to unauthorized modification of time and attendance data at or in transit to the mainframe should not be accepted unless no practical solutions could be identified. After discussions with the mainframe's owning agency, HGA concluded that the owning agency was unlikely to adopt the advanced authentication techniques advocated in the risk assessment. COG, however, proposed an alternative approach that did not require a major resource commitment on the part of the mainframe owner.

The alternative approach would employ digital signatures based on public key cryptographic techniques to detect unauthorized modification of time and attendance data. The data would be digitally signed by the supervisor using a private key prior to transmission to the mainframe. When the payroll application program was run on the mainframe, it would use the corresponding public key to validate the correspondence between the time and attendance data and the signature. Any modification of the data during transmission over the WAN or while in temporary storage at the mainframe would result in a mismatch between the signature and the data. If the payroll application detected a mismatch, it would reject the data; HGA personnel would then be notified and asked to review, sign, and send the data again. If the data and signature matched, the payroll application would process the time and attendance data normally.

HGA's decision to use advanced authentication for Time and Attendance Clerks and Supervisors can be combined with digital signatures by using smart tokens. Smart tokens are programmable devices, so they can be loaded with private keys and instructions for computing digital signatures without burdening the user. When supervisors approve a batch of time and attendance data, the time and attendance application on the server would instruct the supervisor to insert their token in the token reader/writer device attached to the supervisors' PC. The application would then send a special "hash" (summary) of the time and attendance data to the token via the PC. The token would generate a digital signature using its embedded secret key, and then transfer the signature back to the server, again via the PC. The time and attendance application running on the server would append the signature to the data before sending the data to the mainframe and, ultimately, the payroll application.

Although this approach did not address the broader problems posed by the mainframe's I&A vulnerabilities, it does provide a reliable means of detecting time and attendance data tampering. In addition, it protects against bogus time and attendance submissions from systems connected to the WAN because individuals who lack a Time and Attendance Supervisor's smart token will be unable to generate valid signatures. (Note, however, that the use of digital signatures does require increased administration, particularly in the area of key management.) In summary, digital signatures mitigate risks from a number of different kinds of threats.

HGA's management concluded that digitally signing time and attendance data was a practical, cost-effective way of mitigating risks, and directed COG to pursue its implementation. (They also noted that it would be useful as the agency moved to use of digital signatures in other applications.) This is an example of developing and providing a solution in an environment over which no single entity has overall authority.

MITIGATING PAYROLL ERROR VULNERABILITIES

After reviewing the risk assessment, HGA's management concluded that the agency's current safeguards against payroll errors and against accidental corruption and loss of time and attendance data were adequate. However, the managers also concurred with the risk assessment's conclusions about the necessity for establishing incentives for complying (and penalties for not complying) with these safeguards. They thus tasked the Director of Personnel to ensure greater compliance with paperwork-handling procedures and to provide quarterly compliance audit reports. They noted that the digital signature mechanism HGA plans to use for fraud protection can also provide protection against payroll errors due to accidental corruption.

MITIGATING VULNERABILITIES RELATED TO THE CONTINUITY OF OPERATIONS

The assessment recommended that COG institute a program of periodic internal training and awareness sessions for COG personnel having contingency plan responsibilities. The assessment urged that COG undertake a rehearsal during the next three months in which selected parts of the plan would be exercised. The rehearsal should include attempting to initiate some aspect of processing activities at one of the designated alternative sites. HGA's management agreed that additional contingency plan training was needed for COG personnel and committed itself to its first plan rehearsal within three months.

After a short investigation, HGA divisions owning applications that depend on the WAN concluded that WAN outages, although inconvenient, would not have a major impact on HGA. This is because the few time-sensitive applications that required WAN-based communication with the mainframe were originally designed to work with magnetic tape instead of the WAN, and could still operate in that mode; hence courier-delivered magnetic tapes could be used as an alternative input medium in case of a WAN outage. The divisions responsible for contingency planning for these applications agreed to incorporate into their contingency plans both descriptions of these procedures and other improvements.

With respect to mainframe outages, HGA determined that it could not easily make arrangements for a suitable alternative site. HGA also obtained and examined a copy of the mainframe facility's own contingency plan. After detailed study, including review by an outside consultant, HGA concluded that the plan had major deficiencies and posed significant risks because of HGA's reliance on it for payroll and other services. This was brought to the attention of the Director of HGA, who, in a formal memorandum to the head of the mainframe's owning agency, called for (1) a high-level interagency review of the plan by all agencies that rely on the mainframe, and (2) corrective action to remedy any deficiencies found.

HGA's management agreed to improve adherence to its virus-prevention procedures. It agreed (from the point of view of the entire agency) that information stored on PC hard disks is frequently lost. It estimated, however, that the labor hours lost as a result would amount to less than a person year—which HGA management does not consider to be unacceptable. After reviewing options for reducing this risk, HGA concluded that it would be cheaper to accept the associated loss than to commit significant resources in an attempt to avoid it. COG volunteered, however, to set up an automated program on the LAN server that e-mails backup reminders to all PC users once each quarter. In addition, COG agreed to provide regular backup services for about 5 percent of HGA's PCs; these will be chosen by HGA's management based on the information stored on their hard disks.

MITIGATING THREATS OF INFORMATION DISCLOSURE/BROKERING

HGA concurred with the risk assessment's conclusions about its exposure to information-brokering risks, and adopted most of the associated recommendations.

The assessment recommended that HGA improve its security awareness training (e.g., via mandatory refresher courses) and that it institute some form of compliance audits. The training should be sure to stress the penalties for noncompliance. It also suggested installing "screen lock" software on PCs that automatically lock a PC after a specified period of idle time in which no keystrokes have been entered; unlocking the screen requires that the user enter a password or reboot the system.

The assessment recommended that HGA modify its information-handling policies so that employees would be required to store some kinds of disclosure-sensitive information only on PC local hard disks (or floppies), but not on the server. This would eliminate or reduce risks of LAN eavesdropping. It was also recommended that an activity log be installed on the server (and regularly reviewed). Moreover, it would avoid unnecessary reliance on the server's access-control features, which are of uncertain assurance. The assessment noted, however, that this strategy conflicts with the desire to store most information on the server's disks so that it is backed up routinely by COG personnel. (This could be offset by assigning responsibility for someone other than the PC owner to make backup copies.) Since the security habits of HGA's PC users have generally been poor, the assessment also recommended use of hard-disk encryption utilities to protect disclosure-sensitive information on unattended PCs from browsing by unauthorized individuals. Also, ways to encrypt information on the server's disks would be studied.

The assessment recommended that HGA conduct a thorough review of the mainframe's safeguards in these respects, and that it regularly review the mainframe audit log, using a query package, with particular attention to records that describe user accesses to HGA's employee master database.

MITIGATING NETWORK-RELATED THREATS

The assessment recommended that HGA:

- Require stronger I&A for dial-in access or, alternatively, that a restricted version of the mail utility be provided for dial-in, which would prevent a user from including files in outgoing mail messages;
- Replace its current modem pool with encrypting modems, and provide each dial-in user with such a modem; and
- Work with the mainframe agency to install a similar encryption capability for server-to-mainframe communications over the WAN

As with previous risk assessment recommendations, HGA's management tasked COG to analyze the costs, benefits, and impacts of addressing the vulnerabilities identified in the risk assessment. HGA eventually adopted some of the risk assessment's recommendations, while declining others. In addition, HGA decided that its policy on handling time and attendance information needed to be clarified, strengthened, and elaborated, with the belief that implementing such a policy would help reduce risks of Internet and dial-in eavesdropping. Thus, HGA developed and issued a revised policy, stating that users are individually responsible for ensuring that they do not transmit disclosure-sensitive information outside of HGA's facilities via e-mail or other means. It also prohibited them from examining or transmitting e-mail containing such information during dial-in sessions and developed and promulgated penalties for noncompliance.

Summary

This case has illustrated how many of the concepts described in previous chapters might be applied in a federal agency. An integrated example concerning a Hypothetical Government Agency (HGA) has been discussed and used as the basis for examining a number of these concepts. HGA's distributed system architecture and its uses were described. The time and attendance application was considered in some detail.

For context, some national and agency-level policies were referenced. Detailed operational policies and procedures for computer systems were discussed and related to these high-level policies. HGA assets and threats were identified, and a detailed survey of selected safeguards, vulnerabilities, and risk mitigation actions were presented. The safeguards included a wide variety of procedural and automated techniques, and were used to illustrate issues of assurance, compliance, security program oversight, and interagency coordination.

As illustrated, effective computer security requires clear direction from upper management. Upper management must assign security responsibilities to organizational elements and individuals and must formulate or elaborate the security policies that become the foundation for the organization's security program. These policies must be based on an understanding of the organization's mission priorities and the assets and business operations necessary to fulfill them. They must also be based on a pragmatic assessment of the threats against these assets and operations. A critical element is assessment of threat likelihoods. These are most accurate when derived from historical data, but must also anticipate trends stimulated by emerging technologies.

A good security program relies on an integrated, cost-effective collection of physical, procedural, and automated controls. Cost-effectiveness requires targeting these controls at the threats that pose the highest risks while accepting other residual risks. The difficulty of applying controls properly and in a consistent manner over time has been the downfall of many security programs. This case has provided numerous examples in which major security vulnerabilities arose from a lack of assurance or compliance. Hence, periodic compliance audits, examinations of the effectiveness of controls, and reassessments of threats are essential to the success of any organization's security program.

[*The preceding case was extracted in its entirety from* NIST Special Publication 800-12: The NIST Computer Security Handbook *available from* http:// csrc.nist. gov/publications/nistpubs/800-12/handbook.pdf].

CASE C

Random Widget Works

Overview

This case is drawn from Management of Information Security, *a Course Technology textbook (Copyright ©2004, ISBN 0-619-21515-1). This version of the case has been lightly edited and had a few things added.*

Introduction

Mission Statement:

Random Widget Works designs and manufactures quality widgets and associated equipment and supplies for use in modern business environments.

Vision Statement:

Random Widget Works will be the preferred manufacturer of choice for every business's widget equipment needs, with an RWW widget in every machine they use.

Value Statement:

RWW values commitment, honesty, integrity, and social responsibility among its employees, and is committed to providing its services in harmony with its corporate, social, legal, and natural environments.

Random Widget Works was established in 1995, and has grown to be the Southeast's largest manufacturer of widgets, gizmos, and gadgets. The organization, based in Atlanta, Georgia, employs over 350 employees.

Organization or RWW

The organization chart is presented in Figure C-1. Random's CEO, Alex Truman, pioneered the field of widget development, creating a new manufacturing process. RWW's CIO, Mike Edwards, has been with RWW since its formulation. Mike has recently decided to upgrade RWW's information technology security function, creating a separate Chief Information Security

Officer. His first choice for the position was Iris Majwabu, based in no small part on the recommendation of Charlie Moody, a colleague of his from Sequential Label and Supply.

Beginnings

One month into her new job at Random Widget Works, Inc. (RWW), Iris Majwabu left her office early one afternoon to attend a meeting of the Information Systems Security Association (ISSA). The new job was a promotion from her previous position as an information security risk manager.

Although she had paid her organization dues for almost a year, this occasion marked Iris's first ISSA meeting. With a mountain of pressing matters on her cluttered desk, Iris didn't know why she was making this meeting a priority. She sighed. As the first Chief Information Security Officer (CISO) of RWW, she already spent many hours in business meetings, followed by long hours at her desk as she pressed on in defining her new position at the firm.

In the ISSA meeting room she saw Charlie Moody, her supervisor at her previous job at Sequential Label and Supply. Charlie had been promoted to CIO almost a year ago.

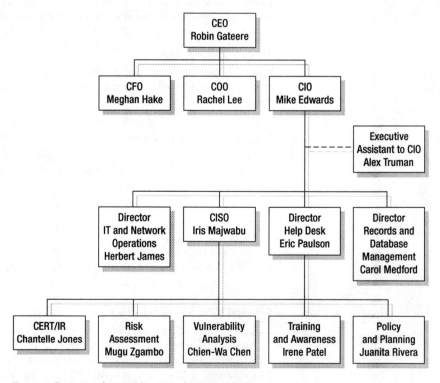

FIGURE C-1 Random Widget Works organization chart

"Hi, Charlie," she said.

"Hello, Iris." They shook hands warmly. "How are things at the new office?"

"So far," she replied, "things are going well—I think."

Charlie noticed her hesitancy. "You think?" he said. "Okay, tell me what's really going on."

Iris explained. "I am struggling to get a consensus from the management team about the problems that we have. I'm told that information security is a priority, but everything is in disarray. Any ideas that are brought up, especially my ideas, are chopped to bits before they're even formally proposed. There's no established policy covering our information security needs, and it seems that we have little hope of getting one approved. The information security budget covers my salary plus funding for one technician in the network department. The IT managers act like I'm a waste of their budget, and they do not seem to take security issues as seriously as I do. It's like trying to drive a herd of cats!"

"It sounds like we need to talk," Charlie said. "But not now; the meeting is about to start. Here's my card—call me tomorrow and we'll arrange to get together for coffee."

Charlie and Iris made an appointment to meet for a working lunch the next week. Charlie sat down the day before the meeting to jot down his thoughts about good advice for Iris.

---

1. What would you recommend if you were Charlie?
2. Among the things listed in your advice to Iris, which one thing is the most important? Which one thing should she try to accomplish first? Are they the same thing?

Planning

Iris was a little uneasy. While this wasn't her first meeting with Mike Edwards, the Chief Information Officer, it was her first planning meeting. Around the table, the other IT department heads were casually chatting, drinking their coffee. Iris stared at her notepad, where she had carefully written "Strategic Planning Meeting" and nothing else.

Mike entered the room followed by his assistants. Alex, his lead executive assistant, was loaded down with stacks of copied documents, which he and the other assistants began handing out around the table. Iris took her copy and scanned the title: Random Widget Works, Inc., Strategic Planning Document, Information Technology Division, FY 2006–2010.

Mike began, "As you know, it's annual planning time again. You just got your copies of the multiyear IT strategic plan. Last month you each received your numbered copy of the company strategic plan." Iris remembered the half-inch–thick document she had carefully read and then filed.

Mike continued, "I'm going to go through the IT vision and mission statements, and then review the details of how the IT plan will allow us to meet the objectives articulated in the strategic plan. In 30 days you'll submit your draft plans back to me for review. Don't hesitate to come by to discuss any issues or questions."

Later that day, Iris dropped by Mike's office to discuss her planning responsibilities. This duty was not something he had briefed her about yet. Mike apologized, "I'm sorry, Iris. I meant to spend some time outlining your role as security manager. I'm afraid I can't do it this week; maybe we can start next week, by reviewing some key points I want you to make sure are in your plan."

The next day Iris and Charlie Moody had planned lunch. After they ordered, Iris said, "We just started on our strategic planning project and I'm developing a security strategic plan. You know, I've never worked up one of these from scratch before. Got any good advice on what to look for?"

Charlie responded, "Sure. Coincidentally, when we're finished eating, I have something for you in my car that might help."

After they finished lunch, the pair went out to the parking lot. Inside Charlie's trunk were two cardboard boxes, marked "BOOKS." He opened one and rummaged around for a few seconds. "Here," he said, handing her a textbook.

Iris read the title out loud. *"Strategic Planning."*

"This one is from a planning seminar I did a while back. I have a later edition, but there really isn't much difference between the two. I was cleaning out some of my redundant books. I was going to donate these to the library book sale. It's yours if you want it. It might help out with your planning project."

Charlie slammed the trunk shut and then said, "Read over the first few chapters—that'll give you the basics. Then sit down with your planning documents from corporate management and from IT. For each goal of the CEO and CIO you can identify, think about what your department needs to do to meet it. Then write up how you think the company as whole and your team in particular could satisfy that objective. Once you've listed the objectives and a way to meet them, you can go back and describe the resources you'll need to make it happen." Iris said, "That's it?"

Charlie shook his head. "There's more to it than that, but this exercise will get you started. Once you reach that point, I can share some of what I know about how to frame your plans and format them for use in the planning process."

During the Random Widget's CIO strategic planning meeting...

CIO Mike Edwards discussed and expanded upon the details of how the Information Technology division would enable RWW to achieve each of its strategic goals. As he was finishing his review of the document, Mike made a crucial point: "Make sure you don't let this planning document get out. These documents are not to leave the building."

Iris asked, "Shouldn't they be labeled 'Confidential' then?"

"What do you mean, Iris?" Mike asked.

Iris replied, "I've been working on a data classification scheme for RWW along with the systems administrators. We have a draft that uses three data classification levels for the company. Every piece of information in the company is categorized as 'Confidential,' 'Sensitive,' or 'Public.' This document should be clearly labeled 'Confidential' to prevent it from being released by mistake."

After a moment's thought Mike exclaimed, "Excellent! Please send copies of the draft data classification scheme to all department heads immediately." He turned to Stan, his assistant, and said, "Please have new covers that label this plan as 'Confidential' prepared by noon today, and have one of your people replace each cover with the revised, properly marked cover before the end of business today."

---

1. Create definitions of "Confidential," "Sensitive," and "Public" for RWW. Create a list of examples of documents that should be labeled with each classification.
2. Design a labeling scheme (cover sheet, stamp, or other scheme) to associate with this classification system.

Incident Response I

A week after the strategic planning meeting, Iris was just finishing a draft of the information security strategic plan. Satisfied with her progress thus far, she activated the calendar on her desktop computer and began reviewing her schedule, hoping to find a good day and time to meet with Mike about contingency planning. During their last luncheon, her friend Charlie had warned her not to let too much time pass before addressing the issue again. She knew he was right. It simply wasn't a good idea to put off discussing such an important project until the end of the month, as Mike had suggested during last week's strategic planning meeting. Having a plan in place in case of an emergency just made good business sense, even if planning for the unexpected was not perceived as a high priority by many of her management peers.

Suddenly, the building's fire alarm went off. Heart pumping, Iris left her office. With or without a contingency plan, it was her responsibility to assess this situation as quickly and as safely as possible. Was there an incident? A disaster? Or was it simply a false alarm? As she quickly moved down the line of cubicles, Iris called for everyone who had not yet left the floor to leave by way of the nearest exit. Then she rushed to the floor's fire control panel, which was located in the elevator lobby. A blinking light showed that one heat-sensitive sprinkler head had been activated. Iris waited a moment to see whether any other blinking lights came on. None did, but the existing light stayed on. It seemed that she was dealing with an incident, and not a disaster.

She headed down the hall to the place shown on the fire panel where the sprinkler had been triggered. Hearing voices coming from the break station, Iris turned the corner, and saw Harry and Joel from the Accounting department. Their offices were located right next to the break station. Harry was inspecting what had once been the coffee pot, while Joel held a fire extinguisher. Both were wet and irritated. The room smelled of scorched coffee and was filled with smoke. To her relief, there was no more fire.

"Is everyone all right?" she asked.

"Yeah," Harry replied, "but our offices are a mess. There's water everywhere."

Joel shook his head in disgust. "What a time for this to happen. We were just getting ready to finish the quarterly reports, too."

"Never mind that. As long as you're both okay. You guys need to make a trip home so you can get changed . . ."

Iris was interrupted by Mike Edwards, who had just joined them. "What happened?" he asked.

Iris shrugged. "It's a minor incident, Mike, everything's under control. The fire department will be here any minute. . ."

"Incident? Incident?" Joel said in dismay as he pointed at his desk, where steam rose from his soaked CPU, and a pile of drenched reports littered the floor. "This isn't an incident. *This* is a disaster!"

Iris tried not to smile. She explained, "Of course, it isn't technically a disaster, but I understand what you mean. How much information is lost?"

Joel looked at her in dismay. "Lost? All of it! We had just saved the report and sent it to the department print server!"

Iris asked, "Where did you save it—to your local drive or to the department share?"

Joel tried to remember. "I think it was to the G: drive. Why?"

"Well, the G: drive is on a machine at the end of the hall, which doesn't have a water-based fire suppression system. It's probably fine. And if you did save it to your local drive, there's about an 80% chance we can get it anyway. I doubt the water damaged the hard drive itself." Iris continued, "We were lucky this time. If the fire had spread to the next room, the paper file storage could have been destroyed."

---

1. Extrapolate on the case. At what point could this incident have been declared a disaster? What would Iris have done differently if it had?
2. Identify the procedures that Joel could have taken to minimize the potential loss in this incident. What would he need to do differently in the event of a disaster, if anything?

Human Resources I

Iris was returning from lunch when she ran into Susan Weinstein, one of RWW's best account executives, who was accompanied by a man whom Iris did not know. Susan introduced him as Bob Watson, a prospective client. As they were chatting, Iris noticed Bob's distracted demeanor and Susan's forced smile and unusually stiff manner.

"We didn't get the account," Iris realized.

A few minutes later, she saw why the meeting between RWW's account executive and new client did not go well. In the cubicle across the hall from Susan's office, two programmers were having lunch. Tim had his feet propped up on the desk. In one hand was a half-eaten hamburger; in the other, he held several playing cards. John had made himself comfortable by taking off his shoes. Next to his elbow was an open container of coffee, which he had placed in the open tray of the PC's CD-ROM driver. On the desk between the two employees was a small pile of coins.

Iris went into her office and pulled the company's policy manual off the shelf. She had already become familiar with RWW's policies, but for the next steps she had in mind, she needed specifics. As she read the sections on workplace behavior, however, Iris found that the policy manual didn't seem to cover Tim's and John's behavior. She did not find policies about alerting employees to meetings with prospective clients, eating and drinking in the workplace, or specifics about practices that supported data protection and other information security necessities.

Before Iris left for home that evening, she typed up her notes and scheduled an early meeting for the morning with her boss, Mike Edwards. Iris had some concrete concerns about the behavior of the staff and the omissions from the policy manual. As she left for home, she thought, "I think seeing Tim and John playing cards and lunching in may have cost us a new account." Her thoughts continued, "Our Company is growing, and things are getting more complicated than they were just a few months ago. I'll suggest to Mike that it's time for us to set up a policy review committee."

Prior to the first meeting of the RWW Enterprise Policy Review Committee, Mike and Iris met in Mike's office to formulate a common IT and information security approach to the coming policy review cycle. Here is part of that conversation:

Mike motioned for Iris to sit down, and then said, "You've convinced me that IT and InfoSec policy are tightly integrated, and that InfoSec policy is critical to the enterprise. I would like you to join me as a member of the Enterprise Policy Review Committee. Okay?"

Iris, who knew how important policy was to her program's success, replied, "Sure. No problem."

Mike continued. "Good. We'll work together to make sure the Enterprise Information Security Policy you've drafted gets equal status with the other top-level enterprise policies and that the second-tier issue and third-tier system policies are also referenced in all other top-level policies, especially those of the HR department."

Iris nodded. Mike went on, "I want you to take the current HR policy document binder and make a 'wish list' of changes you need to be sure we get the right references in place. Let me see your HR policy change plan by the end of the week."

---

1. If the enterprise policy committee is not open to the approach that Mike and Iris want to use for structuring information security policies into three tiers, how should they proceed?
2. Should the CISO (Iris) be assessing HR policies? Why or why not?

Privacy

Iris was looking over the freshly printed first issue of RWW's information security newsletter when Mike Edwards walked into her office.

"What's new, Iris?" he asked.

"See for yourself!" she replied with a grin, as she handed him her latest completed project.

"Very nice," he commented. "How close are you to publication?"

"We've just put it on the intranet, and we're going to run off a few dozen hard copies for our office. That's your copy."

"Thanks!" he said while he scanned the cover article. "What is this privacy situation all about?"

Mike was referring to the recent state law that mandated very specific definitions and penalties for computer-related crimes such as computer trespassing and theft of computer information. What had caught his attention was the clause providing penalties for the disclosure of some types of personal data such as Social Security numbers and account passwords. The penalties ranged from $500 to $5000 per incident, and even up to a year in jail.

Mike whistled and said, "We need to talk about this issue at the senior staff meeting. We should get the other departments involved to make sure we don't have any problems in complying with this law."

Iris nodded and said, "Maybe someone from corporate legal should be there, too."

"Good idea."

Then Mike asked about the newsletter's listing of information security training sessions. "Where did you get the training staff?" he asked.

"I've been meaning to talk to you about that," Iris said. "I'll teach the classes until my security manager, Tom, can take over. But we should ask the corporate training office about getting some of their staff up to speed on our topics."

"Sounds good. I'll get with Jerry tomorrow after the staff meeting," Mike replied. Mike Edwards thanked the attorney from the corporate legal office for his presentation on the newly enacted state computer crime and privacy law, and then asked, "How should we comply and when does it take effect?" The attorney gave a full analysis of RWW's responsibilities.

Mike turned to his staff of department managers and said, "It's important that we comply with the new law. First, however, we need to determine how much it will cost us to comply with the password privacy area. I need from each of you a budget impact analysis that encompasses the effort needed to meet this new requirement."

---

1. What elements will each department manager have to consider to complete Mike's assignment?
2. How will a privacy law affect an organization like RWW? What other laws also affect privacy in the workplace?

Management Models

Iris looked at the mound of documents on her desk. Each one was neatly labeled with its own acronym and number, NIST, ISO, Special Publication, and RFC. Her head was beginning to swim. She had not imagined that it would be quite so difficult to choose a security management model for her review of RWW's ongoing security program. She wanted an independent framework that would allow her to perform a thorough analysis of RWW's program.

Iris was almost finished skimming the stack when she found what she was looking for: a document that contained a self-assessment checklist with page after page of specific items important in the management of information security. She perused the list carefully. Using her Internet connection, Iris downloaded the full document, inserted a few minor changes, made copies for the managers who worked for her, and then scheduled a meeting.

At the meeting, Tom, the Manager of Risk Assessment and Policy, commented, "Gee, Iris, when did you have time to design this checklist?" Iris replied, "I didn't. I was lucky enough to find the perfect one for us. I changed just a few things to make it specific enough for our needs." She quickly outlined her plan. Using the checklist, each manager would indicate the progress that RWW had made in that area—specifically, whether policy had been created and, if so, whether it had been integrated into the company culture. Iris explained how to use the forms and noted when she expected the assessment to be complete.

"What happens once we're done?" one manager asked.

"That's when the real work begins," Iris said. "We'll establish priorities for improving the areas that need improvement, and sustaining the areas that are satisfactory. Then we'll determine whether we have the resources needed to accomplish that work; if not, I'll go to the CIO and request more resources."

Iris sighed as she completed her initial review of her staff's checklist results. She pulled out a notepad and began outlining the projects she foresaw, based on the shortcomings identified via the checklists. She was fortunate to have found a useful model for an information security review of her program.

---

1. Based on your understanding of the case, from which model did Iris draw her checklist?
2. Referring to the section in this case regarding best practices, what do you think Iris should do next?

Risk Management I

Iris Majwabu and Mike Edwards sat side by side on the short flight to the nearby city where the RWW Board of Directors audit committee was meeting that afternoon. The two had been invited to present RWW's IT risk management program to the committee. The board's concerns stemmed from a recent briefing by the National Association of Corporate Directors, which focused on trends affecting the potential liability of board members in the area of information security in general and risk management in particular.

After the plane leveled off, Mike pulled out his copy of the presentation he planned to give that afternoon. He and Iris had been working on it for at least two weeks, and each knew the slides by heart. Iris was along to assist with the question-and-answer period that would follow Mike's presentation.

"They're not going to be happy campers when you're done," said Iris.

"Nope. They are likely to be a little unhappy. The CEO is worried about how they'll respond, and about what might come up at the full board meeting next month," Mike said. "I'm afraid the disconnection between IT and Internal Audit in this briefing may have some unexpected consequences."

Iris considered Mike's comment and what she knew about the weaknesses of the Internal Audit department's approach to the company's non-IT assets. Where Mike and Iris had built a sound, information-based approach to estimating and controlling IT risk, some of the other company divisions used less empirical methods.

"I think we should come out of this okay," Iris told Mike. "After all, the main concern of the audit committee members is the newfound perception of their liability for IT security and the effects it has on the issues of privacy. We have a solid risk management plan in place that's working well, in my opinion."

Mike looked up from his notes and said, "It's not us I'm worried about. I'm afraid we may create some discomfort and unwanted attention for our peers after the board sees the wide variety of risk management approaches used in other divisions."

Later, Mike and Iris were flying home from the meeting. The reaction of the audit committee members had not been as they had discussed on the way to the meeting.

"I'm glad they understood the situation," Mike said to Iris. "I'd like you to start revising our risk management documentation to make it a little more general. It sounds like the board will want to take our approach company-wide soon."

Iris nodded and pulled out her notepad to make herself a to-do-list.

---

1. What will Iris have on her to-do-list?
2. What resources can Iris call upon to assist her?

Risk Management II

Iris opened the door to the manager's lounge and walked up to the counter to pick up a soda. Leaving the lounge, she saw Jane Harris—accounting supervisor of RWW—at a table, poring over a spreadsheet that Iris recognized.

"Hi, Jane," she said. "Can I join you?"

"Sure, Iris," she said. "Perhaps you can help me with this form Mike wants us to fill out."

Jane was working on the asset valuation worksheet that Iris had sent to all of the company managers. The worksheet contained a list of all of the information assets in Jane's department. Mike had asked each manager to provide four values for each item: its cost, its replacement value, its criticality to the company's mission, and a rank order, with the most important item being ranked number one. Mike hoped that Iris and the rest of the risk management team could use the data to build a consensus about the relative importance of various assets to the company.

"What's the problem?" Iris asked.

"I understand these first two columns. But how am I supposed to decide what's the most important?"

"Well," Iris began, "with your accounting background, you could base your answers on some of the data you collect about each of these information assets. For this quarter, what's more important to senior management—revenue or profitability?"

"Profitability is almost always more important," Jane replied. "We have some systems that have lots of revenue, but operate at a loss."

"Well, there you go," Iris said. "Why not calculate the profitability margin for each listed item and use that to rate and rank them?"

"Oh, okay, Iris. Thanks for the idea." Jane started to make notes on her copy of the form. Mike and Iris were meeting to review the asset valuation worksheets that had been collected from all over the company. After a few minutes of review, Mike said, "Iris, the problem as I see it is that no two managers used the same criteria to assess the asset values or rank the priority of their asset lists."

Iris nodded and said, "I agree. Some of the worksheets have only one of the four asset valuations filled in. This is going to be very difficult to merge into a single, uniform list of information assets. We're going to have to visit each manager and figure out what basis was used and how the assets were ranked."

---

1. If you could have spoken to Mike Edwards before he distributed the asset valuation worksheets, what advice would you have given him to make the consolidation process easier?
2. How would you advise Mike and Iris to proceed with the worksheets they already have in hand?

Incident Response II

One night toward the end of his shift, a technician at RWW, Inc., received a call from his wife; one of his children was ill, and she wanted the technician to pick up some medicine on his way home from work. He decided to leave a few minutes early.

Like all watch-standing employees in the operations center, he had a procedures manual, which was organized sequentially. He used the checklists for everyday purposes, and had an index to look up anything else he needed. Only one unchecked box remained on the checklist when he snapped the binder closed and hurriedly secured his workstation.

Since he was the second-shift operator and RWW did not have a third shift in its data center, the technician carefully reviewed the shutdown checklist next to the door, making sure all the room's environmental, safety, and security systems were set correctly. He activated the burglar alarm, exited the room and the building, and was soon on his way to the drugstore.

At about the same time, a seventh-grader in San Diego was up late, sitting at her computer. Her parents assumed that she was listening to 311 tunes while "chatting" with school friends online. In fact, she had become bored with chatting and had discovered some new friends on the Internet—friends who shared her interest in programming and Perl script writing. One of these new friends had sent the girl a link to a new warez (illegally copied software) site.

From this site the seventh-grader downloaded a kit called Blendo, which helped hackers create attack programs that combined a mass e-mailer with a worm, a macro virus, and a network scanner. She clicked her way through the configuration options, clicked a button labeled "custom scripts," and then pasted in a script that one of her new friends had e-mailed to her. This script was built to exploit a brand-new vulnerability (announced only a few hours before). Although she didn't know it, the anonymous middle-schooler had created new malware that was soon to bring the Internet to a standstill. She exported the attack script, attached it to an e-mail, and sent it out to an anonymous remailer service to be forwarded to as many e-mail accounts as possible. She had naively set up a mailback option to an anonymous e-mail account so she could track the progress of her creation.

Thirty minutes later, she checked that anonymous e-mail account. She had more than 8000 new messages, and her mailbox was full.

Back at RWW, the e-mail gateway was hard at work sorting and forwarding all of the incoming e-mail. The account sales@rww.biz always received a lot of traffic, as did service@rww.biz. Tonight was no exception. Unfortunately for RWW, and for the second-shift operator who had failed to install the patch download that fixed the new vulnerability announced by the vendor, the seventh-grader's attack code tricked the RWW mail server into running the program. The RWW mail server, with its high-performance server and high-bandwidth Internet connection, began to do three things at once: It sent an infected e-mail to everyone with whom RWW had ever traded e-mail, it infected every RWW server that the e-mail server could reach, and it started deleting files, randomly, from every folder on each infected server.

Within seconds, the network intrusion detection system had determined that something was afoot. By then, it was too late to stop the infection, but the system sent a message to Iris's PDA anyway.

Iris's PDA beeped. Frowning, she glanced at the screen, expecting to see another junk e-mail. "We've really got to do something about the spam!" she muttered to herself. She scanned the header of the message. "Uh-oh!" She looked at her watch, grabbed her cell phone, and while looking at her incident response pocket card, dialed the home number of the on-call systems administrator. When he answered, she asked "Seen the alert yet? What's up?"

"Wish I knew—some sort of virus," he replied. "A user must have opened an infected attachment."

Iris made a mental note to remind the awareness program manager to restart the refresher training program for virus control. Her users should know better, but some new employees had not been trained yet.

"Why didn't the firewall catch it?" Iris asked.

"It must be a new one," he replied. "It slipped by the pattern filters."

"What are we doing now?" Iris was growing more nervous by the minute.

"I'm ready to cut our Internet connection remotely, then drive down to the office and start our planned recovery operations—shut down infected systems, clean up any infected servers, recover data from tape backups, and notify our peers that they may receive this virus from us in our e-mail. I just need your go-ahead." The admin sounded uneasy. This was not a trivial operation, and he was facing a long night of intense work.

"Do it. I'll activate the incident response plan and start working the notification call list to get some extra hands in to help." Iris knew this situation would be the main topic at the weekly CIO's meeting. She just hoped her colleagues would be able to restore the systems to safe operation quickly. She looked at her watch: 12:35 A.M.

---

1. What can be done to minimize the risk of the situation recurring? Can these types of situations be completely avoided?
2. If you were in Iris's position, how would you approach your interaction with the second-shift operator?
3. How should RWW go about notifying its peers? What other procedures should Iris have the technician perform?
4. When would be the appropriate time to begin the forensic data collection process to analyze the root cause of this incident? Why?

Human Resources II

Mike Edwards stuck his head into Iris's office and said, "Iris, are you free for the next hour or so?"

Iris glanced at her calendar and said, "Sure. What's up?"

Mike was standing in the hall with Erik Paulson, the manager of RWW's help desk. Both men looked grave. Mike said. "Can you bring the human resources policy manual with you?" Without asking any further questions, Iris pulled the manual from her bookshelf and joined the pair. As they walked down the hall, Mike filled her in on the brewing situation.

In the meeting room that adjoined the CEO's office, three people were already seated. Mike and Paul took seats at the table, and Iris took a chair along the wall. Robin Gateere, RWW's CEO, cleared her throat and said, "Okay. Let's get started."

Jerry Martin from Legal was facilitating the meeting. The other person in the room was Gloria Simpson, Senior Vice President of Human Resources. Mike had asked Iris to join this upper-level management meeting because of her familiarity with human resources policy regarding information security.

Jerry began, "Recent events have caused us to revisit our hiring policies. Last week, one of our employees was arrested, and our company name was plastered all over the newspapers and on television. It turns out that the employee was on parole for sexual assault. He was hired into our IT department to work at the help desk. The police have since discovered that he is running a Web-based pornography site. His parole was revoked, and he's now in the state prison. The questions are, how did he come to be an employee of this company in the first place, and what do we do now?"

Robin said, "As to the second question, we terminated his employment for cause since he did not report to work because he is in jail. As to the first question, . . ." She looked pointedly at Erik and said, "What do you know?"

Erik looked uneasy. He said, "This is the first time I became aware that Sam had trouble with the law. As a matter of fact, I was the hiring manger who recruited him, and all of this is news to me. Of course, we followed the usual human resources procedures when we hired him, although I have always wondered why hiring managers don't get to see the whole personnel file for new hires."

Gloria spoke up. "I agree that practice seems odd in light of this case. According to his file, Sam did write about his conviction and parole status on his application. In fact, we did an identity check and received a criminal background report that confirmed the conviction and his parole status. He didn't lie on his application, but it's beyond me how Erik was ever cleared to make him a job offer."

Erik lifted the folder he was holding. "Here's the whole manager's file on Sam. The standard clearance to extend an offer is right here." He slid it down the table to Gloria, who looked at the approval signature on the form.

Iris realized several things: Some of the byzantine practices in human resources were about to change, somebody in human resources was in a lot of trouble, and it was time for her to revisit all of the company's personnel information security policies.

Iris reviewed the scant stack of applications for the newly created security manager position and frowned. There should have been many more than just three applicants for the position.

After the human resources incident earlier in the month, she had been extremely careful in crafting the job description, and was elated when Mike Edwards approved the hire. The new security manager was to assist in the drafting of security policies and plans, a need that had been highlighted by the recent problem.

Iris called Cheryl in Human Resources. "I'm worried about the number of applicants we've had," she said. "I really thought there would be more than three given the way the economy's slowed down."

Cheryl replied, "Oh, there were dozens, but I prescreened them for you."

"What do you mean?" Iris asked. "Prescreened how?"

Cheryl elaborated. "Well, we pass on only the most qualified applicants. According to our criteria, applicants for information security positions must have a CISA certification or some level of GIAD."

"You mean GIAC?" Iris asked, her uneasiness building.

"No, the file says GIAD," Cheryl replied confidently.

"Well, for this position we need a CISSP or CISM, not a GIAD or CISA. Those certifications don't match the job description I wrote, and I don't remember specifying any required certifications."

"You don't have to," Cheryl said. "We've determined that the best people for the jobs are the ones who have the most certifications. We don't really look at anyone who isn't certified. Is there a problem?"

---

1. If you were Iris, how would reply to Cheryl's question?
2. What, if anything, is wrong with the human resources focus depicted here? Examine the relationship between certifications and experience. Do certifications alone identify the job candidates with the most appropriate expertise and work experience?

Incident Response III

Iris was just over halfway through her morning e-mail ritual when she came to a message that used the standard subject line of the anonymous ethics mailbox. Just a few weeks ago RWW had set up a new Web server that allowed anyone, anywhere, to send anonymous e-mail to the company's most senior executive. The message had in fact been sent by the CEO's executive assistant. It read as follows:

```
To: Iris Majwabu
From: RWW Anonymous Ethics Mailbox
Date: 2005-11-18 07:45 AM
Subject: FW: Anonymous Ethics Report-2005-11-17
02:46 AM
Iris, you better look at this. I pulled the text out
and encrypted it. I am briefing a special executive
meeting with Robin, Jerry, and Mike at 10:00. You
should be there too. Meeting invitation follows...
— Cassandra
```

Iris opened her safe and mounted her secure document drive, then exported the file to it. She opened the decryption program, fumbling with her badge carrier to read the randomized key from her security token. The text of the anonymous e-mail appeared on her screen:

```
To: RWW Anonymous Ethics Mailbox
From: A Friend
Date: 2005-11-17 02:46 AM
Subject: Anonymous Ethics Report-2005-11-17 02:46 AM
You might want to look at the nile.com auction site at
www.nile.com/auctions/ref=19085769340
Iris opened her browser window and typed in the URL.
She saw:
Item #19085769340
RWW, Inc. Customer and key accounts list
Starting bid: US $10,000.00
Time left: 2 days 22 hours 50 mins 3-day listing
History: 0 bids
Location: Cityville WI
```

Iris reached for her incident response plan binder. She knew it was going to be a busy morning and a busy afternoon, too.

Iris was a little unsure of what to do next. She had just left the meeting with the other executives of RWW, Inc. At that meeting they confirmed the need for action on the matter of the critical information offered for sale on a public auction site. That was the last point of agreement. This was a risk they had simply not planned for and they were completely unprepared.

Just before the meeting broke up, they had made assignments to various people in the meeting. Robin, the CEO, was going to contact the members of the Board of Directors to brief them, so that if the story became public they would not be surprised. Jerry, the corporate counsel, was going to start an intensive effort to discover what peer companies had done in situations like this. Mike, the CIO, was assigned to contact the auction site to get the auction shut down and lay the groundwork for working with whatever authorities were brought in for the criminal aspects of the case.

Iris was assigned to investigate which law enforcement agency should be involved in the investigation. She reached for her business card box and began thumbing through the contacts she had.

---

1. With which agency do you think she should start? On what factors do you base that recommendation?
2. What criminal acts do you think are involved in this? What do you think the relationship of the perpetrator to RWW, Inc. might be?

Project Management

"Come in," said Iris to Maria Rodriguez, one of the technicians in the Information Security department. "Have a seat, please." As Iris closed her office door, Maria settled at the small table by the window.

Iris began. "Maria, we've been working together since I joined RWW. I've been very happy with your work as the team lead for the network vulnerability assessment team. You and the others have done a good job finding holes and fixing them across the company. I know how much collaboration and teamwork goes into that process. Now I'm ready to offer you another opportunity in a different part of the security group. Are you ready for some new challenges?"

"Yes!" said Maria.

"Good." Iris continued. "I think it would be good for you to start training Marion on the vulnerability team to be the team leader while we get you started as project manager for the deployment of our upgraded intrusion-detection system."

Maria said, "I don't have any experience with project management, but I'm willing to learn." Iris nodded. "Maria, you have a great track record as a developer and a systems administrator here at RWW. You've got the right attitude for this job, and I'm here to make sure you get the right skills. I would like you to take the next week to work out the transition of your team lead role, and then you'll spend a week at a project management class that I asked the RWW Training Department to arrange for you. I've already ordered you a license for Microsoft Project, which is the software that you'll need for the class."

Maria thought about it for just a second, and then said, "I'm ready."

Later that day, Iris met with Charlie for their usual coffee chat. Charlie looked up from his coffee as Iris sat down across from him. "How's it going?" he asked.

"I don't know how much longer I'll be able to squeeze time in for these coffee meetings," she replied, looking exhausted.

"Why's that?" Charlie asked.

"It seems I spend all my time in meetings, and when I'm not in a meeting I'm explaining some aspect of the job to one of my security managers."

"Really?" Charlie asked, concealing a smile.

"Really!" Iris replied. "Just today I spent half an hour with Maria going over the basics of project management, much of which I had to dredge up from my old college textbook. I mean, I know how to manage a project, but I don't remember all of the technical components."

"A project management text? What in the world are you doing that requires a project management text?" Charlie asked.

"I've assigned Maria to head the deployment of our new IDS. I felt it was a perfect opportunity for her to show me what she can do, and complete some of her background education at the same time."

"So you're the master now, Grasshopper?" Charlie laughed.

Iris looked confused for a second, and then began to laugh. "Yes, sensei . . . and my Kung Fu is strong."

For the next hour Iris explained how she integrated project management techniques into the development and implementation of key security components. Before long Charlie pulled out a yellow pad and began scribbling notes. Iris was proud that she had mastered the lessons offered by her former boss and was now able to teach him something in return.

---

1. What other components of information security could Iris have used project management techniques to control?
2. How could Charlie have made it as far as he has in the IT and information security industry without any formal project management education?

Sequential Label and Supply

Introduction

The Sequential Label and Supply Company (often referred to as SLS) is a national supplier of stock labels as well as a manufacturer of custom labels and distributor of supplies often used in conjunction with labels, such as envelopes, adhesive tape, mailing cartons, and related office supplies. The company was founded by Fred Chin in 1992 and has grown steadily in the intervening years.

As the case study begins, the company has recognized its growing dependence on information technology and has organized its information technology group as shown in Figure D–1.

Trouble

It started out like any other day for Amy Windahl at Sequential Label and Supply Company. She liked her technical support job at the help desk. Taking calls and helping the office workers with PC problems was not glamorous, but it was challenging and paid pretty well. Some of her friends worked at bigger companies, some at higher-tech companies, but everyone kept up with each other, and they all agreed that technology jobs were a good way to pay the bills.

The phone rang. This was not a big deal for Amy. She answered her phone about 35 times an hour, 315 times a day, nine days every two weeks. The first call of the day started out the same as usual, with a worried user hoping Amy could help him out of a jam. The call display on her screen gave her all the facts: the user's name, his phone number, the department in which he worked, where his office was on the company campus, and a list of all the calls he'd made in the past.

"Hi, Bob," she said. "Did you get that document formatting problem squared away after our last call?"

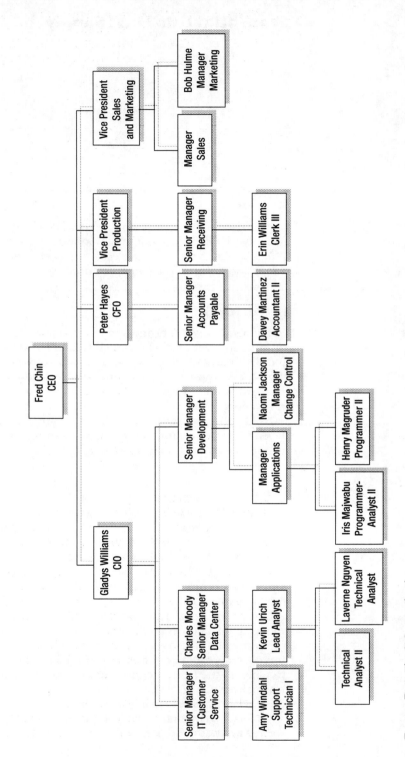

Figure D-1 The SLS organization

"Sure did, Amy. Hope we can figure out what's going on today."

"We'll try, Bob. Tell me about it."

"Well, my PC is acting weird," Bob said. "When I go to the screen that has my e-mail program running, it doesn't respond to the mouse or the keyboard."

"Did you try a reboot yet, Bob?"

"Sure did. But the window wouldn't close, and I had to turn it off. Once it finished the reboot, and I opened the e-mail program, it's just like it was before—no response at all. The other stuff is working OK, but really, really slowly. Even my Internet browser is sluggish."

"OK, Bob. We've tried the usual stuff we can do over the phone. Let me open a case, and I'll dispatch a tech over as soon as possible."

Amy looked up at the LED tally board on the wall at the end of the room. She saw that there were only two technicians dispatched to deskside support at the moment, and since it was the day shift, there were four available.

"Shouldn't be long at all, Bob."

She clicked off the line from Bob and typed her notes into ISIS, the company's Information Status and Issues System. She assigned the newly generated case to the deskside dispatch queue, knowing the roving deskside team would be paged with the details and would attend to Bob's problem in just a few minutes.

A moment later, Amy looked up to see Charles Moody walking briskly down the hall. Charlie was the senior manager of the server administration team. He was being trailed by three of his senior technicians as he made a beeline from his office to the door of the server room where the company servers were kept in a controlled environment. They all looked worried.

Just then, Amy's screen beeped to alert her of a new e-mail. She glanced down. It beeped again—and again. It started beeping constantly. She clicked on the envelope icon, and after a short delay, the mail window opened. She had 47 new e-mails in her inbox. She opened one from Davey Martinez, an acquaintance from the Accounting Department. The subject line said, "Wait till you see this." The message body read, "Look what this has to say about our managers' salaries..." There was an icon for a file attachment that Amy did not recognize. But, she knew Davey, he often sent her interesting and funny e-mails. She clicked on the icon.

Her PC showed the hourglass pointer icon for a second and then resumed showing its normal pointer. Nothing happened. She clicked on the icon for the next e-mail message. Nothing happened. Her phone rang again. She clicked on the ISIS icon on her computer desktop to activate the call management software, and activated her headset. "Hello, Tech Support, how can I help you?" She couldn't greet the caller by name because ISIS had not yet opened the screen on her PC.

"Hello, this is Erin Williams in Receiving."

Amy glanced down at her screen. Still no ISIS. She glanced up to the tally board and was surprised to see the inbound call counter tallying up waiting calls like digits on a stopwatch. Amy had never seen so many calls come in at one time.

"Hi, Erin," Amy said. "What's up?"

"Nothing," Erin answered. "That's the problem." The rest of the call was an exact replay of Bob's earlier call, except Amy couldn't type the notes into ISIS and had to jot them down on a legal pad. She also couldn't dispatch the deskside support team either. She looked at the tally board. It had gone dark. No numbers at all.

Then she saw Charlie running down the hall from the server room. He didn't look worried anymore. He looked frantic.

Amy picked up the phone. She wanted to check with her supervisor about what to do now. There was no dial tone.

The next day at SLS found everyone in technical support busy restoring computer systems to their former state and installing new virus and worm control software. Amy found herself learning how to install desktop computer operating systems and applications as SLS made a heroic effort to recover from the previous day's attack.

---

1. Do you think this event was caused by an insider or outsider? Why do you think this?
2. Other than installing virus and worm control software, what can SLS do to be ready for the next incident?
3. Do you think this attack was the result of a virus, or a worm? Why do you think this?

Starting Out

Fred Chin, CEO of Sequential Label and Supply, leaned back in his leather chair. He propped his feet up on the long mahogany table in the conference room where the SLS Board of Directors had just adjourned their quarterly meeting.

"What do you think about our computer security problem?" he asked Gladys Williams, the company's chief information officer, or CIO. He was referring to last month's outbreak of a malicious worm on the company's computer network.

Gladys replied, "I think we have a real problem this time, and we need to put together a real solution, not just a quick patch like the last time." Eighteen months ago someone had brought an infected floppy disk in from home and infected the network. To prevent this from happening again, all the floppy drives were removed from the company computers.

Fred wasn't convinced. "Let's just add another thousand dollars in the next budget to fix it up."

Gladys shook her head. "You've known for some time now that this business runs on computers. That's why you hired me as CIO. I've been researching information security, and my staff and I have some ideas to discuss with you. I've asked Charlie Moody to come in today to talk about it. He's waiting to speak with us."

Charlie joined the meeting, and Fred said, "Hello, Charlie. As you know the Board of Directors met today. They received a report on the expenses and lost production from the virus outbreak last month, and they directed us to improve the security of our computers. Gladys says you can help me understand what we need to do about it."

"To start with," Charlie said, "instead of setting up a computer security solution, we need to develop an information security program. We need a thorough review of our policies and practices, and we need to establish an ongoing risk management program. There are some other things that are part of the process as well, but these would be a good start."

"Sounds expensive," said Fred.

Charlie looked at Gladys, then answered,"Well, there will be some extra expenses for specific controls and software tools, and we may have to slow down our product development projects a bit, but the program will be more of a change in our attitude about security than a spending spree. I don't have accurate estimates yet, but you can be sure we will put cost-benefit worksheets in front of you before we spend any money."

Fred thought about this for a few seconds. "OK. What is our next step?"

Gladys answered, "To start with, we need to initiate a project plan to develop our new information security program. We'll use our usual systems development and project management approach. There are a few differences, but we can adapt our current models easily. We will need to appoint or hire a person to be responsible for information security."

"Information security? What about computer security?" asked Fred.

Charlie responded, "Information security includes all the things we use to do business: software, procedures, data, networks, our staff, and computers."

"I see," Fred said. "Bring me the draft project plan and budget in two weeks. The audit committee of the board meets in four weeks, and we'll need to report our progress."

Soon after the board of directors meeting, Charlie was promoted to chief information security officer, a new position that reports to the CIO Gladys Williams, and that was created to provide leadership for SLS's efforts to improve its security profile.

---

1. How do Fred, Gladys, and Charlie perceive the scope and scale of the new information security effort?
2. How will Fred measure success when he evaluates Gladys' performance for this project? How about Charlie's performance?
3. Which of the threats discussed in this chapter should receive Charlie's attention early in his planning process?

Industrial Espionage

Henry Magruder made a mistake: he left a CD at the coffee station. Later, Iris Majwabu was at the coffee station, topping off her coffee cup, hoping to wrap up her work on the current SQL code module before it was time to go home. As she turned to leave, she saw the unlabeled CD on the counter. Being the helpful sort, she picked it up, intending to return it to the person who'd left it behind.

Expecting to find perhaps the latest device drivers, or someone's work from the development team's office, Iris slipped the disk into the drive of her computer and ran a virus scan against its contents. She then opened the file explorer program. She had been correct in assuming the CD contained data files, lots of them. She opened a file at random, and names, addresses, and Social Security numbers scrolled down her screen. These were not the test records she expected; instead they looked more like critical payroll data. Concerned, she found a readme.txt file and opened it. It read:

Jill, see files on this disc. Hope they meet your expectations. Wire money to my account as arranged. Rest of data sent on payment.

Iris realized that someone was selling sensitive company data to an outside information broker. She looked back at the directory listing and saw that the files spanned the range of every department at Sequential Label and Supply—everything from customer lists to shipping invoices. She saw one file that she knew contained the credit card numbers for every Web customer the company supplied. She opened another file and saw that it stopped about halfway through the data. Whoever did this had split the data into two parts. That made sense: payment on delivery of the first half.

Now, who did this belong to? She opened up the file properties option on the readme.txt file. The file owner was listed as "hmagruder." That must be Henry Magruder, the developer two cubes over in the next aisle. Iris pondered her next action.

Iris called the company security hotline. The hotline was an anonymous way to report any suspicious activity or abuse of company policy, although Iris chose to identify herself. The next morning, she was called to a meeting with an investigator from corporate security, which led to more meetings with others in corporate security, and then finally a meeting with the Director of Human Resources and Gladys Williams, the CIO of SLS.

---

1. Was Iris justified in determining who the owner of the CD was?
2. Should Iris have approached Henry directly, or was the hotline the most effective way to take action?
3. Should Iris have placed the CD back at the coffee station and forgotten the whole thing? Would that response have been ethical on her part?

Deciding What to Protect

Charlie Moody called the meeting to order. The conference room was full of developers, systems analysts, IT managers, business users, and business managers.

"All right everyone, let's get started. Welcome to the kick-off meeting of the Sequential Label and Supply Information Security Task Force. That's the name of our new project team, and we're here today to talk about our objectives and to review the initial work plan."

"Why are all of the users here?" asked the manager of sales. "Isn't security a problem for the IT Department?"

Charlie explained, "Well, that used to be the case, but we've come to realize that information security is about managing the risk of using automated systems, which involves almost everyone in the company. In order to make our systems more secure, we will need the participation of people from all departments."

Charlie continued, "I hope everyone has read the packets we sent out last week with the legal requirements we face in our industry and the background articles on threats and attacks. Today we'll begin the process of identifying and classifying all of the information technology risks that face our organization. This includes everything from fires and floods that could disrupt our business to criminal hackers who might try to steal or destroy our data. Once we identify and classify the risks facing our assets, we can discuss how to reduce or eliminate these risks by establishing controls. Which controls we actually apply will depend on the costs and benefits of each control."

"Wow, Charlie!" said Amy Windahl from the back of the room. "I'm sure we need to do it—I was hit by the last attack, just as everyone here was—but we have hundreds of systems."

"It's more like thousands," said Charlie. He went on, "That's why we have so many people on this team and why the team includes members of every department."

Charlie continued, "Okay, everyone, please open your packets and take out the project plan with the work list showing teams, tasks, and schedules. Any questions before we start reviewing the work plan?"

As Charlie wrapped up the meeting, he ticked off a few key reminders for everyone involved in the asset identification project.

"Okay, everyone, before we finish, please remember that you should try to make your asset lists complete, but be sure to focus your attention on the more valuable assets first. Also, remember that we evaluate our assets based on business impact to profitability first, and then economic cost of replacement. Make sure you check with me about any questions that come up. We will schedule our next meeting in two weeks, so please have your draft inventories ready."

---

1. Did Charlie effectively organize the work before the meeting? Why or why not? Make a list of the important issues you think should be covered by the work plan. For each issue, provide a short explanation.
2. Will the company get useful information from the team it has assembled? Why or why not?
3. Why might some attendees resist the goals of the meeting? Does it seem that each person invited was briefed on the importance of the event and the issues behind it?

Plans

Charlie Moody flipped his jacket collar up to cover his ears. The spray blowing over him from the fire hoses was cold and was icing the cars that lined the street where he stood watching his office building burn. The warehouse and shipping dock were not gone, only severely damaged by smoke and water. He tried to hide his dismay by turning to speak to Fred Chin.

"Look at the bright side," said Charlie. "At least we can get the new server that we have been putting off."

Fred shook his head. "Charlie, you must be dreaming. We don't have enough insurance for a full replacement of everything we've lost."

Charlie was stunned. The offices were gone, and all the computer systems, servers, and desktops were melted slag, and he was going to have to try to rebuild without all the resources he needed. At least he had good backups, or so he hoped. He thought hard, trying to remember the last time the off-site backup tapes had been tested.

He wondered where all the network design diagrams were. He knew he could call his network provider to order new circuits as soon as Fred found some new office space. But where were all the circuit specs? The only copy had been in a drawer in his office, the office that wasn't there anymore. This was not going to be fun. He would have to call directory assistance just to get the phone number for his boss, Gladys Williams, the CIO.

Charlie heard a buzzing noise off to his left. He turned to see the flashing numbers of his alarm clock. Relief flooded over him as he realized it was just another nightmare and Sequential Label and Supply had not really burned down. He turned on the light to make himself some notes to go over with his staff later in the morning. Charlie was going to make some changes to the company contingency plans today.

Charlie sat at his desk the morning after his nightmare. He had answered the most pressing e-mail in his Inbox and had a piping hot cup of coffee at his elbow. He looked down at a blank legal pad ready to make notes about what to do in case his nightmare became reality.

---

1. What would be the first note you would write down if you were Charlie?
2. What else should be on Charlie's list?

Politics

Kelvin Urich came into the meeting room a few minutes late. He took an empty chair at the conference table, flipped open his notepad, and went straight to the point. "Okay, folks, I am scheduled to present the plan to Charlie Moody and the IT planning staff in two weeks. I noticed from the last project status report that you still do not have a consensus for the Internet connection architecture. Without that, we have not selected a technical approach and have not even started costing the project and planning for deployment. We cannot make acquisition and operating budgets, and I will look very silly at the presentation. What seems to be the problem?"

Laverne Nguyen replied, "Well, we seem to have developed a difference of opinion among the members of the architecture team. Some of us want to set up a screened subnet with bastion hosts, and some of the others want to use a screened subnet with proxy servers. That decision will affect the way we specify the new application and Web servers."

Miller Harrison, a contractor brought in to help with this project, picked up where Laverne had left off. "We can't seem to be able to move beyond this impasse, but we have done all the planning up to that point."

"Laverne, what does the consultant's report say?"

Laverne answered. "She proposed two alternative designs and noted that a decision will have to be made between them 'at a later date'."

Miller looked sour.

Kelvin said, "Sounds like we need to make a decision, and soon. Get a conference room reserved for tomorrow, ask the consultant if she can come in for a few hours first thing, and let everyone on the architecture team know we will meet from 8 to 11 on this matter. Now, here is how I think we should prepare for the meeting."

The next morning at 8 o'clock, Kelvin called the meeting to order.

The first person to address the group was the network design consultant, Susan Hamir. She reviewed the critical points from her earlier design report, going over the options it had presented and outlining the tradeoffs in those design choices.

When she finished, she sat down and Kelvin addressed the group again: "We need to break the logjam on this design issue. We have all the right people in this room to make the right choice for the company. Now here are the questions I want us to consider over the next three hours." Kelvin hit the key on his PC to show a slide with a list of discussion questions on the projector screen.

---

1. What questions do you think Kelvin should have included on his slide to start the discussion?
2. If the questions to be answered were broken down into two categories, they would be cost vs. maintaining high security while keeping flexibility. Which is most important for SLS?

Payback Denied

Miller Harrison was going to make them sorry, and make them pay. Earlier today, his contract at SLS had been terminated, and he'd been sent home. Oh sure, the big shot manager, Charlie Moody, had said Miller would still get paid for the two weeks remaining in his contract, and that the decision was based on "changes in the project and evolving needs as project work continued," but Miller knew better. He knew he'd been let go because of that know-nothing Kelvin and his simpering lapdog Laverne Nguyen. And now he was going to show them and everyone else at SLS who knew more about security.

Miller remembered from the days before he became an information security consultant that the secret to hacking into a network successfully was knowing that it required the same patience, attention to detail, and dogged determination that defending a network did. He also remembered that the first step in a typical hacking protocol was footprinting—that is, getting a fully annotated diagram of the network. Luckily for him, Miller could skip this first step, because, as he had been working at SLS for a number of weeks, he had been given a network diagram, and even though this diagram was not supposed to leave the workplace, he had brought a copy home last week when Laverne first started trying to tell him how to do his job.

After they let him go today, Miller's supervisor from the consulting firm had made him turn in his company laptop right away and then actually had the nerve to search his briefcase. By this time, however, Miller had—again, luckily for him—already stashed all the files and access codes he needed to wage an attack.

Ready to start, he activated his VPN client to connect to the SLS network. He realized almost immediately that Charlie Moody had also confiscated the crypto-token that enabled him to use the VPN for remote access to SLS. No problem, Miller decided. If the front door was locked, he would try the back door. He opened up a modem dialing program and typed in the dial-up number for SLS he had gotten from the network administrator last week. After the usual caterwauling sounds, the dialer established the connection. Miller readied himself to begin his retribution against the SLS servers. His fingers were poised above the keyboard when he saw a prompt:

```
SLS Inc. Company Use Only. Unauthorized use is
prohibited and subject to prosecution.
Enter Passphrase:
```

Miller realized that the SLS security team had rerouted all dial-up requests to be authenticated through the same RADIUS services that the VPN used. Thus, he was locked out of the back door too. But Miller moved on to his next option, which was to use another back door of his very own. This was also another little "precaution" he'd taken last week before he'd been booted from his job. The back door consisted of a zombie program he'd installed to run on the company's extranet Quality Assurance server. No one at SLS took the QA server seriously since it did not store any production data. In fact, the server wasn't even subject to all the change control procedures that were applied to other systems on the extranet. Miller activated the control program he used to remotely control the zombie program and typed in the IP address of the computer where the zombie was running. No response. He opened up a command window and Pinged the zombie. The computer at that address answered each Ping promptly, which meant the computer itself was alive and well. Miller checked the UDP port number the zombie in his notebook used and ran an Nmap scan against that single computer for that port. The UDP port the zombie control dialogue used was closed tight. He cursed the firewall, the policy that controlled it, and the technicians that kept it up to date.

With all of his pre-planned payback cut off at the edge of SLS's network, he decided to continue his hack by going back to the usual first step in his hacking protocol—in other words, to get a detailed fingerprinting of all SLS Internet addresses. Since the front and both back doors were locked, it was time to get a new floor plan. His next action was to launch a simple network port scanner on his Linux laptop. He restarted Nmap and configured it to scan the entire IP address range for SLS's extranet. With a single keystroke, he unleashed the port scanner against the SLS network.

Nmap started out as it usually did: giving the program identification and version number. Then it started reporting back on the first host in the SLS network. It reported all of the open ports on this server. Then the program moved on to a second host and began reporting back the open ports on that system, too. Once it reached the third host, however, it suddenly stopped.

Miller restarted Nmap, using the last host IP as the starting point for the next scan. No response. He opened up another command window and tried to Ping the first host he had just port-scanned. No luck. He tried to Ping the SLS firewall. Nothing. He happened to know the IP address for the SLS edge router. He Pinged that and got the same result. He had been black-holed—meaning his IP address had been put on a list of addresses from which the SLS edge router would no longer accept packets. This was, ironically, his own doing. The IDS he had been helping SLS configure seemed to be working just fine at the moment. His attempt to hack the SLS network was shut down cold.

1. Do you think Miller is out of options as he pursues his vendetta? If you think there are additional actions he could take in his effort to damage the SLS network, what are they?
2. Suppose a system administrator at SLS happened to read the details of this case. What steps should he or she take to improve the company's information security program?

Safe, for a Long, Long Time

Peter Hayes, CFO of Sequential Label and Supply, opened an e-mail from the manager of the Accounting Department. He saw that the e-mail had an attachment—probably a spreadsheet or a report of some kind. From the icon associated with the attached file, he knew it was an encrypted file. He saved the file to his computer's hard drive and then double-clicked on the icon to open it.

The operating system of his computer recognized that the file he was opening was encrypted and started the encryption program, which promptly asked Peter for his passphrase. Peter's mind went blank. He couldn't remember the passphrase. "Oh, good grief!" he said to himself aloud, reaching for his phone.

"Charlie, good, you're still here. I'm having trouble with a file in my e-mail program. My computer is prompting me for my passphrase, and I think I forgot it."

"Uh-oh," said Charlie Moody.

"What do you mean 'Uh-oh'?" Peter asked.

"I mean you're S - O - L," Charlie replied. "Simply outta luck."

"Out of luck?" said Peter. "Why? Can't you do something? I have quite a few files saved on my computer that are encrypted with this PGP program. I need my files."

Charlie let him finish, then said, "Peter, do you recall how I told you it was important to remember your passphrase?" Charlie heard a sigh on the other end of the line, but decided to ignore it. "And do you remember I said that PGP is only free for individuals and that you weren't supposed to use it for company files since we didn't buy a license for the company? We only set that program up on your PC for your personal mail-for when your sister wanted to send you some financial records. When did you start using it for company business?"

"Well," Peter answered, "one of my staff had some financials that were going to be ready a few weeks ago while I was traveling. I swapped public keys with him before I left, and then he sent the files to me securely by e-mail while I was in Dallas. It worked out great. So that week I encrypted quite a few files. Now I can't get to any of them just because I can't seem to remember my passphrase." There was a long pause, when he said, "Can you hack it for me?"

Charlie chuckled a bit and then said, "Sure, Peter, no problem. Send me the files and I'll put the biggest server we have to work on it. Since we set you up in PGP with 128-bit 3DES, I should be able to apply a little brute force and crack the key to get the plaintext in two or three hundred million years or so."

Charlie was just getting ready to head home when the phone rang. Caller ID showed it was Peter.

"Hi, Peter," he said into the receiver. "Want me to start the file cracker on your spreadsheet?"

"No, thanks," Peter answered, taking the joke well. "I finally remembered my passphrase. But I want to get your advice on what we need to do to make the use of encryption more effective and to get it properly licensed for the whole company to use. I see the value in using it for certain kinds of information, and I think we need to plan for its use. I'm just worried about the next time I forget a passphrase, or even worse, what if someone gets hurt or leaves the company, how would we get their files back?"

"We'd use a feature called key recovery, which is usually part of PKI software," said Charlie. "Actually, if we invest in PKI software, we could solve that problem as well as several others."

"OK," said Peter. "Can you see me tomorrow at 10 o'clock to talk about this PKI solution, and how we can make better use of encryption?"

> 1. Was Charlie exaggerating when he gave Peter an estimate for the time that would be required to crack the encryption key using a brute force attack?
> 2. Are there any tools that an individual like Peter can use safely to avoid losing his or her passphrase without using key recovery?

Amy Windahl was back early from lunch. As she was walking toward the SLS building from the parking lot, she saw one of the accounting clerks go through the building's double glass doors. After him, a person she didn't recognize, a tall, blond man in nondescript business casual clothes, went in. The two of them walked past the security guard station in the lobby and headed for the elevator. Amy waited for the next elevator and pressed the button for her floor.

When the elevator doors opened, she saw the blond man again, this time standing in the second floor elevator lobby and looking at the company's phone list. She walked over to the doors to the hallway that led to that floor's offices and cocked her right hip, where her badge was clipped, toward the sensor for the locks. When she heard the magnetic lock release, Amy pulled the door open and went through. As the door began to shut, the stranger grabbed it and came through behind her.

Amy realized now that she had a "tailgater," a person who follows the people who manage to remember to bring their badges to work. She had seen the security bulletin just last week emphasizing tailgaters should be reported. Everyone in the staff meeting had had a good laugh about turning each other in the next time any two of them came through the door together. But now she was beginning to understand the seriousness of the bulletin.

Amy turned around quickly, to head back into the lobby, and found herself face-to-face with the blond man. "Excuse me," she said. The stranger stepped back to let her pass and then continued down the hall. Amy picked up the lobby phone and dialed the number for building security.

"Security," a voice answered.

"Hi, Amy Windahl here. I work in the IT Department on the second floor. I just had a stranger tailgate into the second floor offices. Do you guys want to check it out?"

"Yes, ma'am. We have someone on the floor already. I'll have him meet you in the lobby in two minutes," said the security dispatcher.

When the security officer appeared, Amy said, "He went down the hall, toward the programming offices. He's tall, heavy, has green slacks, a tan shirt, a leather jacket—oh, and he has blond hair."

The guard said, "Wait here. If he comes through here without me, call dispatch at extension 3333. I'll be right back."

Amy sat down in the chair by the phone. After three or four minutes, she saw the blond man walking briskly toward the doors. The guard was right behind him. As the stranger opened the door, the guard called out, "Sir, please stop. I need to speak with you. What's your name?" Before the blond man could answer, the elevator opened, and two more guards came into the lobby.

The stranger responded, "Alan Gaskin."

The guard asked, "What's your business here?"

"Just visiting a friend," said the stranger.

"And who would that be?" the guard asked.

The stranger looked a bit surprised, and then said, "Uh, William Walters, uh, in the Accounting Department, I think."

The guard reached for his wireless handheld terminal and punched a few buttons. Then he said, "Mr. Gaskin, there are no employees with that name working here, in Accounting or any other department. Do you want to try another answer?"

The stranger looked a little confused and took a few steps toward the stairwell. But the other two guards moved up and cut him off. As the guards took the blond man by the upper arms to keep him from escaping, a brown paper bag dropped to the floor from under his jacket, it contents spilling out on the carpet. Amy saw several office badges, a watch, two PalmPilots, and several cell phones.

The first guard immediately radioed dispatch. "Contact the city police and advise them we have a trespasser. We will press charges." The other guards led the man toward the elevators, while the first guard told Amy, "You need to call your supervisor and tell her you will be delayed. We have to take a statement from you."

Amy walked into her office cubicle and sat down. The entire episode with the blond man had taken her over two hours. Plus, the police officers had told her the district attorney would also be calling to make an appointment to speak to her, which meant she would have to spend even more time dealing with this episode. She hoped her manager would understand.

---

1. What security awareness and training documents and posters seem to have an impact regarding this event?
2. Do you think Amy should have done anything differently? What?

Politics

Kelvin Urich arrived early for the change control meeting. Sitting in the large conference room, he reviewed his notes and then flipped through the handouts one final time. After the meeting last week where the technical review committee members approved his project plan, he felt he had a tight, well-ordered project plan.

Once this meeting was over, he knew that the series of change requests this project would generate would keep the technical analysts across the company busy for months to come. He was hopeful the scope and scale of the project, and the vast improvement it would bring to the SLS information security program would inspire his colleagues. At this moment, he felt everything was under control. His handouts were loaded with columns of tasks, subtasks, and action items. He had assigned dates to every action step, and he had also already assigned which people would implement each required task.

Naomi Jackson, the change control supervisor, also arrived a few minutes early. She saw Kelvin and gave him a nod as she placed a stack of revised agendas in the middle of the conference table. Everyone attending had received the detailed report of planned changes the previous day. Charlie Moody came in, also nodding to Kelvin, and took his usual seat.

Once the room filled, Naomi said, "Time to get started." She picked up her copy of the planned change report and announced the first change control item for discussion, Item 742.

One of the members of the UNIX support team responded, "As planned." This short statement meant to all of the regular attendees that this item was a routine maintenance check that was going to happen in the upcoming planned maintenance window—that is, next Sunday afternoon.

Since no one else said anything, Naomi continued down the list in numeric order. Most items received the response, "As planned," from the sponsoring team member. Once in a while, someone answered "Cancelled" or "Will be rescheduled," but for the most part, the review of the change items proceeded as usual until they came to Kelvin's group of change requests for information security.

Naomi said, "Items 761 through 767. Kelvin Urich from the security team is here to discuss these items as a package with the whole change control group."

Kelvin started by sending his handouts around the table. He waited, a little nervously, until everyone had a copy, and then began speaking: "I'm sure most of you are already aware of the information security upgrades we have been working on for the past few months. We've created an overall strategy based on the revised policies that were published last year and a detailed analysis of the threats we face with the systems we have. Since becoming project manager, I have created what I think is a very workable plan. First, the seven change requests on the list today are all network changes and are all top priority. I have more changes planned for coming weeks and I will be sending each department head a complete list of all planned changes and the expected dates. Of course, detailed change requests will be filed in advance for these change control meetings, but using the master list, each department knows what is coming up next. As I said, there are more changes coming, and I hope we can all work together to make this a success." He looked at Naomi to indicate he was finished.

"Uh, comments or questions?" asked Naomi.

Instantly six hands shot into the air. All of them belonged to senior technical analysts. Kelvin realized belatedly that none of these analysts were on the technical review committee that had approved his plan last week. He noticed also that half the people in the room, like Amy Windahl from the user group and training committee, were busy pulling calendars and PDAs out of briefcases and bags, and that Davey Martinez from Accounting was engaged in a private but heated discussion with Charlie Moody, Kelvin's boss. Charlie did not look pleased.

Above the noise, Kelvin heard someone ask, "Who does he think he is to dump this much work on us all at once?" Someone else was heard to say, "This isn't going to happen on this schedule."

This sudden state of chaos during an otherwise orderly meeting made Kelvin realize that his plan was not as simple as he'd thought. He braced himself—it was going to be a very long afternoon.

Later, Kelvin was in Charlie's office to discuss the change control meeting that occurred earlier that day. Charlie looked across his desk at Kelvin, who was absorbed in the sheaf of handwritten notes from the technical review meeting.

"So what do you think?" he asked.

"I think I was blindsided by a bus!" Kelvin replied sheepishly. "I thought I had thought the project plan and the change management impacts through, but everyone acted as if I had threatened their job."

"In a way you did," Charlie stated. "Some people believe that change is the enemy."

"But these changes are important."

"I agree," Charlie nodded. "But successful change usually occurs in small steps. What's your top priority?"

"All the items on this list are top priorities," Kelvin stressed. "I haven't even gotten to the second tier."

"So what should you do to accomplish these top priorities?" Charlie asked.

"I guess I should reprioritize within my top tier, but what then?"

"The next step is to build support before the meeting, not during it." Charlie smiled. "Never go into a meeting where you haven't done your homework, especially when other people in the meeting can reduce your chance of success."

1. What project management tasks should Kelvin perform before his next meeting?
2. What change management tasks should Kelvin perform before his next meeting, and how do these tasks fit within the project management process?
3. Had you been in Kelvin's place, what would you have done differently to prepare for this meeting?

Opportunities

While she drank her coffee, Iris browsed her e-mail. Mixed in among the newsletters and unsolicited offers for travel deals and mortgage loans was a message from Charlie Moody. As she opened the message, Iris worried about what a note from the senior manager of IT could mean. The e-mail read:

From: Charles Moody [cmoody@slsco.com]
To: Iris Majwabu [imajwabu@slsco.com]
Subject: I need to see you
Iris,
I wanted to tell you that the managers in IT and the whole information security team appreciate your diligence and attitude in the Magruder affair. We completed all of the personnel actions on this matter yesterday, and it is now behind us.
You might like to know that the best guess from the Corporate Security Department is that you helped us catch this in the early stages, and so no company assets were compromised.
Please set up an appointment with me in the next few days to discuss a few things.
/CM

"Uh-oh," she thought. As she opened her calendar program to set up the appointment, Iris couldn't imagine what Charlie, who was her boss's boss, could want. Iris was a database administrator, and she hoped he wasn't going to give her more work.

A week later, Iris entered Charlie Moody's office. He was sitting behind his desk and stood as she entered.

"Come in," Charlie said. "Have a seat."

After Iris made herself comfortable in one of the many chairs in the office, Charlie came around his desk and sat down next to her. She took a deep breath, eyeing the folder in his hand, which looked like her personnel file.

"I'm sure you're wondering why I asked you here," said Charlie smiling. "Because you did so well in the Magruder affair, I am offering you a transfer to Kelvin Urich's information security group. You were right to bring that issue to your manager's attention and avoid confronting Magruder directly. You made the right choice, you acted quickly, showed a positive attitude throughout the whole situation, and I think you have demonstrated an information security mindset. You are someone I want on Urich's team."

"I'm not sure what to say," she began. "I've been a DBA for three years here. I really don't know much about information security other than what I learned from the company training and awareness sessions."

"That's not a problem," Charlie said. "You can learn. So how about it, are you interested in the job?"

Iris said, "It sounds interesting, but I hadn't thought of a career change just now. I am willing to think about it, but have a few questions . . . ."

After their meeting, Iris returned to her office. After finishing up her daily assignments, she pulled out a blank notepad and began to make some notes about the information security position Charlie had asked her about.

---

1. What questions should Iris ask Charlie about the new job, about Kelvin's team, and about the future of the company?
2. Do you think Iris has the right stuff for a job in information security? Why? Why not?
3. Do you think Charlie is making the right choice in transferring Iris to his information security group, or would he be better served by other options? Think of at least three of those options. What are the advantages and disadvantages of each?

Iris takes the new job, and coupled with other changes at SLS, Figure D-2 now shows the new IT organization chart.

Conversions

Charlie Moody leaned back in his chair. It was Monday morning after the biggest conversion weekend for the implementation of the information security project. Charlie had just completed his review of the results of the implementation steps. Everything was working as expected. The initial penetration tests run on Sunday afternoon were clean. Charlie was eager for everything to return to normal, that is, to the way things had been before the attack on the SLS network had triggered the changes of the past few months.

Kelvin Urich tapped on the open door of Charlie's office. "Hey Charlie," he said. "Have you seen the e-mail I just sent? There's an urgent vulnerability report on Bugtraq about the version of UNIX we use. The vendor just released a critical patch to be applied right away. Should I get the system programming team started on an acceptance test for the patch?"

"Oh yes. Get them to pull a download from the vendor's FTP site as soon as they can," said Charlie. "Then get them to patch the test lab servers. If that looks okay, have them patch the development servers for the HQ development team. Oh, and get these into change control ASAP, and add the production server change request for the overnight change window tonight."

"Okay," Kelvin said.

Kelvin left Charlie's office as Charlie pulled up the CERT home page on his PC. He was reading about the new vulnerability when there was another knock on the doorjamb. It was Iris Majwabu.

When Charlie looked up, Iris said, "Hi Charlie. Got a second?"

"Sure, Iris. How have you been? Settling in with Kelvin's team, okay?"

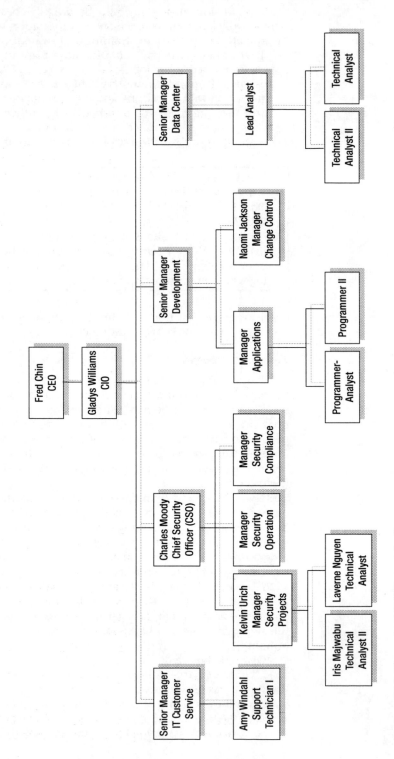

Figure D-2 The revised SLS IT organization

She smiled. "Oh sure. They are a good group. They have me studying the documentation trail from the time before the security program was implemented. I came to see you about the reassessment of the information asset inventory and the threat-vulnerability update."

Charlie looked a little confused for a second, and then his memory kicked in and he grimaced just a little. "Oh, yes. I had put the quarterly asset and threat review out of my mind while we were busy with the implementation of the blueprint. I suppose it's time to start planning for the regular reviews, isn't it?"

Iris handed him a folder and said, "Here's the first draft of the plan for the review project. Kelvin has already seen it and suggested I review it with you. Let me know when you would like to go over it."

After their meeting, Iris returned to her office. After finishing up her daily assignments, she pulled out a blank notepad and began to make some notes about the information security position Charlie had asked her about.

1. What information should be included in the planning document that Iris gave Charlie?
2. Since the maintenance effort at SLS never stops, when should the management team assess the progress of the maintenance effort? Should this assessment be linked to the SLS corporate, IT, and information security budget process?
3. Kelvin mentioned BUGTRAQ as an information service that informs professionals about vulnerabilities. Use the Internet to identify other sources of valuable vulnerability information. Be sure to include US-CERT in your search. Why is US-CERT deserving of special attention?

A Different Day

Remember how Amy's day started at the beginning of this case, and imagine how it could have been. It started out like any other day for Amy at the Sequential Label and Supply Company. She liked her technical support job at the help desk. Taking calls and helping the office workers with PC problems was not glamorous, but it was challenging and paid pretty well.

The phone rang. That was not a big deal for Amy; after all, that was her job. She answered the phone about 35 times an hour, eight to ten hours a day, 20 days a month. This call began like so many others, with a worried user hoping Amy could help him out of a jam. The call display on her screen gave her all the facts: the user's name, his phone number, the department, the location of his office on the company campus, and a list of all the support request calls he'd made in the past.

"Hi, Bob," she said. "Did you get that document-formatting problem squared away after our last call?"

"Sure did, Amy. Hope we can figure out what's going on today."

"I'll try, Bob. Tell me about it."

"Well, I need help setting a page break in this new spreadsheet template I'm working on," Bob said.

Amy smiled to herself. She knew spreadsheets well, so she could probably close this call on first contact. That would help her call statistics, which was one of the ways her job performance was measured.

Roughly four minutes before Amy's phone had rung, a specially programmed computer out at the edge of the SLS network had made a programmed decision. This computer was known to the world as postoffice.seqlbl.com, but was called the e-mail gateway by the networking, messaging, and information security teams at SLS. The decision it had made, just like many thousands of other decisions in a typical day, was to block the transmission of a file that had been attached to an e-mail addressed to *Bob.Hulme@seqlbl.com*. The gateway had determined that Bob didn't need an executable program attached to an e-mail from somewhere on the Internet that contained a forged reply-to address from Davey Martinez at SLS.

The attachment didn't go through.

The e-mail came to Bob Hulme, who had seen that another unsolicited commercial e-mail with an unwanted executable had been blocked. He had deleted the nuisance message without a second thought.

Amy looked up to see Charles Moody walking calmly down the hall. Charlie, as he liked to be called, was the senior manager of the server administration team and also the company's chief information security officer. Kelvin Urich and Iris Majwabu were trailing him as he walked from his office to the door of the conference room. Amy thought, "It must be time for the weekly security status meeting."

She was the user representative on the company information security oversight committee. She was due at that meeting, and would join them for coffee and bagels as soon as she finished her call with Bob.

1. What area of the ISO-based security management model addresses the actions of the content filter described here?

2. What recommendations would you give Sequential for selection of a security management model?

Brightington Academy

Overview

This case provides a different perspective on the need for information security, taking the form of an educational institution. While private industry has more control over its computing resources, academic institutions typically desire to sponsor academic freedom and the creative pursuits of scholarly work. As such there are typically fewer restrictions on faculty, staff, and student computer uses. This must be reflected in the policies and technologies of the academic environment. This is not to suggest that it is impossible to secure academic technologies, but rather to recommend selective restraint in implementing security technologies, and crafting strategic plans and policies.

Introduction

The Brightington Academy (BA), founded in 1965, was named for its founder, and first headmaster, William Farnsworth Brightington. Brightington began with the simple mission of providing the highest quality college preparatory education. The Academy is committed to developing young minds and bodies, creating distinguished and productive members of society ready for the rigors of the College or University. Stretching for more than 150 acres, Brightington's beautiful campus is nestled in the foothills of the Yoknapatopha Mountain Range in Cheetaw, Georgia, a community of 130,000. The Academy is located only a short drive from metropolitan Atlanta, but enjoys the advantages of a rural campus, with the advanced curriculum, facilities, and technology sponsored by its affluent stakeholders.

The Academy averages an annual enrollment of 300–350 students, with an average class size of 15 and a faculty of 30. The Academy is accredited by the Southern Association of Colleges and Schools.

Strategic Plan & Vision for Brightington Academy

During the summer of 2005, the Brightington Board of Trustees mandated a comprehensive strategic planning process to chart the course of the school through the year 2012. The board appointed a steering committee, which began its work in August 2005. The steering committee and the Board of Trustees recognize that a strategic plan is a guide for direction subject to modification as conditions may warrant.

Brightington Academy

The resulting guidance represents the input of hundreds of members of the Brightington community and is offered not as a policy directive to the administration, but as recommendations for the headmaster. As such, the recommendations do not establish priorities; however, it will be necessary to establish priorities among those goals selected for implementation.

A VISION FOR BRIGHTINGTON

The Strategic Plan through the Year 2010 establishes as goals for the Academy to:

- Establish its position as one of the top college-prep school in the Southeast
- Increase opportunities for student intellectual and spiritual development
- Increase the recruitment and retention of underrepresented students
- Effectively manage expenses, while maintaining state-of-the-art educational facilities and remaining competitive in faculty salaries
- Emphasize the development of character, ethics, and values at each grade level
- Increase alumni giving to fund further capital development, including the creation of a high-technology computer lab wing

Academics

Brightington Academy has four academic departments providing strong curriculum development and academic rigor across the basics. Each department is headed by a tenured Ph.D. in a related field, and contains high-quality faculty dedicated to the promotion of their respective disciplines.

DEPARTMENTS

Each department offers a number of specialized courses designed to place the student in good standing for college-level performance.

Arts & Sciences
Chair: Dr. Mary Worth

The Arts & Sciences Department offers courses in traditional arts (humanities, fine arts, drama, and music) as well as the sciences (anatomy, biology, chemistry, and earth science). It also provides many advanced placement courses allowing students to earn college credits, including AP-Biology and AP-Chemistry.

English & Foreign Languages
Chair: Dr. Laura Kingsley

The English & Foreign Languages Department offers courses in traditional English, literature, Spanish, and French. It also provides many advanced placement courses allowing students to earn college credits, including AP-English, AP-Literature, and AP-French and Spanish.

Mathematics & Information Technology
Chair: Dr. Isaac Axiom

The Mathematics & Information Technology Department offers courses in traditional mathematics and computer-based education, including algebra, geometry, calculus, and computer science. It also provides many advanced placement courses allowing students to earn college credits, including AP-Calculus 1, AP-Calculus 2, and AP-Computer Science.

History & Social Studies
Chair: Dr. William Jackson

The History & Social Studies Department offers courses in traditional history (ancient history, modern world history, European history, American history, Georgia history, and U.S. government). It also provides many advanced placement courses allowing students to earn college credits, including AP-Modern World History, AP-European History, AP-American History, and AP-U.S. Government.

Facilities

Brightington Academy constructed its state-of-the-art building in 1995. It consists of a two-story structure, with six classrooms on the first floor and 35 faculty offices, plus two secretarial positions on the second floor. The first-floor classrooms consist of two large 75-seat auditoriums, and four smaller 45-seat classrooms. The offices on the second floor are comfortably equipped with modern furniture. Currently only 31 of the 35 offices are staffed. The second floor also hosts the conference room, and a 25-seat computer lab. The building also has several empty rooms currently being used for short-term storage. When the building was constructed it was expected that staff support and technology equipment would occupy these spaces.

TECHNOLOGY

Currently each of the faculty offices in the Brightington Academy building has its own 2.4 GHz personal computer with a color inkjet printer. The headmaster, vice-headmaster, and each department chair each have a laser printer. The Academy also has a 25-seat computer lab equipped with comparable computers and two laser printers. The lab has recently purchased a large capacity laser printer, to support lab and campus printing needs. Each classroom also has a computer, which is currently connected to overhead data projectors. All systems are networked to the Internet via a high-speed connection (approx 1.5 Mbps) through a local ISP.

The Academy has a Fast Ethernet network, with a Windows 2000 file server. The technology support staff (consisting of two full time administrators) provide Internet-based e-mail for all faculty, and Internet connectivity in all offices, labs, and classrooms. There are no formal security policies, and the only protection for the network comes from NAT services provided by the file server that connects the network to the Internet.

NEEDS

Based on the current and projected needs of the Academy, the headmaster has authorized the issuance of a Request for Proposal (this document) to allow potential vendors to offer solutions to the Academy's security needs. Based on the recommendations of the faculty, the following needs have been determined to support future growth and expansion of the Academy:

- Strategic plan for the implementation and management of an information security program
- Policies for the overall information security program, and specific issues facing the Academy
- Security Education, Training, and Awareness program for faculty, staff, and students
- Protection for the network connectivity between all computers
- Protection for e-mail capability, which facilitates internal and external communications
- Protection for Internet connectivity, which allows all faculty, lab, and classroom computers to access the WWW and external resources
- Protection for shared information storage resources, which allows faculty to store and exchange electronic copies of documents, grades, etc. and access them from off campus

CONSTRAINTS

It is understood that there will need to be additional staff hiring to support the security technology to solve these needs. However, the budget of the Academy will only allow the hiring of one manager, and two administrator/technicians. In addition, the Academy realizes that some of these needs are extremely technical in nature. The headmaster has a philosophy of "stick to the knitting," meaning that we should focus on what we do best, and hire someone else to do the rest. So any task that requires high degrees of technical expertise, beyond the capability of the three hires just mentioned, should have external contracts for support.

BUDGET

While no definitive budget for this project has been established, based on current and projected revenues, the administration anticipates that a

(Text continued on Page E-8)

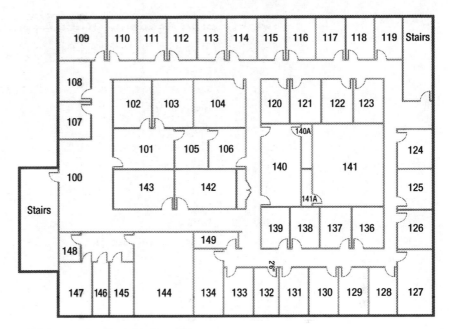

Brightington Academy 1st floor plan

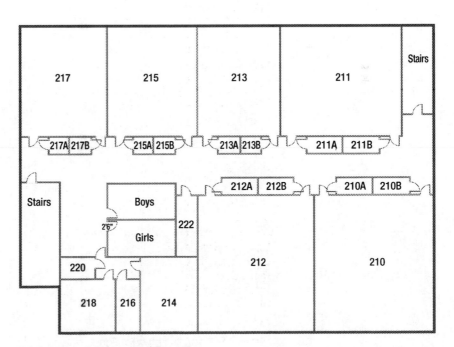

Brightington Academy 2nd floor plan

Brightington Academy Office Assignments

Office	Occupant	# of Computers	Need Computers?
100	Foyer	0	N
101	Secretary	3	3
102	Headmaster	2	2
103	Vice-Headmaster	2	2
104	Chair, Arts & Sciences	2	2
105	Mailroom	0	Y
106	Workroom	0	Y
107	Faculty	1	1
108	Faculty	1	1
109	Chair, History & Social Studies	2	2
110	Faculty	1	1
111	Faculty	1	1
112	Faculty	1	1
113	Faculty	1	1
114	Faculty	1	1
115	Faculty	1	1
116	Faculty	1	1
117	Faculty	1	1
118	Faculty	1	1
119	Faculty	1	1
120	Faculty	1	1
121	Faculty	1	1
122	Faculty	1	1
123	Faculty	1	1
124	Faculty	1	1
125	Faculty	1	1
126	Faculty	1	1
127	Chair, Mathematics & Information Technology	2	2
128	Faculty	1	1
129	Faculty	1	1
130	Faculty	1	1
131	Faculty	1	1
132	Faculty	1	1
133	Faculty	1	1
134	Chair, English & Foreign Languages	2	2

Continued

Brightington Academy Office Assignments—cont'd

Office	Occupant	# of Computers	Need Computers?
135	Faculty	1	1
136	Faculty	1	1
137	Faculty	1	1
138	Faculty	1	1
139	Faculty	1	1
140	Conference Room	0	Y
140a	Conference Room Storage Closet	0	N
141	Computer Lab	20	20
141a	Computer Lab Storage Closet	0	N
142	Ladies' Room	0	N
143	Men's Room	0	N
144	Empty	0	?
145	Empty	0	?
146	Empty	0	?
147	Empty	0	?
148	Empty	0	?
210	Classroom A	1	1
211	Classroom B	1	1
211a	Classroom Storage Closet	0	N
211b	Classroom Storage Closet	0	N
212	Classroom C	1	1
213	Classroom D	1	1
213a	Classroom Storage Closet	0	N
213b	Classroom Storage Closet	0	N
214	Sciences Lab	2	2
215	Classroom E	1	1
215a	Classroom Storage Closet	0	N
215b	Classroom Storage Closet	0	N
216	Sciences Lab Storage Closet	0	N
217	Classroom F	1	1
217a	Classroom Storage Closet	0	N
217b	Classroom Storage Closet	0	N
218	Arts Lab	2	2
220	Arts Lab Storage Closet & Kiln	0	N
222	Classroom Storage Closet	0	N

budget of no more than $200,000 initial, and $20,000 annual, will be available (not including personnel costs). This is not to suggest that vendors aim for this as a target figure, but to provide a *maximum* cap for recommended expenditures.

PROPOSAL FORMAT FOR BRIGHTINGTON ACADEMY INFORMATION SECURITY RFP RESPONSE

The following sections should guide the development and submission of the proposal. The final document will be submitted in a three-ring binder, and single-spaced, with standard margins and fonts. Each section should be properly tabbed, organized, and structured with appropriate headers. Each new section and subsection should begin on a fresh page. All pages should be numbered, and an index placed at the beginning of the document. The group members' names should be prominently displayed on the front cover. For each section, address the subjects or components outlined beneath it. If a component requires a separate binder or document, create it as needed.

OVERVIEW OF BA

Provide an overview of the BA company history, including an organization chart, physical plant layout (blank), and general description of organization computing and in-place security resources.

PROBLEM DEFINITION

Create a summary of the situation leading to the issuance of the RFP. Specify specific organizational needs, and situations demanding resolution.

ENTERPRISE INFORMATION SECURITY POLICY

Create an Enterprise Information Security Policy for BA, based on the template in the text. Feel free to use assumptions to fill the policy with information as if you are the CISO of BA, just beginning a new Security SDLC.

ISSUANCE OF SPECIFIC POLICIES

Create a list outlining the ISSPs that BA will need, and specify what each policy should address (one paragraph each). As an example, create an issue-specific security policy for the BA case, based on the template in the text. The issue you are to address is fair and responsible use of office e-mail. Feel free to use assumptions to fill the policy with information as if you are the CISO of BA, just beginning a new Security SDLC.

RISK MANAGEMENT

Create an assessment of the risks inherent in BA's current security profile. Include an assessment of threats facing BA, along with estimated vulnerabilities in the BA systems. Include weighted tables: a) prioritizing threats and b) prioritizing assets. Make recommendations as to general improvements in the information security posture. Basically perform a Risk Assessment/Business Impact Analysis on BA.

INFORMATION SECURITY AWARENESS PROGRAM

Create an information security awareness program overview document, outlining a projected implementation of awareness in BA. Feel free to use assumptions to fill the policy with information as if you are the CISO of BA, just beginning a new Security SDLC. As part of your program include:

- Two examples of Security Awareness Posters in PowerPoint
- A training calendar for needed security training (one month)
- A sample newsletter (two-to-four pages) providing security awareness information to BA employees

CONTINGENCY PLANNING

Provide a planning framework for BA's contingency planning. Design a contingency planning program, including specifications for the program team, deliverables, timelines, etc. Provide a template for each of the following components:

- Incident Response Plan
- Disaster Recovery Plan
- Business Continuity Plan

This does not require you to complete these components; only provide a detailed outline that BA can fill in to create these plans, and a project management plan for the design and development of both the team, and the actual plans.

SECURITY STAFF

Design a security team for this size organization (organization chart) including specifications for the numbers and types of security professionals needed. Develop a job advertisement for each position with qualifications and requirements.

SECURITY TECHNOLOGIES

Design a security architecture to protect the Academy's network and computers. Include specifications for the Total Cost of Ownership for all technology recommended.

The 9/11 Commission Report

Overview

A defining event in the political and cultural landscape of the 21st century occurred on September 11, 2001. The terrorist attack on that date has served not only as an alarm about national security in general but also to underscore several issues in the realm of information security, specifically the critical role of the incident response plan. This chapter addresses those sections of the report from the 9/11 Commission that are concerned with that end. Each excerpt will be introduced with a short description in italics and followed with suggestions for classroom discussion and/or short writing assignments.

Introduction

This book's editors, Whitman and Mattord, have added commentary to each selected section of the report. The commentary can also be used to stimulate discussion. The authors strongly recommend that the report should be read in its entirety. The complete report includes many footnotes that document key facts and explain important details. The footnotes have been removed from this excerpt for brevity.

Excerpt 1

The following excerpt is from the preamble and preface of the 9/11 Commission report. Like any effective incident after-action report, the 9/11 Commission Report establishes the reasons for writing the report and provides pertinent background information regarding the incident.

THE 9/11 COMMISSION INVESTIGATION

We present the narrative of this report and the recommendations that flow from it to the President of the United States, the United States Congress, and the American people for their consideration. Ten Commissioners—five Republicans and five Democrats chosen by elected leaders from our nation's capital at a time of great partisan division—have come together to present this report without dissent. We have come together with a unity of purpose because our nation demands it. September 11, 2001, was a day of unprecedented shock and suffering in the history of the United States. The nation was unprepared. How did this happen, and how can we avoid such tragedy again? To answer these questions, the Congress and the President created the National Commission on Terrorist Attacks Upon the United States (Public Law 107–306, November 27, 2002).

Our mandate was sweeping. The law directed us to investigate "facts and circumstances relating to the terrorist attacks of September 11, 2001," including those relating to intelligence agencies, law enforcement agencies, diplomacy, immigration issues and border control, the flow of assets to terrorist organizations, commercial aviation, the role of congressional oversight and resource allocation, and other areas determined relevant by the Commission. In pursuing our mandate, we have reviewed more than 2.5 million pages of documents and interviewed more than 1,200 individuals in 10 countries. This included nearly every senior official from the current and previous administrations who had responsibility for topics covered in our mandate. We have sought to be independent, impartial, thorough, and nonpartisan. From the outset, we have been committed to share as much of our investigation as we can with the American people. To that end, we held 19 days of hearings and took public testimony from 160 witnesses.

▓ What are the elements of the introduction to an effective after-action incident report?

▓ Discuss the necessity for these types of reviews in general and this incident review in particular. In other words, why have one?

Our aim has not been to assign individual blame. Our aim has been to provide the fullest possible account of the events surrounding 9/11 and to identify lessons learned. We learned about an enemy who is sophisticated, patient, disciplined, and lethal. The enemy rallies broad support in the Arab and Muslim world by demanding redress of political grievances, but its hostility toward us and our values is limitless. Its purpose is to rid the world of religious and political pluralism, the plebiscite, and equal rights for women. It makes no distinction between military and civilian targets. *Collateral damage* is not in its lexicon.

We learned that the institutions charged with protecting our borders, civil aviation, and national security did not understand how grave this threat could be, and did not adjust their policies, plans, and practices to deter or defeat it. We learned of fault lines within our government— between foreign and domestic intelligence, and between and within agencies. We learned of the pervasive problems of managing and sharing information across a large and unwieldy government that had been built in a different era to confront different dangers.

▓ Discuss the specific components mentioned here that comprise an effective incident-response plan.

▓ Discuss incident-response plan components that are not mentioned above.

▓ What policies, plans, and practices are referred to in above paragraphs? Do the 9/11 Commissioners feel these policies, plans, and practices are sufficient? Why or why not?

Excerpt 2

The physical security practices in place on 9/11/2001 were not designed to counter the threats posed by the 9/11 attackers. While the technology-based controls in place on 9/11/01 triggered alerts on the hijackers, given the degree of training and awareness demonstrated by the security employees, the security measures, as implemented, appear to have been inadequate. This is a significant point; the technical controls in place at the screening locations worked as expected. Even so, the failure of the human elements of the security systems to perform as required by policy and as they were most likely trained did not function correctly.

The complex nature of interdependent components in systems (physical security systems or information systems) points out that even when one component works as expected, a failure in another can result in a failure of the whole system. Information systems security is faced with an identical issue when technical controls, such as intrusion detection or e-mail filtering technical controls, work but the human component fails and the whole system is compromised.

FROM CHAPTER 1 – "WE HAVE SOME PLANES"

Tuesday, September 11, 2001, dawned temperate and nearly cloudless in the eastern United States. Millions of men and women readied themselves for work. Some made their way to the Twin Towers, the signature structures of the World Trade Center complex in New York City. Others went to Arlington, Virginia, to the Pentagon. Across the Potomac River, the United States Congress was back in session. At the other end of Pennsylvania Avenue, people began to line up for a White House tour. In Sarasota, Florida, President George W. Bush went for an early morning run. For those heading to an airport, weather conditions could not have been better for a safe and pleasant journey. Among the travelers were Mohamed Atta and Abdul Aziz al Omari, who arrived at the airport in Portland, Maine.

INSIDE THE FLIGHTS

Boston: American 11 and United 175. Atta and Omari boarded a 6:00 A.M. flight from Portland to Boston's Logan International Airport. When he checked in for his flight to Boston, Atta was selected by a computerized prescreening system known as CAPPS (Computer Assisted Passenger Prescreening System), created to identify passengers who should be subject to special security measures. Under security rules in place at the time, the only consequence of Atta's selection by CAPPS was that his checked bags were held off the plane until it was confirmed that he had boarded the aircraft. This did not hinder Atta's plans.

Atta and Omari arrived in Boston at 6:45. Seven minutes later, Atta apparently took a call from Marwan al Shehhi, a longtime colleague who was at another terminal at Logan Airport. They spoke for three minutes. It would be their final conversation. Between 6:45 and 7:40, Atta and Omari, along with Satam al Suqami, Wail al Shehri, and Waleed al Shehri, checked in and boarded American Airlines Flight 11, bound for Los Angeles. The flight was scheduled to depart at 7:45.

In another Logan terminal, Shehhi, joined by Fayez Banihammad, Mohand al Shehri, Ahmed al Ghamdi, and Hamza al Ghamdi, checked in for United Airlines Flight 175, also bound for Los Angeles. A couple of

Shehhi's colleagues were obviously unused to travel; according to the United ticket agent, they had trouble understanding the standard security questions, and she had to go over them slowly until they gave the routine, reassuring answers. Their flight was scheduled to depart at 8:00.

The security checkpoints through which passengers, including Atta and his colleagues, gained access to the American 11 gate were operated by Global Security under a contract with American Airlines. In a different terminal, the single checkpoint through which passengers for United 175 passed was controlled by United Airlines, which had contracted with Hunt-leigh USA to perform the screening.

In passing through these checkpoints, each of the hijackers would have been screened by a walk-through metal detector calibrated to detect items with at least the metal content of a .22-caliber handgun. Anyone who might have set off that detector would have been screened with a hand wand—a procedure requiring the screener to identify the metal item or items that caused the alarm. In addition, an X-ray machine would have screened the hijackers' carry-on belongings. The screening was in place to identify and confiscate weapons and other items prohibited from being carried onto a commercial flight. None of the checkpoint supervisors recalled the hijackers or reported anything suspicious regarding their screening.

While Atta had been selected by CAPPS in Portland, three members of his hijacking team—Suqami, Wail al Shehri, and Waleed al Shehri—were selected in Boston. Their selection affected only the handling of their checked bags, not their screening at the checkpoint. All five men cleared the checkpoint and made their way to the gate for American 11. Atta, Omari, and Suqami took their seats in business class (seats 8D, 8G, and 10B, respectively). The Shehri brothers had adjacent seats in row 2 (Wail in 2A, Waleed in 2B), in the first class cabin. They boarded American 11 between 7:31 and 7:40. The aircraft pushed back from the gate at 7:40.

Shehhi and his team, none of whom had been selected by CAPPS, boarded United 175 between 7:23 and 7:28 (Banihammad in 2A, Shehri in 2B, Shehhi in 6C, Hamza al Ghamdi in 9C, and Ahmed al Ghamdi in 9D). Their aircraft pushed back from the gate just before 8:00.

> ▦ In an incident-response plan, discuss how much importance should be given to technology-based controls and how much stress placed in the human factors of the system.
> ▦ When faced with management who has a philosophy that "technology is the solution to every problem," what should you do as an incident-response planner?

Excerpt 3

The role of the individuals involved in response to an incident remains a critical success factor. While the importance of the planning process is great, the preparation of individuals who will be expected to work within the plan is equally so. Note that in the following passage, individuals achieved results when they go beyond the boundaries of established procedure to take action outside the scope of the plan and their training. This point should not be lost on the incident-response planner. When creating a training program for incident-detection and response, the need to remain alert and proactive should be communicated along with the training of the team to respond to expected (and unexpected) events with prepared actions.

THE HIJACKING OF AMERICAN 11

American Airlines Flight 11 provided nonstop service from Boston to Los Angeles. On September 11, Captain John Ogonowski and First Officer Thomas McGuinness piloted the Boeing 767. It carried its full capacity of nine flight attendants. Eighty-one passengers boarded the flight with them (including the five terrorists).

The plane took off at 7:59. Just before 8:14, it had climbed to 26,000 feet, not quite its initial assigned cruising altitude of 29,000 feet. All communications and flight profile data were normal. About this time the "Fasten Seatbelt" sign would usually have been turned off and the flight attendants would have begun preparing for cabin service.

At that same time, American 11 had its last routine communication with the ground when it acknowledged navigational instructions from the FAA's air traffic control (ATC) center in Boston. Sixteen seconds after that transmission, ATC instructed the aircraft's pilots to climb to 35,000 feet. That message and all subsequent attempts to contact the flight were not acknowledged. From this and other evidence, we believe the hijacking began at 8:14 or shortly thereafter.

Reports from two flight attendants in the coach cabin, Betty Ong and Madeline "Amy" Sweeney, tell us most of what we know about how the hijacking happened. As it began, some of the hijackers—most likely Wail al Shehri and Waleed al Shehri, who were seated in row 2 in first class—stabbed the two unarmed flight attendants who would have been preparing for cabin service.

We do not know exactly how the hijackers gained access to the cockpit; FAA rules required that the doors remain closed and locked during flight. Ong speculated that they had "jammed their way" in. Perhaps the terrorists stabbed the flight attendants to get a cockpit key, to force one of them to open the cockpit door, or to lure the captain or first officer out of the cockpit. Or the flight attendants may just have been in their way. At the same time or shortly thereafter, Atta—the only terrorist on board trained to fly a jet—would have moved to the cockpit from his business-class seat, possibly accompanied by Omari. As this was happening, passenger Daniel Lewin, who was seated in the row just behind Atta and Omari, was stabbed by one of the hijackers—probably Satam al Suqami, who was seated directly behind Lewin. Lewin had served four years as an officer in the Israeli military. He may have made an attempt to stop the hijackers in front of him, not realizing that another was sitting behind him.

The hijackers quickly gained control and sprayed Mace, pepper spray, or some other irritant in the first-class cabin, in order to force the passengers and flight attendants toward the rear of the plane. They claimed they had a bomb.

About five minutes after the hijacking began, Betty Ong contacted the American Airlines Southeastern Reservations Office in Cary, North Carolina, via an AT&T airphone to report an emergency aboard the flight. This was the first of several occasions on 9/11 when flight attendants took action outside the scope of their training, which emphasized that in a hijacking, they were to communicate with the cockpit crew. The emergency call lasted approximately 25 minutes, as Ong calmly and professionally relayed information about events taking place aboard the airplane to authorities on the ground.

At 8:19, Ong reported: "The cockpit is not answering, somebody's stabbed in business class—and I think there's Mace—that we can't breathe—I don't know, I think we're getting hijacked." She then told of the stabbings of the two flight attendants.

At 8:21, one of the American employees receiving Ong's call in North Carolina, Nydia Gonzalez, alerted the American Airlines operations center in Fort Worth, Texas, reaching Craig Marquis, the manager on duty. Marquis soon realized this was an emergency and instructed the airline's dispatcher responsible for the flight to contact the cockpit. At 8:23, the dispatcher tried unsuccessfully to contact the aircraft. Six minutes later, the air traffic control specialist in American's operations center contacted the FAA's Boston Air Traffic Control Center about the flight. The center was already aware of the problem.

Boston Center knew of a problem on the flight in part because just before 8:25 the hijackers had attempted to communicate with the passengers. The microphone was keyed, and immediately one of the hijackers said, "Nobody move. Everything will be okay. If you try to make any moves, you'll endanger yourself and the airplane. Just stay quiet." Air traffic controllers heard the transmission; Ong did not. The hijackers probably did not know how to operate the cockpit radio communication system correctly, and thus inadvertently broadcast their message over the air traffic control channel instead of the cabin public-address channel. Also at 8:25, and again at 8:29, Amy Sweeney got through to the American Flight Services Office in Boston but was cut off after she reported someone was hurt aboard the flight. Three minutes later, Sweeney was reconnected to the office and began relaying updates to the manager, Michael Woodward.

[. . .]

At 8:44, Gonzalez reported losing phone contact with Ong. About this same time Sweeney reported to Woodward, "Something is wrong. We are in a rapid descent. . . we are all over the place." Woodward asked Sweeney to look out the window to see if she could determine where they were. Sweeney responded: "We are flying low. We are flying very, very low. We are flying way too low." Seconds later she said, "Oh my God we are way too low." The phone call ended.

At 8:46:40, American 11 crashed into the North Tower of the World Trade Center in New York City. All on board, along with an unknown number of people in the tower, were killed instantly.

※ In the passage above, find an example of an individual who performed an action outside the scope of their training, and in fact outside the scope of any incident-response plan. Why were they motivated to take these actions?

※ What steps can an incident-response planner take to allow for individual initiative and proactive behavior without compromising the overall plan?

Excerpt 4

In general, incident-response plans are activated when sufficient uncertainty about future events reaches some triggering threshold. Observe in the following passage that the containment phase of American Airlines incident response begins as soon as the second anomalous event has been recognized. Without detailed knowledge of the scope of the attack against its aircraft, management has already begun to make the effort to contain the incident to the degree possible. As soon as additional information made it apparent that the threat was continuing (or even escalating), additional containment actions were invoked.

THE HIJACKING OF AMERICAN 77

American Airlines Flight 77 was scheduled to depart from Washington Dulles for Los Angeles at 8:10. The aircraft was a Boeing 757 piloted by Captain Charles F. Burlingame and First Officer David Charlebois. There were four flight attendants. On September 11, the flight carried 58 passengers.

American 77 pushed back from its gate at 8:09 and took off at 8:20. At 8:46, the flight reached its assigned cruising altitude of 35,000 feet. Cabin service would have begun. At 8:51, American 77 transmitted its last routine radio communication.

The hijacking began between 8:51 and 8:54. As on American 11 and United 175, the hijackers used knives (reported by one passenger) and moved all the passengers (and possibly crew) to the rear of the aircraft (reported by one flight attendant and one passenger). Unlike the earlier flights, the Flight 77 hijackers were reported by a passenger to have box cutters. Finally, a passenger reported that an announcement had been made by the "pilot" that the plane had been hijacked. Neither of the firsthand accounts mentioned any stabbings or the threat or use of either a bomb or Mace, though both witnesses began the flight in the first-class cabin.

At 8:54, the aircraft deviated from its assigned course, turning south. Two minutes later the transponder was turned off and even primary radar contact with the aircraft was lost. The Indianapolis Air Traffic Control Center repeatedly tried and failed to contact the aircraft. American Airlines dispatchers also tried, without success.

At 9:00, American Airlines Executive Vice President Gerard Arpey learned that communications had been lost with American 77. This was now the second American aircraft in trouble. He ordered all American Airlines flights in the Northeast that had not taken off to remain on the ground. Shortly before 9:10, suspecting that American 77 had been hijacked, American headquarters concluded that the second aircraft to hit the World Trade Center might have been Flight 77. After learning that United Airlines was missing a plane, American Airlines headquarters extended the ground stop nationwide.

[...]At 9:34, Ronald Reagan Washington National Airport advised the Secret Service of an unknown aircraft heading in the direction of the White House. American 77 was then five miles west-southwest of the Pentagon and began a 330-degree turn. At the end of the turn, it was descending through 2,200 feet, pointed toward the Pentagon and downtown Washington. The hijacker pilot then advanced the throttles to maximum power and dove toward the Pentagon.

At 9:37:46, American Airlines Flight 77 crashed into the Pentagon, traveling at approximately 530 miles per hour. All on board, as well as many civilian and military personnel in the building, were killed.

> ▓ As an incident-response planner, what criteria should be used to establish the threshold for escalation and containment actions?
> ▓ In the passage above, can you infer the criteria used by American Airlines?

Excerpt 5

Early and aggressive incident containment may often reduce losses or even prevent elements of a multipart attack. This belief encourages incident-response planners to strive for instant notification and rapid escalation to the broadest group consistent with the scope of the attack. Note the lack of these behaviors in the excerpt below.

UNITED FLIGHT 93

At 8:42, United Airlines Flight 93 took off from Newark (New Jersey) Liberty International Airport bound for San Francisco. The aircraft was piloted by Captain Jason Dahl and First Officer Leroy Homer, and there were five flight attendants. Thirty-seven passengers, including the hijackers, boarded the plane. Scheduled to depart the gate at 8:00, the Boeing 757's takeoff was delayed because of the airport's typically heavy morning traffic.

The hijackers had planned to take flights scheduled to depart at 7:45 (American 11), 8:00 (United 175 and United 93), and 8:10 (American 77). Three of the flights had actually taken off within 10 to 15 minutes of their planned departure times. United 93 would ordinarily have taken off about 15 minutes after pulling away from the gate. When it left the ground at 8:42, the flight was running more than 25 minutes late.

As United 93 left Newark, the flight's crew members were unaware of the hijacking of American 11. Around 9:00, the FAA, American, and United were facing the staggering realization of apparent multiple hijackings. At 9:03, they would see another aircraft strike the World Trade Center. Crisis managers at the FAA and the airlines did not yet act to warn other aircraft.

At the same time, Boston Center realized that a message transmitted just before 8:25 by the hijacker pilot of American 11 included the phrase, "We have some planes."

No one at the FAA or the airlines that day had ever dealt with multiple hijackings. Such a plot had not been carried out anywhere in the world in more than 30 years, and never in the United States. As news of the hijackings filtered through the FAA and the airlines, it does not seem to have occurred to their leadership that they needed to alert other aircraft in the air that they too might be at risk.

> ▓ While it is impossible to know, could earlier involvement of a broader cross-section of the airlines and government agencies have lessened the impact of these events?

Excerpt 6

One way to improve an incident-response plan is to create an after-action report using the benefit afforded from hindsight. In the passage that follows, it is clear that if United Airlines had established an incident-containment response to increase cockpit security, and had the activation of that containment been practiced as a part of the standard procedures, it is possible that the crew could have been able to retain control of the aircraft.

THE HIJACKING OF UNITED 175

United 175 was hijacked between 8:42 and 8:46, and awareness of that hijacking began to spread after 8:51. American 77 was hijacked between 8:51 and 8:54. By 9:00, FAA and airline officials began to comprehend that attackers were going after multiple aircraft. American Airlines' nationwide ground stop between 9:05 and 9:10 was followed by a United Airlines ground stop.

FAA controllers at Boston Center, which had tracked the first two hijackings, requested at 9:07 that Herndon Command Center "get messages to airborne aircraft to increase security for the cockpit." There is no evidence that Herndon took such action. Boston Center immediately began speculating about other aircraft that might be in danger, leading them to worry about a transcontinental flight—Delta 1989—that in fact was not hijacked. At 9:19, the FAA's New England regional office called Herndon and asked that Cleveland Center advise Delta 1989 to use extra cockpit security.

Several FAA air traffic control officials told us it was the air carriers' responsibility to notify their planes of security problems. One senior FAA air traffic control manager said that it was simply not the FAA's place to order the airlines what to tell their pilots. We believe such statements do not reflect an adequate appreciation of the FAA's responsibility for the safety and security of civil aviation.

The airlines bore responsibility, too. They were facing an escalating number of conflicting and, for the most part, erroneous reports about other flights, as well as a continuing lack of vital information from the FAA about the hijacked flights. We found no evidence, however, that American Airlines sent any cockpit warnings to its aircraft on 9/11. United's first decisive action to notify its airborne aircraft to take defensive action did not come until 9:19, when a United flight dispatcher, Ed Ballinger, took the initiative to begin transmitting warnings to his 16 transcontinental flights: "Beware any cockpit intrusion- Two a/c [aircraft] hit World Trade Center." One of the flights that received the warning was United 93. Because Ballinger was still responsible for his other flights as well as Flight 175, his warning message was not transmitted to Flight 93 until 9:23.

By all accounts, the first 46 minutes of Flight 93's cross-country trip proceeded routinely. Radio communications from the plane were normal. Heading, speed, and altitude ran according to plan. At 9:24, Ballinger's warning to United 93 was received in the cockpit. Within two minutes, at 9:26, the pilot, Jason Dahl, responded with a note of puzzlement: "Ed, confirm latest mssg plz—Jason."

The hijackers attacked at 9:28. While traveling 35,000 feet above eastern Ohio, United 93 suddenly dropped 700 feet. Eleven seconds into the descent, the FAA's air traffic control center in Cleveland received the first of two radio transmissions from the aircraft. During the first broadcast, the captain or first officer could be heard declaring "Mayday" amid the sounds of a physical struggle in the cockpit. The second radio transmission, 35 seconds later, indicated that the fight was continuing. The captain or first officer could be heard shouting: "Hey get out of here—get out of here—get out of here."

■ Of course, even if the established containment response were in place, the attackers may have been able to exploit the weak state of the cockpit access controls as they were implemented before 9/11/2001. How have recent changes to airline security reduced the odds of a repeat of this specific type of attack?

Excerpt 7

The incident-response planner should note that while planning, training, and rehearsal are critical, the application of initiative and ad hoc implementation must always be part of the preparation of the response team.

THE HIJACKING OF UNITED 93

On the morning of 9/11, there were only 37 passengers on United 93-33 in addition to the 4 hijackers. This was below the norm for Tuesday mornings during the summer of 2001. But there is no evidence that the hijackers manipulated passenger levels or purchased additional seats to facilitate their operation.

The terrorists who hijacked three other commercial flights on 9/11 operated in five-man teams. They initiated their cockpit takeover within 30 minutes of takeoff. On Flight 93, however, the takeover took place 46 minutes after takeoff and there were only four hijackers. The operative likely intended to round out the team for this flight, Mohamed al Kahtani, had been refused entry by a suspicious immigration inspector at Florida's Orlando International Airport in August.

Because several passengers on United 93 described three hijackers on the plane, not four, some have wondered whether one of the hijackers had been able to use the cockpit jump seat from the outset of the flight. FAA rules allow use of this seat by documented and approved individuals, usually air carrier or FAA personnel. We have found no evidence indicating that one of the hijackers, or anyone else, sat there on this flight. All the hijackers had assigned seats in first class, and they seem to have used them. We believe it is more likely that Jarrah, the crucial pilot-trained member of their team, remained seated and inconspicuous until after the cockpit was seized; and once inside, he would not have been visible to the passengers.

At 9:32, a hijacker, probably Jarrah, made or attempted to make the following announcement to the passengers of Flight 93: "Ladies and Gentlemen: Here the captain, please sit down keep remaining sitting. We have a bomb on board. So, sit." The flight data recorder (also recovered) indicates that Jarrah then instructed the plane's autopilot to turn the aircraft around and head east.

The cockpit voice recorder data indicate that a woman, most likely a flight attendant, was being held captive in the cockpit. She struggled with one of the hijackers who killed or otherwise silenced her.

Shortly thereafter, the passengers and flight crew began a series of calls from GTE airphones and cellular phones. These calls between family, friends, and colleagues took place until the end of the flight and provided those on the ground with firsthand accounts. They enabled the passengers to gain critical information, including the news that two aircraft had slammed into the World Trade Center.

- In the passage above, what initiative was taken to thwart the attempted hijacking? Were any of the participants formal members of any response team?
- Which federal regulations were violated but can be seen as necessary initiative in the face of extraordinary circumstance?
- When creating an incident-response plan, what are the boundaries for appropriate action? Should these be written into the plan or left for the initiative of the responders?
- What criterion separates a "normal" incident response from an "extreme" incident response? Who makes that determination? Should planners anticipate and incorporate "extreme" responses into the plan? Why or why not?
- Who should establish the boundaries for appropriate action within an incident-response plan?

Excerpt 8

When the worst has come to pass, the attackers have compromised our systems and gained access to our infrastructure. Examine the passage below for how this came to be and what can be learned from this experience. Incident planners may want to note that guidance about the use of in-band communications may be needed in an incident-response plan and that, in times of heightened alert or during an incident response, additional or more frequent authentication actions may be needed.

THE CLEVELAND AIR ROUTE TRAFFIC CONTROL CENTER

At 9:39, the FAA's Cleveland Air Route Traffic Control Center overheard a second announcement indicating that there was a bomb on board, that the plane was returning to the airport, and that they should remain seated. While it apparently was not heard by the passengers, this announcement, like those on Flight 11 and Flight 77, was intended to deceive them. Jarrah, like Atta earlier, may have inadvertently broadcast the message because he did not know how to operate the radio and the intercom. To our knowledge, none of them had ever flown an actual airliner before. At least two callers from the flight reported that the hijackers knew that passengers were making calls but did not seem to care. It is quite possible Jarrah knew of the success of the assault on the World Trade Center. He could have learned of this from messages being sent by United Airlines to the cockpits of its transcontinental flights, including Flight 93, warning of cockpit intrusion and telling of the New York attacks. But even without them, he would certainly have understood that the attacks on the World Trade Center would already have unfolded, given Flight 93's tardy departure from Newark. If Jarrah did know that the passengers were making calls, it might not have occurred to him that they were certain to learn what had happened in New York, thereby defeating his attempts at deception.

▓ Did the successful compromise of the cockpit give the attackers access to the in-band communications systems of the airline? How did they exploit it?

▓ If you were creating an incident-response plan for an airline company, how would you implement the steps needed to handle the incident from the above passage?

Excerpt 9

When an incident escalates beyond the immediate ability to contain, communication becomes key. Without proper communication, coordinated response becomes impossible.

NATIONAL CRISIS MANAGEMENT

When American 11 struck the World Trade Center at 8:46, no one in the White House or traveling with the President knew that it had been hijacked. While that information circulated within the FAA, we found no evidence that the hijacking was reported to any other agency in Washington before 8:46.

Most federal agencies learned about the crash in New York from CNN. Within the FAA, the administrator, Jane Garvey, and her acting deputy, Monte Belger, had not been told of a confirmed hijacking before they learned from television that a plane had crashed. Others in the agency were aware of it . . . .

Inside the National Military Command Center, the deputy director of operations and his assistant began notifying senior Pentagon officials of the incident. At about 9:00, the senior NMCC operations officer reached out to the FAA operations center for information. Although the NMCC was advised of the hijacking of American 11, the scrambling of jets was not discussed.

In Sarasota, Florida, the presidential motorcade was arriving at the Emma E. Booker Elementary School, where President Bush was to read to a class and talk about education. White House Chief of Staff Andrew Card told us he was standing with the President outside the classroom when Senior Advisor to the President Karl Rove first informed them that a small, twin-engine plane had crashed into the World Trade Center. The President's reaction was that the incident must have been caused by pilot error.

At 8:55, before entering the classroom, the President spoke to National Security Advisor Condoleezza Rice, who was at the White House. She recalled first telling the President it was a twin-engine aircraft—and then a commercial aircraft—that had struck the World Trade Center, adding "that's all we know right now, Mr. President."

At the White House, Vice President Dick Cheney had just sat down for a meeting when his assistant told him to turn on his television because a plane had struck the North Tower of the World Trade Center. The Vice President was wondering "how the hell could a plane hit the World Trade Center" when he saw the second aircraft strike the South Tower.

Elsewhere in the White House, a series of 9:00 meetings was about to begin. In the absence of information that the crash was anything other than an accident, the White House staff monitored the news as they went ahead with their regular schedules.

THE AGENCIES CONFER

When they learned a second plane had struck the World Trade Center, nearly everyone in the White House told us, they immediately knew it was not an accident. The Secret Service initiated a number of security enhancements around the White House complex. The officials who issued these orders did not know that there were additional hijacked aircraft, or that one such aircraft was en route to Washington. These measures were precautionary steps taken because of the strikes in New York.

The FAA and White House Teleconferences

The FAA, the White House, and the Defense Department each initiated a multiagency teleconference before 9:30. Because none of these teleconferences—at least before 10:00—included the right officials from both the FAA and Defense Department, none succeeded in meaningfully coordinating the military and FAA response to the hijackings.

At about 9:20, security personnel at FAA headquarters set up a hijacking teleconference with several agencies, including the Defense Department. The NMCC officer who participated told us that the call was monitored only periodically because the information was sporadic, it was of little value, and there were other important tasks. The FAA manager of the teleconference also remembered that the military participated only briefly before the Pentagon was hit.

Both individuals agreed that the teleconference played no role in coordinating a response to the attacks of 9/11. Acting Deputy Administrator Belger was frustrated to learn later in the morning that the military had not been on the call.

At the White House, the video teleconference was conducted from the Situation Room by Richard Clarke, a special assistant to the president long involved in counterterrorism. Logs indicate that it began at 9:25 and included the CIA; the FBI; the departments of State, Justice, and Defense; the FAA; and the White House shelter. The FAA and CIA joined at 9:40. The first topic addressed in the White House video teleconference—at about 9:40—was the physical security of the President, the White House, and federal agencies.

Immediately thereafter it was reported that a plane had hit the Pentagon. We found no evidence that video teleconference participants had any prior information that American 77 had been hijacked and was heading directly toward Washington. Indeed, it is not clear to us that the video teleconference was fully under way before 9:37, when the Pentagon was struck.

Garvey, Belger, and other senior officials from FAA headquarters participated in this video teleconference at various times. We do not know who from Defense participated, but we know that in the first hour none of the personnel involved in managing the crisis did. And none of the information conveyed in the White House video teleconference, at least in the first hour, was being passed to the NMCC. As one witness recalled, "[It] was almost like there were parallel decision-making processes going on; one was a voice conference orchestrated by the NMCC...and then there was the [White House videoteleconference]...[I]n my mind they were competing venues for command and control and decision making."

At 10:03, the conference received reports of more missing aircraft, "two, possibly three, aloft," and learned of a combat air patrol over Washington. There was discussion of the need for rules of engagement. Clarke reported that they were asking the President for authority to shoot down aircraft. Confirmation of that authority came at 10:25, but the commands were already being conveyed in more direct contacts with the Pentagon.

The Pentagon Teleconferences

Inside the National Military Command Center, the deputy director for operations immediately thought the second strike was a terrorist attack. The job of the NMCC in such an emergency is to gather the relevant parties and establish the chain of command between the National Command Authority—the president and the secretary of defense—and those who need to carry out their orders.

On the morning of September 11, Secretary Rumsfeld was having breakfast at the Pentagon with a group of members of Congress. He then returned to his office for his daily intelligence briefing. The Secretary was informed of the second strike in New York during the briefing; he resumed the briefing while awaiting more information. After the Pentagon was struck, Secretary Rumsfeld went to the parking lot to assist with rescue efforts.

Inside the NMCC, the deputy director for operations called for an all-purpose "significant event" conference. It began at 9:29, with a brief recap: two aircraft had struck the World Trade Center, there was a confirmed hijacking of American 11, and Otis fighters had been scrambled. The FAA was asked to provide an update, but the line was silent because the FAA had not been added to the call. A minute later, the deputy director stated that it had just been confirmed that American 11 was still airborne and heading toward D.C. He directed the transition to an air threat conference call. NORAD confirmed that American 11 was airborne and heading toward Washington, relaying the erroneous FAA information already mentioned. The call then ended, at about 9:34.

It resumed at 9:37 as an air threat conference call, which lasted more than eight hours. The President, Vice President, Secretary of Defense, Vice Chairman of the Joint Chiefs of Staff, and Deputy National Security Advisor Stephen Hadley all participated in this teleconference at various times, as did military personnel from the White House underground shelter and the President's military aide on Air Force One.

Operators worked feverishly to include the FAA, but they had equipment problems and difficulty finding secure phone numbers. NORAD asked three times before 10:03 to confirm the presence of the FAA in the teleconference. The FAA representative who finally joined the call at 10:17 had no familiarity with or responsibility for hijackings, no access to decision makers, and none of the information available to senior FAA officials.

We found no evidence that, at this critical time, NORAD's top commanders, in Florida or Cheyenne Mountain, coordinated with their counterparts at FAA headquarters to improve awareness and organize a common response. Lower-level officials improvised—for example, the FAA's Boston Center bypassed the chain of command and directly contacted NEADS after the first hijacking. But the highest-level Defense Department officials relied on the NMCC's air threat conference, in which the FAA did not participate for the first 48 minutes.

At 9:39, the NMCC's deputy director for operations, a military officer, opened the call from the Pentagon, which had just been hit. He began: "An air attack against North America may be in progress. NORAD, what's the situation?" NORAD said it had conflicting reports. Its latest information was "of a possible hijacked aircraft taking off out of JFK en route to Washington, D.C." The NMCC reported a crash into the mall side of the Pentagon and requested that the Secretary of Defense be added to the conference.

At 9:44, NORAD briefed the conference on the possible hijacking of Delta 1989. Two minutes later, staff reported that they were still trying to locate Secretary Rumsfeld and Vice Chairman Myers. The Vice Chairman joined the conference shortly before 10:00; the Secretary, shortly before 10:30. The Chairman was out of the country.

At 9:48, a representative from the White House shelter asked if there were any indications of another hijacked aircraft. The deputy director for operations mentioned the Delta flight and concluded that "that would be the fourth possible hijack." At 9:49, the commander of NORAD directed all air sovereignty aircraft to battle stations, fully armed.

At 9:59, an Air Force lieutenant colonel working in the White House Military Office joined the conference and stated he had just talked to Deputy National Security Advisor Stephen Hadley. The White House requested (1) the implementation of continuity of government measures, (2) fighter escorts for Air Force One, and (3) a fighter combat air patrol over Washington, D.C.

By 10:03, when United 93 crashed in Pennsylvania, there had been no mention of its hijacking and the FAA had not yet been added to the teleconference.

- How would you describe the federal government's response to the 9/11 attacks from the time of the first news until 10:00 AM?
- Do you believe mistakes were made? Where and how so?
- As an incident-response planner, create your own theoretical communications plan with the information given in the passage above. Pretend you are making a presentation to the President and defend your plan

---

Excerpt 10

We have been led to believe, whether by films or novels, that the President of the United States is always in close contact with his aides and other government officials. The following passage indicates that this may not in fact be the case.

THE PRESIDENT AND THE VICE PRESIDENT

The President was seated in a classroom when, at 9:05, Andrew Card whispered to him: "A second plane hit the second tower. America is under attack." The President told us his instinct was to project calm, not to have the country see an excited reaction at a moment of crisis. The press was standing behind the children; he saw their phones and pagers start to ring. The President felt he should project strength and calm until he could better understand what was happening. [...]

THE SHOOT-DOWN ORDER

On the morning of 9/11, the President and Vice President stayed in contact not by an open line of communication but through a series of calls. The President told us he was frustrated with the poor communications that morning. He could not reach key officials, including Secretary Rumsfeld, for a period of time. The line to the White House shelter conference room—and the Vice President—kept cutting off.

The Vice President remembered placing a call to the President just after entering the shelter conference room. There is conflicting evidence about when the Vice President arrived in the shelter conference room. We have concluded, from the available evidence, that the Vice President arrived in the room shortly before 10:00, perhaps at 9:58. The Vice President recalled being told, just after his arrival, that the Air Force was trying to establish a combat air patrol over Washington.

The Vice President stated that he called the President to discuss the rules of engagement for the CAP. He recalled feeling that it did no good to establish the CAP unless the pilots had instructions on whether they were authorized to shoot if the plane would not divert. He said the President signed off on that concept. The President said he remembered such a conversation, and that it reminded him of when he had been an interceptor pilot. The President emphasized to us that he had authorized the shoot-down of hijacked aircraft...

- If the President has trouble staying in touch with the Secretary of Defense during an incident, how likely do you think it will be for your organization's incident responders to stay in touch when your incident-response plan is activated?
- How can your incident-response plan deal with this issue?

Conclusion

And so, the United States and the world continue to grapple with the geopolitics of terrorism and how best to mount a meaningful homeland defense. It is established that cyber-defense is part of this response, and even the seemingly mundane tasks of securing commercial information systems and control systems of the national and local infrastructure are an important part of the response.

Given the post-9/11 political climate, it is likely that information security practitioners will find themselves a part of or the leader of an incident-response process. The time to plan is before the incident, just as it is also the time to train. But every plan, no matter how well crafted, how rigorously trained, or how well executed will ever survive contact with reality unaltered. As was seen in the unfolding of the events on 9/11, the characteristic of flexibility in planning and the encouragement of initiative among responders has to be a part of each incident-response plan.

The aftermath of the events of 9/11 and the outcomes of the incident-response plans that were in place prior to the attacks were subject to an extreme degree of scrutiny. When you are involved in an actual incident-response, you will probably not find that level of after-action review. But in order to improve, every incident should be followed by an open and honest review of what happened and how the planning for incidents can be improved. Just as needed changes in national defense planning are achieved by these types of review, your incident-response plans will need to be improved as well.